iMovie

the missing manual®

The book that should have been in the box®

David Pogue & Aaron Miller

O'REILLY®

Beijing | Boston | Farnham | Sebastopol | Tokyo

iMovie: The Missing Manual

by David Pogue and Aaron Miller

Copyright © 2014 David Pogue. All rights reserved.
Printed in Canada.

Published by O'Reilly Media, Inc.,
1005 Gravenstein Highway North, Sebastopol, CA 95472.

O'Reilly books may be purchased for educational, business, or sales promotional use. Online editions are also available for most titles (*http://safaribooksonline.com*). For more information, contact our corporate/institutional sales department: (800) 998-9938 or *corporate@oreilly.com*.

May 2014:   First Edition.

Revision History for the First Edition:

2014-05-05	First release
2014-09-05	Second release
2015-05-08	Third release
2015-12-11	Fourth release
2017-02-24	Fifth release

See *http://www.oreilly.com/catalog/errata.csp?isbn=0636920032809* for release details.

ISBN-13: 978-1-4919-4732-6

[TI]

Contents

Part One: iMovie Basics

Part Two: **Build Your Movie**

Part Five: **Appendixes**

The Missing Credits

ABOUT THE AUTHORS

 David Pogue (coauthor, editor) is the founder of Yahoo Tech, having been groomed for the position by 13 years as the tech columnist for the New York Times. He's a monthly columnist for Scientific American, Emmy-winning correspondent for "CBS Sunday Morning," and host of science shows on PBS's "NOVA." He's the creator of the Missing Manual series and the author of 75 books. He lives in Connecticut with his wife and three awesome kids.

Links to his columns and weekly videos await at *www.davidpogue.com*. He welcomes feedback about his books at *david@pogueman.com*.

 Aaron Miller (author, '09 and '11 updates) is a part-time lawyer and part-time professor. He also authors the blog Unlocking iMovie (*http:// unlockingimovie.blogspot.com*), his own little way of trying to make the Mac world a better place. If he's not at his computer, he's probably playing Ultimate Frisbee or "tickle monster" with his kids. Email: *ilifer08@gmail.com*.

ABOUT THE CREATIVE TEAM

Peter McKie (editor) has a master's degree in journalism from Boston University. He lives in New York City and can be found exploring abandoned buildings and researching the history of old structures. Email: *pmckie@oreilly.com*.

Kara Ebrahim (production editor) lives, works, and plays in Cambridge, MA. She loves graphic design and all things outdoors. Email: *kebrahim@oreilly.com*.

Julie Van Keuren (proofreader) quit her newspaper job in 2006 to move to Montana and live the freelancing dream. She and her husband (who is living the novel-writing dream) have two hungry teenage sons. Email: *little_media@yahoo.com*.

Ron Strauss (indexer) specializes in the indexing of information technology publications of all kinds. Ron is also an accomplished classical violist and lives in Northern California with his wife and fellow indexer, Annie, and his miniature pinscher, Kanga. Email: *rstrauss@mchsi.com*.

ACKNOWLEDGMENTS

This book is a new edition of *iMovie: The Missing Manual*—the sixth edition, actually—so it represents a lot of effort by some gifted collaborators over the years. I offer my gratitude to those whose contributions live on in these pages: Teresa

Noelle Roberts, Tim Geaney, and Lesa Snider. I'm also grateful to David Rogelberg, my agent; our O'Reilly liaison Peter McKie; and especially to Aaron Miller, who has once again updated this book so skillfully, it's impossible to tell his prose from mine. He did a seamless, witty, professional job.

Above all, thanks to my lovely bride Nicki and my amazing kids, Kell, Tia, and Jeffrey. They make these books—and everything else—possible.

—David Pogue

Many thanks to David Pogue for another great opportunity to collaborate and for his masterful writing and editing (even if keeping up with his writing prowess felt like chasing an Olympic sprinter). Thanks as well to Peter McKie for expert support and guidance, and to the O'Reilly professionals behind the scenes who make it all look incredible.

Thanks to Peter Miller for great advice, and to all the friends and family members whose smiling faces appear throughout the book. Great thanks as well to my colleagues in the Romney Institute of Public Management and the Marriott School of Management at BYU, where I am surrounded by great thinkers and talented writers.

I also join with Mac owners everywhere in giving thanks to Randy Ubillos and the entire iMovie team, whose abilities turn our home movies into treasures. Warmest thanks, in particular, to Randy for kindly and patiently answering questions.

Finally, my deepest gratitude to Katie, Luke, Sam, Thomas, and Seth for love, support, and antics that make great home movies.

—Aaron Miller

THE MISSING MANUAL SERIES

Missing Manuals are witty, superbly written guides to computer products that don't come with printed manuals (which is just about all of them). Each book features a handcrafted index.

Recent and upcoming titles include:

WordPress: The Missing Manual, Second Edition by Matthew MacDonald

iPhoto: The Missing Manual by David Pogue and Lesa Snider

iWork: The Missing Manual by Jessica Thornsby and Josh Clark

Switching to the Mac: The Missing Manual, Mavericks Edition by David Pogue

OS X Mavericks: The Missing Manual by David Pogue

HTML5: The Missing Manual, Second Edition by Matthew MacDonald

Dreamweaver CC: The Missing Manual by David Sawyer McFarland and Chris Grover

Windows 8.1: The Missing Manual by David Pogue

iPad: the Missing Manual, Sixth Edition by J.D. Biersdorfer

Quickbooks 2014: The Missing Manual by Bonnie Biafore

iPhone: the Missing Manual, Seventh Edition by David Pogue

Photoshop Elements 12: The Missing Manual by Barbara Brundage

Galaxy S4: The Missing Manual by Preston Gralla

Photoshop CC: The Missing Manual by Lesa Snider

Office 2013: The Missing Manual by Nancy Connor and Matthew MacDonald

Excel 2013: The Missing Manual by Matthew MacDonald

Microsoft Project 2013: The Missing Manual by Bonnie Biafore

Access 2013: The Missing Manual by Matthew MacDonald

For a full list of all Missing Manuals in print, go to *www.missingmanuals.com/library.html*.

Introduction

Whether this is your first time using iMovie or you're an old hand, you have a lot to look forward to. iMovie is incredibly powerful software, but you might not know it from the surface. Under the hood, it does intensely complex things (like stabilizing shaky footage) that video editors in the past would've sold their children for.

And that's the whole point of iMovie, to do amazing things with your footage without requiring years (or even days) of expertise. Still, when you first open the software, you won't realize all of iMovie's full power. This book will introduce you to iMovie, diving into all its features (and even into a few nooks and crannies), so you can draw on all its abilities.

The Difficult Birth of the New iMovie

Within six months of its release in October 1999, iMovie had become, in the words of beaming iMovie papa (and Apple CEO) Steve Jobs, "the most popular video-editing software in the world."

Apple only fanned the flames when it released iMovie 2 in July 2000 (for $50), iMovie 3 in January 2003 (for free), and then—as part of the iLife software suite—iMovie 4, iMovie HD, and iMovie 6 in successive Januaries.

Then, in August 2007, Apple dropped a bombshell. Or, rather, it dropped iMovie.

The company's new consumer video-editing program, called iMovie '08, was, in fact, not iMovie at all. It was a totally different program, using all-new code and a different design, and built by different people. It was conceived, according to Steve

Jobs, by Randy Ubillos, an Apple programmer who wanted to edit down his vacation footage—but found the old iMovie too slow and complicated. So the guy sat down and wrote his own little program, focused primarily on editing speed above all. Jobs loved it and decided that it would replace the old iMovie.

Many people were stunned by Apple's move—and I, your humble author, was among them. In my *New York Times* column, I wrote about just how different iMovie '08 was from its predecessors:

> iMovie '08 has been totally misnamed. It's not iMovie at all. It's designed for an utterly different task.
>
> The new iMovie, for example, is probably the only video-editing program on the market with no timeline—no horizontal, scrolling strip that displays your clips laid end to end, with their lengths representing their durations. You have no indication of how many minutes into your movie you are.
>
> The new iMovie also gets a D for audio editing. You can't manually adjust audio levels during a scene (for example, to make the music quieter when someone is speaking). All the old audio effects are gone, too. No pitch changing, high-pass and low-pass filters, or reverb.
>
> The new iMovie doesn't accept plug-ins, either. You can't add chapter markers for use in iDVD, which is supposed to be integrated with iMovie. Bookmarks are gone. Themes are gone. You can no longer export only part of a movie. And you can't export a movie back to tape—only to the Internet or to a file.
>
> All visual effects are gone—even basic options like slow motion, reverse motion, and fast motion. Incredibly, the new iMovie can't even convert older iMovie projects. All you can import is the clips themselves. None of your transitions, titles, credits, music, or special effects are preserved.
>
> On top of all that, this more limited iMovie has steep horsepower requirements that rule out most computers older than about two years old.

Pretty harsh, I know. But listen, I was an absolute whiz at iMovie 6. I knew it like the back of my mouse. And it looked to me like Apple was junking that mature, powerful program for what amounted to a video slideshow program.

Fortunately, Apple restored many of those "doesn't haves" in iMovie '09. The last major missing feature, detailed audio editing, showed up in another version of the program, iMovie '11. Furthermore, iMovie '11 came with so many useful features of its own that it changed the focus from what was missing to what was added.

Well, now Apple has swung the simplify hammer again. Realizing that the software was getting more complex with each new feature, it went back to the drawing board. The goal this time wasn't a complete redo, but something more like a spring cleaning. The result is a dramatically streamlined iMovie.

The new iMovie still has all the cool features the old iMovie could only dream about. Image-stabilizing, color-correction, and frame-cropping tools are unprecedented in a consumer program. The trailer-builder is downright awesome. And it's all hooked up to the Web, so you can post your masterpiece on Facebook, YouTube, or Vimeo with a single command.

iMovie also creates titles, crossfades, and color adjustments instantly. There's no "rendering" time, as there was in the old iMovie. So you gain an exhilarating freedom to play, to fiddle with the timing and placement of things, without having to watch your computer crunch the effect for 5 minutes only to decide you don't like it.

But a lot of features hit the chopping block, too. You can't tag video with keywords anymore. Your export options have been reduced. And if you used iMovie's Space Saver feature to free up hard drive space from unused, unwatched footage, I'm sorry to tell you that ability is gone, too.

Time will tell if Apple starts filling in more features again or keeps iMovie lean and trim. Just know that what you have now is all muscle.

iMovie for iOS

As you may have noticed, this book comes with a free bonus book: *iMovie for iOS: The Missing Manual*, which constitutes Chapters 18 through 24. See, iMovie's little brother works on iPhones, iPads, and iPod Touches, and it's no slouch. Those chapters will cover everything iMovie can do on a touchscreen.

A Crash Course in Video Recording

For decades, when you said "camcorder," people understood that you meant *tape* camcorder. And until about 10 years ago, that meant recording onto MiniDV cassettes.

The popularity of digital tape camcorders has permanently crashed, however. These days it's hard to even find one to watch old tapes on. Now if you buy a camcorder, it's tapeless—your footage gets saved to a memory card or hard drive. And today's cameras record in high-definition format.

But if you're like most people, you don't even own a camcorder. That's because still cameras and smartphones have taken over the world of home video.

The Switch to Tapeless Camcorders

At some point, camcorder manufacturers realized that what the world wants in a video camera is the ability to jump directly to any scene without having to wait. In theory, a tapeless camcorder also saves time because, when you transfer your video to your computer to edit it, you don't have to play the camcorder tape back from start to finish in real time. The camcorder stores your video on a memory card or hard drive as a regular computer file, which you can simply drag and drop onto your Mac's hard drive.

It used to be that tapeless camcorders couldn't match the incredible video quality of MiniDV tape cameras. To store a reasonable amount of video on a tiny memory card, hard drive, or DVD, the camera had to *compress* it to an alarming degree, using less information to describe each frame of video. Video recorded onto MiniDV tapes, on the other hand, is essentially uncompressed. What you record is what you see on playback.

Everything changed with the advent of high-definition, or HD, compression techniques. Camera manufacturers figured out a multitude of ways to compress very high-quality video onto small storage media. Today, most tapeless HD camcorders match or surpass MiniDV picture quality.

> **TIP** The world of tapeless camcorders is filled with alphabet-soup model numbers. Apple identifies all iMovie-compatible cameras at *http://help.apple.com/imovie/10/cameras*. But you should also run a Google search before you buy any camcorder to ensure that other owners of the same model have had a good experience with iMovie. (Search for *Sony HDR-CX190 iMovie*, for example.)

High Definition

The other huge change in the past decade is that camcorders now film in gorgeous, widescreen, ultrasharp *high-definition* format. The video looks absolutely incredible on an HDTV set. Your own life looks like a Hollywood movie crew filmed it. Standard definition now looks as quaint as daguerreotype photographs.

Still Cameras and Smartphones

This brings us to the latest chapter of our camcorder history class. It used to be that people carried both a digital still camera *and* a camcorder on every vacation. That's because neither one was good at doing what the other one did well. Still cameras shot only low-quality video clips that were limited in length. Camcorders could shoot only low-resolution still images that looked even worse in bad lighting.

Then still cameras started getting better. Expensive DSLRs with exchangeable lenses could shoot full-quality HD video. And what expensive cameras could do one day, inexpensive cameras could do the next. Soon enough, every digital still camera was capable of the same video quality as bulkier camcorders.

Enter the iPhone. In one fell swoop, the world of personal photography changed forever. Sure, the original iPhone took low-quality pictures, but in a few short years, it and its Android competitors were shooting HD video. They say the best camera is the one you have with you. Well, we always have our smartphones with us. And now the majority of home video is captured on a smartphone.

Lucky for you, iMovie can work with video from all these cameras.

H.264, MPEG-4, AVCHD, and Other Jargon

Tapeless camcorders store videos as ordinary computer files—on a hard drive or a memory card—that you can copy to your Mac and edit in iMovie. But what are those files? Every computer document gets stored in some kind of standardized format, whether it's JPEG image (the usual format for photos) or TXT document (a text file). So what format do video files come in?

■ H.264

Today, most smartphones record in a format called H.264. It's the same format Blu-ray disks use. It's relatively lightweight and fast, file-wise, making it appealing for smaller cameras. Because H.264 is less data intensive—meaning it compresses the video more at the cost of some quality—more expensive cameras opt for the MPEG 4 and AVCHD formats instead.

■ MPEG

Many still cameras and camcorders record in MPEG-4 format. (The abbreviation stands for Motion Picture Experts Group, the association of geeks who dream up these standards.) iMovie recognizes and imports all MPEG formats—usually. Unfortunately, there are multiple flavors of MPEG-2, used in older camcorders, and iMovie doesn't recognize them all.

> **TIP**   It's worth repeating: If you're tempted to buy a certain camcorder but you're not sure if it uses a file format that iMovie works with, Google it.

■ AVCHD

iMovie also edits *AVCHD* footage, which is the most popular file format for high-definition tapeless camcorders. (It stands for Advanced Video Coding/High Definition, and yes, it's an annoying acronym. Do they really think they're going to make video editing more attractive by dreaming up names like this?)

Anyway, AVCHD is a high-def format concocted by Sony and Panasonic in 2006, and it is now standard on camcorders from Sony, Panasonic, Canon, Samsung, and others. It offers roughly the same video quality as MPEG-4 but takes up less space on your camcorder's memory card or hard drive.

■ IFRAME

Back when HD was still on its way to becoming standard, Apple itself developed this video format in an effort to create easy-to-edit, reasonably sized video files. It doesn't record in HD (it composes the image from 540 rows of pixels instead of 720 or 1080) but it edits more smoothly on slower Macs. The underlying format is based on industry standards, so you don't need any special software to play iFrame video on a computer. That said, there's not much point to the format anymore, with HD video so ubiquitous.

Camcorder Features: Which Are Worthwhile?

So how do you know which camcorder to buy? Here's a rundown of the most frequently advertised camcorder features, along with a frank assessment of their value to the quality-obsessed iMovie fan.

■ HD CONNECTION

Most HD camcorders now let you connect your camera directly to your HDTV. Using HD connections means you can see your camera's footage at full-quality resolution on your TV.

Some cameras have jacks for component cables, which have three ends (red, blue, and green) for the video signal and two (red and white) for the sound. The jacks on your HDTV, if there, will match in color.

More and more, HD camcorders have HDMI connectors, a convenient, high-quality connection that sends video and audio signals through a single cable. The connectors are flat and rectangular and look like oversized USB connectors.

■ IMAGE STABILIZER

Certain film techniques scream "Amateur!" to audiences. One of them is the instability of handheld filming. In a nutshell, directors shoot professional video using a camera on a tripod (Woody Allen's "handheld" period notwithstanding). Most home camcorder footage, in contrast, is shot from the palm of your hand.

A stabilizing feature (which may have a marketing name, such as Sony's SteadyShot) takes a half step toward solving that problem. As shown in Figure I-1, this feature neatly eliminates the tiny, jittery moves that show up in handheld video. (It can't do anything about bigger jerks and bumps, which are especially difficult to avoid when you zoom in on a subject.) The stabilizer also uses up your battery faster.

FIGURE I-1

A digital stabilizer works by "taking in" more image than it actually uses in your final footage. The stabilizer analyzes your clip and identifies its subject. It then shifts the focus of the clip's individual frames to keep your subject centered and moving smoothly. To make this process work, the stabilizer zooms in on your image a bit. That's why you need the extra-large image capture—to compensate for the zoom-in. On less expensive camcorders, unfortunately, this zooming in means that your clip's final frames will have less video information in them than normal, to the detriment of picture quality.

This kind of anti-shake feature comes in two forms:

- **Electronic, or digital, stabilization** is what you get on cheaper camcorders. Figure I-1 describes how it works.

- **Optical stabilization** is much more preferable. It involves two transparent plates separated by a special optical fluid. As the camera shakes, these plates create a prism effect that keeps handheld shots clearer and steadier than electronic (digital) stabilizers. The images are clearer because optical stabilizers don't have to crop out part of the picture as a buffer, unlike the stabilizers illustrated in Figure I-1.

TIP What could possibly be better than image stabilization on your camcorder? Image stabilization in your editing software. You'll find iMovie's amazing stabilizing feature described on page 130.

■ MANUAL CONTROLS

Better camcorders let you turn off the camera's automatic focus, automatic exposure control, automatic white balance, and even its automatic sound level. You'll find this feature useful in certain situations, like when you want to change focus from one object to another in the same shot (known to the pros as a focus pull). If you decided to pay extra for this feature, look for a model that lets you focus manually by turning a ring on the lens casing, which is much easier than the alternative—sliders.

■ OPTICAL ZOOM

When you read the specs for a camcorder—or read the logos painted on its body—you frequently encounter phrases like "12X/300X ZOOM!" The number before the slash tells you how many times the camera can magnify a distant image, much like a telescope does. That number measures the *optical* zoom, which is the amount of magnification you get through the camcorder's lenses themselves. Such zooming, of course, is useful when you want to film something far away. (As for the number *after* the slash, see page xxiii.)

You should know, however, that the more you zoom in, the shakier your footage is likely to be, since the camera magnifies every microscopic wobble by, say, 12 times. You also have to be much more careful about focusing. When you're zoomed out all the way, everything is in focus—things near you and things far away. But when you zoom in, very near and very far objects go out of focus. Put into photographic terms, the more you zoom in, the shorter the *depth of field* (the range of distance from the camera that can be kept in focus simultaneously).

Finally, remember that magnifying the picture doesn't magnify the sound. If you rely on your camera's built-in microphone for sound, always get as close as you can to the subject, both for the sound and for the wobble.

TIP Professional video and film work includes very little zooming in, unlike most amateur videos. The best zooming is subtle zooming, such as when you very slowly "move toward" the face of somebody you're interviewing.

For this reason, when you shop for a camcorder, test its zoom feature if at all possible. Find out if the camcorder has *variable-speed* zooming, where the zooming speed increases the harder you press the Zoom button. Some camcorders offer only two speeds—fast and faster—but that's still better than having no control at all. (The standard camcorder literature doesn't usually mention whether a camera has variable-speed zooming or not; you generally have to go to the store and try it out to see how it performs.)

■ MINUTES-REMAINING READOUT

Fortunately, the problems exhibited by camcorder batteries of old are a thing of the past. One of most bothersome problems was the "memory effect." That occurred when you halfway depleted an old camcorder battery several times in a row, and the battery adopted that *halfway-empty* point as its new *completely* empty point, effectively halving the battery's capacity. The lithium-ion batteries today's camcorders use eliminate the problem.

Some video cameras—mostly from Sony, JVC, and Canon—even display, in minutes, how much recording or playback time you have left—a worthy feature.

NOTE The number of minutes' worth of recording time advertised for camcorder batteries is *continuous* recording time—that is, the time you'll get if you turn the camcorder on, press Record, and go out to lunch. If you stop and start the camera to capture shorter scenes, as almost everyone does, you'll get much less than the advertised time out of each battery charge.

■ BUILT-IN LIGHT

Insufficient lighting is one of the leading causes of "amateuritis," a telltale form of poor video quality that lets viewers know that the footage is homemade. In the best—and most expensive—of all possible worlds, you'd get your scene correctly lit before filming, or you'd attach a light to the "shoe" (light connector) on top of the camera. Those few cameras that have such a shoe, or even have a built-in light, give you a distinct advantage in capturing colors accurately.

■ SCENE MODES

Many camcorders come with a number of canned focus/shutter speed/aperture settings for different indoor and outdoor environments: Sports Lesson, Beach and Snow, Twilight, and so on. They're a useful compromise between the all-automatic operation of less expensive models and the all-manual operation of professional cameras.

■ REMOTE CONTROL

Some camcorders come with a pocket-sized remote control. It serves two purposes. First, its Record and Stop buttons let you record *yourself*, with or without other people, in a shot. Second, when you play back footage with the camcorder connected to your TV or VCR, the remote lets you control playback without needing to have the camcorder on your lap. You may be surprised at how useful the remote can be.

■ FLEXIZONE OR PUSH FOCUS

All camcorders offer automatic focus. Most work by focusing on the image in the center of your frame as you line up a shot.

That's fine if your subject is in the center of the frame. But if it's off-center, you have no choice but to turn off the autofocus feature and use the manual-focus ring. (Using a camcorder isn't like using a still camera, where you can point the camera directly at the subject for focusing purposes, and then—before taking the shot—shift the angle so that the subject is no longer in the center. Camcorders continually refocus, so pointing the camera slightly away from your subject makes you lose the off-center focus you established.)

Some Canon, Sony, and Sharp camcorders let you specify the spot in a frame that you want to serve as the focus point, even if it's not the center of the picture. (Canon calls this feature FlexiZone; Sony calls it Push Focus. On Sony cams with touchscreen LCD panels, it's especially easy to indicate which spot in the frame should get the focus.) If the model you're eyeing has this feature, it's worth having.

■ NIGHT-VISION MODE

Most Sony camcorders offer a mode called NightShot that works like night-vision goggles. You can actually film (and see, as you watch the LCD screen) in total darkness. The infrared transmitter on the front of the camcorder measures the heat given off by various objects in its path, letting you capture an eerie, greenish night scene. Rent *The Silence of the Lambs* for an idea of how creepy night-vision filming can be. Or watch any episode of *Survivor*.

The transmitter's range is only about 15 feet or so. Still, you may be surprised how often it comes in handy: on campouts, during sleepovers, on nighttime nature walks, and so on.

■ STILL PHOTOS

All modern camcorders can take still photos. The camera freezes one frame of what it's seeing and records it as a regular JPEG file on a memory card.

The still-photo image quality, unfortunately, is pretty terrible. The resolution may be OK (some camcorders offer up to 5-megapixel resolution), but the quality isn't anywhere near what you'd get using a dedicated digital still camera.

Useless Features

Here are some features you'll see in camcorder advertising that you should ignore (and definitely not pay extra for).

■ TITLE GENERATOR

Some camcorders let you superimpose *titles* (that is, text) on your video as you film. In your case, dear iMovie owner, a title-generating feature is useless. Your Mac can add gorgeous, smooth-edged type, with a selection of sizes, fonts, colors, and even scrolling animations, to your finished movies, with far more precision and power than the blocky text available on your camcorder. (Chapter 10 shows you how.)

NOTE A title generator on a camcorder is actually *worse* than useless, because it permanently stamps your original footage with something you may wish you could amend later. In fact, as a general rule, you should avoid using (or paying for) *any* of the in-camera editing features described in this chapter—title generator, fader, special effects—because you can do this kind of editing much more effectively in iMovie. Not only are the in-camera features redundant, but they also commit you to an editing choice in advance, thus limiting how you can use your footage.

◼ SPECIAL EFFECTS

Most camcorders offer a selection of six or seven cheesy-looking special effects. They can make your footage look solarized, or digitized, or otherwise processed (see Figure I-2).

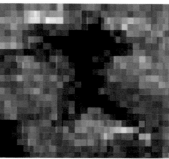

FIGURE I-2

Using the stock collection of special effects built into your camcorder, you can create special, hallucinogenic visuals. The question is: Why?

Avoid using these effects. iMovie has its own special-effects options, and it gives you far greater control over when they start, when they end, and how intensely they affect the video.

In fact, unless you're shooting a documentary about nuclear explosions or bad drug episodes, consider avoiding these effects altogether.

◼ DATE/TIME STAMP

Every camcorder offers the ability to stamp the date and time directly onto your footage. As you've no doubt seen (on *America's Funniest Home Videos* or *World's Wildest Police Videos*), the result is a blocky, typographically hideous stamp that permanently mars your footage. Few things take the romance out of a wedding video, or are more distracting in spectacular weather footage, than a huge **20 NOV 14 12:34 PM** stamped in the corner.

Nor do you have to worry that you'll one day forget when you filmed some event. As it turns out, digital camcorders automatically and invisibly date- and time-stamp *all* your footage. You'll be able to see this information when you connect the camera to your Mac; then you can choose whether or not to add the stamp to the finished footage (and with much more control over its timing, location, and typography).

■ DIGITAL ZOOM

Much as camera owners mistakenly jockey for superiority by comparing the mega-pixel ratings of their cameras (more megapixels doesn't necessarily make for sharper pictures), camcorder makers seem to think that what consumers want most in a camcorder is a powerful digital zoom. Your camcorder's packaging may "boast" digital zoom ratings of "50X," "100X," or "500X!"

When a camcorder uses its *digital* zoom—the number after the slash on the camcorder box tells you its maximum magnification—it simply enlarges the individual dots that compose an image. Yes, the image gets bigger, but it doesn't get any *sharper*. As the dots get larger, the image gets chunkier, coarser, and less recognizable, until it ends up looking like the blocky areas you see superimposed over criminals' faces to conceal their identities on *Cops*. After your digital zoom feature has blown up the picture by 3X, the image falls to pieces. Greater digital zoom is not something worth paying for.

The Long-Term Storage Problem

No matter which kind of camcorder you choose, you have more to think about than features and price; you have the future to consider. Once the memory card or drive is full, you're finished shooting for the day. The camera is worthless until you offload the video to a computer, thereby freeing up space to continue shooting.

Once it's on your computer, what do you do with all of this footage? Backing up to DVDs is no longer a feasible option. (Newer Macs don't even come with DVD drives.) You could, of course, just keep the video on hard drives. Here again, though, you have to wonder: Will the hard drive you buy today still work 50 years from now?

The solution to all these problems is, of course, simple vigilance. Every five or so years, you should copy your masterworks onto newer hard drives, or whatever the latest storage format happens to be.

■ About This Book

Don't let the rumors fool you. iMovie may be simple, but it's not simplistic. Unfortunately, many of the best techniques aren't covered in the only "manual" you get with iLife—its electronic help screens.

This book is designed to serve as the iMovie manual, as the book that should have been in the box. It explores each iMovie feature in depth, offers illustrated catalogs of the various title and transition effects, provides shortcuts and workarounds, and unearths features that iMovie's online help doesn't even mention.

TIP Your camcorder and iMovie produce video of stunning visual and audio quality, giving you the *technical* tools to produce amazing videos. But most people don't have much experience with the *artistic* side of shooting—lighting, sound, and composition—or even how to use the dozens of buttons found on modern camcorders. If you visit this book's Missing CD page at *http://oreilly.com/missingmanuals/cds/imovie2014/* (see page xxvii), you'll find a bonus appendix in PDF form: three chapters designed to give you the basics of lighting, composition, and camera technique.

About the Outline

iMovie: The Missing Manual is divided into four parts, each with several chapters:

- **Part One** introduces iMovie with a tour, shows you how to transfer your footage into iMovie, manage events, and work with projects.

- **Part Two** covers every aspect of making a movie, from the basics of piecing together clips to advanced features like video effects, cutaways, music, titles, and iMovie's incredible trailers feature.

- **Part Three** helps you share your cinematic masterpiece with the world. iMovie excels at exporting your work to the Web, to YouTube, to an iPhone or an iPad, to an Apple TV, or to just a QuickTime file on your hard drive. This part of the book offers step-by-step instructions for each method and shows you how to use QuickTime Player to supplement the editing tools in iMovie.

- **Part Four** is dedicated to iMovie for iOS, iMovie's little brother that runs on iPhones, iPads, and iPod Touches.

At the end of the book, four appendixes await:

- **"Appendix A: iMovie, Menu by Menu"** provides a menu-by-menu explanation of iMovie's commands.

- **"Appendix B: Troubleshooting"** is a comprehensive handbook for solving problems.

- **"Appendix C: Master Keyboard Shortcut List"** is a master cheat sheet of iMovie's shortcuts.

- **"Appendix D: Visual Cheat Sheet"** is a visual reference to all the little symbols, stripes, and color-coded doodads that, sooner or later, will clutter up your iMovie window and leave you bewildered. Turn to this two-page cheat sheet in times of panic.

◼ The Very Basics

You'll find very little jargon or nerd terminology in *iMovie: The Missing Manual*. You will, however, encounter a few terms and concepts you'll see frequently in your computing life:

- **Clicking.** This book offers three kinds of instructions that require you to use the mouse or trackpad attached to your Mac. To *click* means to point the arrow cursor at something onscreen and then—without moving the cursor at all—press and release the clicker button on the mouse (or laptop trackpad). To *double-click*, of course, means to click twice in rapid succession, again without moving the cursor at all. And to *drag* means to move the cursor while keeping the button continuously pressed.

> **NOTE** In the iMovie for iOS part of this book, the lingo changes from clicking to *tapping*. There's no mouse cursor; you do everything with your fingers and the touchscreen of your iPhone, iPad, or iPod Touch.

When you're told to ⌘-*click* something, you click while pressing the ⌘ key (next to the space bar). Such related procedures as *Shift-clicking*, *Option-clicking*, and *Control-clicking* work the same way—just click while pressing the corresponding key on the bottom row of your keyboard.

> **NOTE** Apple has officially changed the name it uses for the little menu that pops up when you Control-click (or right-click) something on the screen. It's still a *contextual* menu, in that the menu choices depend on what you click—but it's now called a *shortcut* menu. That term not only matches what Windows calls pop-up menus, but it's also slightly more descriptive of its function. "Shortcut menu" is the term you'll find used in this book.

- **Menus.** The *menus* are the words at the top of your screen: File, Edit, and so on. Click one to make a list of commands appear, as though they're written on a window shade you just pulled down. Some people click to open a menu and then release the mouse button; then, after reading the menu choices, they click the command they want. Other people like to press the mouse button and go down the list of commands to the desired one; only then do they release the button. Both methods work, so use whichever you prefer.

> **NOTE** On Windows PCs, the mouse has two buttons. The left one is for clicking normally; the right one produces a tiny shortcut menu of useful commands. (See the previous Note.) But new Macs come with either a single-button trackpad or a Apple's Magic Mouse, a mouse that is just one big button but can actually detect which side of its rounded top you press. If you turn on this feature in System Preferences, you, too, can right-click things on the screen.
>
> That's why, all through this book, you'll see the phrase, "Control-click the photo (or right-click it)." That tells you that Control-clicking will do the job—but if you've got a two-button mouse or if you turned on the two-button feature of the Magic Mouse, right-clicking might be more efficient.

- **Keyboard shortcuts.** Every time you take your hand off the keyboard to move the mouse, you lose time and potentially disrupt your creative flow. That's why many experienced Mac fans use keystroke combinations instead of menu commands wherever possible. ⌘-P opens the Print dialog box, for example, and ⌘-M minimizes the current window to the Dock.

When you see a shortcut like ⌘-Q (which closes the current program), it's telling you to hold down the ⌘ key, and, while it's down, type the letter Q, and then release both keys.

If you've mastered this much information, you have all the technical background you need to enjoy *iMovie: The Missing Manual*.

About→These→Arrows

Throughout this book, and throughout the Missing Manual series, you'll find sentences like this one: "Open your Home→Library→Preferences folder." That's shorthand for a much longer instruction that directs you to open three nested folders in sequence, like this: "In the Finder, choose Go→Home. In your Home folder, you'll find a folder called Library. Click it to open it. Inside the Library window is a folder called Preferences. Click it, too."

Similarly, this kind of arrow shorthand helps to simplify the business of choosing commands in menus, as shown in Figure I-3.

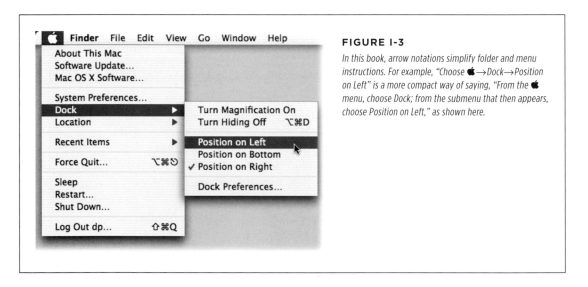

FIGURE I-3

In this book, arrow notations simplify folder and menu instructions. For example, "Choose ⌘→Dock→Position on Left" is a more compact way of saying, "From the ⌘ menu, choose Dock; from the submenu that then appears, choose Position on Left," as shown here.

■ Online Resources

As the owner of a Missing Manual, you've got more than just a book to read. At the Missing Manuals' website, you'll find example files as well as tips, articles, and maybe even a video or two. You can also communicate with the Missing Manual team and tell us what you love (or hate) about the book. Head over to *www.missingmanuals. com*, or go directly to one of the following sections.

The Missing CD

This book doesn't have a CD pasted inside the back cover, but you're not missing out on anything. Go to *http://oreilly.com/missingmanuals/cds/imovie2014/* to download additional information mentioned in this book.

Registration

If you register this book at the O'Reilly Media website (*www.oreilly.com*), you'll be eligible for special offers—like discounts on future editions of this book. Registering takes only a few clicks. Type *http://tinyurl.com/registerbook* into your browser to hop directly to the Registration page.

Feedback

Got questions? Need more information? Fancy yourself a book reviewer? On our Feedback page, you can get expert answers to questions that come to you while reading, share your thoughts on this Missing Manual, and find groups for folks who share your interest in iMovie. To have your say, go to *www.missingmanuals.com/feedback*.

Errata

To keep this book as up to date and accurate as possible, each time we print more copies, we'll make any confirmed corrections you suggest. We also note such changes on the book's website, so you can mark important corrections into your own copy of the book, if you like. Go to *http://tinyurl.com/imovieerrata* to report an error and to view existing corrections.

▇ Safari® Books Online

Safari Books Online is an on-demand digital library that lets you easily search over 7,500 technology and creative reference books and videos to find the answers you need quickly.

With a subscription, you can read any page and watch any video from our library online. Read books on your cell phone and mobile devices. Access new titles before they are available for print, and get exclusive access to manuscripts in development and post feedback for the authors. Copy and paste code samples, organize your favorites, download chapters, bookmark key sections, create notes, print out pages, and benefit from tons of other time-saving features.

O'Reilly Media has uploaded this book to the Safari Books Online service. To have full digital access to this book and others on similar topics from O'Reilly and other publishers, sign up for free at *http://safaribooksonline.com*.

iMovie Basics

Introducing iMovie

Whether you've been an iMovie fan since the program debuted way back in 1999 or you're taking your first foray into editing home movies, you'll be impressed by iMovie's features and your ability to edit video on both your Mac desktop and any iOS device you have.

In brief, iMovie is video-editing software that grabs the raw footage from your camcorder, camera, phone, or computer and lets you edit it easily, quickly, and creatively. In this chapter, you'll learn the many ways you can use iMovie (some of which may surprise you) and take a look at the iMovie workspace.

■ The iMovie Revolution

Over the decades, home movies have gotten a bad rap. Do some random browsing on YouTube and you'll find all kinds of offenders: unending shots of cats sleeping on sofas, high-school plays filmed from the back of the auditorium, and random vacation moments where the camera shakes enough to simulate an earthquake.

Most people know that you can improve home movies by editing out the bad parts and concentrating on the good, but until iMovie came along, that was an expensive and time-consuming undertaking. You needed several thousand dollars' worth of digitizing cards, complicated editing software, and the highest-powered computer equipment available. Unless you were getting a paycheck at the end of the process, editing your own movies just wasn't worth it.

Then along came iMovie, the world's least expensive version of what Hollywood pros call *nonlinear* editing software. In the old days, your recorded footage sat on a videotape, and you edited your clips in linear fashion—you laboriously rewound and fast-forwarded through every frame of the tape to get to the parts you wanted. Nowadays, you don't do any rewinding or fast-forwarding; you can instantly jump to any piece of footage you want.

Why does this history lesson matter? Because it feels pretty dang cool to know that, right there on your Mac, you have video-editing powers that not long ago would've left trained professionals drooling. Little old you can take the cats, the high-school plays, and the vacations and make them look downright epic. With iMovie and a camera, you're ready to go.

iMovie's Many Roles

If you're reading this book, you probably have some idea of the kind of movies you want to make. Here are a few possibilities you may not have thought of. All are natural projects for iMovie:

- **Home movies.** Plain old home movies—casual documentaries of your life, your kids' lives, your school life, your trips—are the single most popular use for iMovie. Using the program, you can delete all but the best scenes (and cut that unending shot of the ground when you forgot to turn off your camcorder). And using the shooting tips you'll find in this book, you can improve the quality of that footage even before you shoot.

- **Web movies.** But why limit your aspirations to people you know? If you've got something funny or interesting on "film," why not share it with the Internet at large? In iMovie, posting to YouTube, Vimeo, and Facebook are only a menu command away—and that's just the beginning. New film festivals, websites, and magazines, all dedicated to independent makers of *short* movies, are springing up everywhere.

- **Business videos.** Because it's so easy to post and share your iMovie creations on the Internet, you should consider video a useful tool in whatever you do. If you're a real estate agent, blow away your rivals (and save your clients time) by showing movies, not still photos, of the properties you represent. If you're an executive, quit boring your comrades with stupefying PowerPoint slides and make your point with video instead.

- **Video photo albums.** A video photo album can be much more exciting, accessible, and engaging than one on paper. Take your digital photos and assemble them in sequence, and then add some crossfades, titles, and music. The result is a much more interesting display than a book of motionless images, thanks in part to iMovie's Ken Burns effect (page 217).

- **Just-for-fun projects.** Never again can anyone over the age of 8 complain that there's "nothing to do." Set your kids loose with a camera and instructions to make a fake rock video, commercial, or documentary.

- **Training films.** If there's a better use for video than how-to instruction, you'd be hard-pressed to name it. Make a video for new employees to show them the ropes. Create a video that ships with your product to humanize your company and to help customers make the most of their purchases. Post videos on the Web to teach newcomers how to play the banjo, grow a garden, kick a football, or use a computer program—and then market it.

- **Interviews.** You're lucky enough to live in an age when you can manipulate video clips in a movie just as easily as you do words in a word processor. Capitalize on this. Create family histories. Film relatives who still remember the War, the Birth, the Immigration. Or create a time-capsule, time-lapse film: Ask your kids or parents the same four questions every year on their birthdays (such as, "What's your greatest worry right now?" or "If you had one wish...?" or "Where do you want to be in 5 years?"). Then, after 5 or 10 or 20 years, splice together the answers for an enlightening fast-forward through a human life.

- **Broadcast segments.** Want a taste of the real world? Call your cable TV company about its public-access channels. (As required by law, every cable company offers a channel or two for ordinary citizens to use for their own programming.) Find out the time and format restraints, and then make a documentary, short film, or other piece for actual broadcast. Advertise the airing to everyone you know. It's a small-time start, but it's real broadcasting.

  Of course, you could skip the small time and upload your videos straight from iMovie to CNN's iReport website. Here, amateur reporters post their own news items for all the world to watch. On occasion, CNN even turns to these videos for its nationwide broadcasts.

- **Analyze performance.** There's no better way to improve your golf swing, tennis form, musical performance, or public speaking style than to study footage of yourself. If you're a teacher, camp counselor, or coach, then film your students, campers, or players so that they can benefit from self-analysis, too.

■ iMovie, the Program

Although you need a Mac and a camera to capture your adventures, the iMovie story is really all about *software*, both the footage as it exists on your Mac and the iMovie program itself. So a few basics about iMovie are in order.

iMovie on a New Mac

If you bought a Mac after October 2013, the latest version of iMovie is probably already on your hard drive. To see, open the Mac's Finder, select Applications, and then look for the iMovie entry. If iMovie is indeed preinstalled, you'll probably find its star-shaped icon (⭐) sitting in your Mac's Dock, too.

iMovie for an Existing Mac

If your Mac didn't come with iMovie, you can get it from Apple's App Store, a built-in software shop that every Mac links to—find it quickly by clicking ✿→App Store. Once in the virtual store, type *iMovie* into the search box. There you can read all about the program and start downloading and installing it (Figure 1-1).

FIGURE 1-1

To install the latest version of iMovie, go to the App Store (✿→App Store). If you have iMovie '11, you'll get the upgrade for free. If not, get ready to shell out $14.99.

If you bought your previous versions of iMovie from the App Store, or if you have iMovie '11 already on your Mac, you'll get the newest version as a free upgrade. If not, Apple will ask you to pony up $14.99. (If that seems steep, consider that previous versions of iMovie came in a software bundle called iLife that cost anywhere from $50 to $80.)

Apple says iMovie requires a Mac running OS X Mavericks (version 10.9) or later. Apple also recommends at least 4 GB of memory. It goes without saying, of course, that the more memory you have (and the bigger your screen and the faster your processor), the happier you and iMovie will be. This program is *seriously* hungry for horsepower.

TIP   Consider installing GarageBand from the App Store, too, even if you're not a musician. It can help you edit the sound for your movie, and it's free for everyone.

iMovie takes up almost 2 GB of your hard drive. When you finish downloading it, you'll find iMovie in your Applications folder and the iMovie icon in your Dock.

NOTE   Installing the new version of iMovie doesn't replace or remove older versions. Once you install the new version, you'll find the older version in a folder called "iMovie 9.0.9" (or whatever iMovie version you had) in your Applications folder, ready to run when necessary.

Keep this older version around for a while. The latest version of iMovie might be missing some features that you counted on in the past. These features may find their way back into the program with future updates, but in the meantime you can always go back to the older software.

".1" Updates

Like any other software company, Apple occasionally releases new versions of iMovie: version 10.1, version 10.2, and so on (or even 10.1.1, then 10.1.2, and so on). Each "point" upgrade (as in "iMovie ten-point-one") is free and improves the program's reliability. Upgrades are well worth installing for any program, but they're especially important for iMovie—they do more than squash bugs; they often add features you want.

You don't have to look far to find these updates. One day you'll be online and a notification will pop up onscreen, letting you know that there's a new "point" update for your version of iMovie, and offering to install it for you. (If you set your App Store preferences to install updates automatically, your Mac will download and install the update without any input from you. You can turn on this option at →System Preferences→App Store.)

When the updater finishes, your original copy of iMovie has morphed into the updated version of the program. (One way to find out what version of iMovie you have is to open the program and then choose iMovie→About iMovie.)

This book assumes that you have at least iMovie 10.0.3.

◼ Getting into iMovie

After you install iMovie, open it by double-clicking its icon in the Applications folder, or by single-clicking the star-shaped icon (✷) in the Dock.

Now, just in case you had somehow forgotten that iMovie is a totally new program, a special starter screen appears to let you know. Click Continue to get a rundown of iMovie's new features (Figure 1-2).

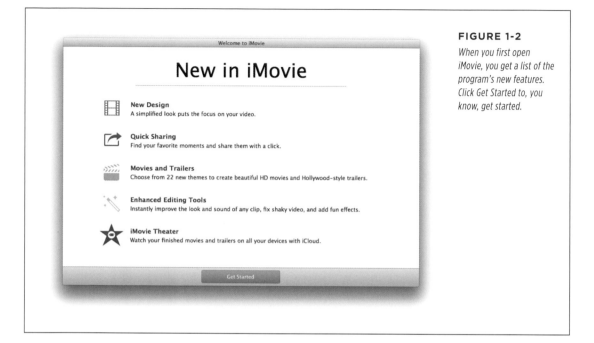

FIGURE 1-2

When you first open iMovie, you get a list of the program's new features. Click Get Started to, you know, get started.

Tour iMovie

The latest version of iMovie boasts a shiny new appearance. If you've used a prior version of the program over the past few years, you'll see a *mostly* familiar layout. Although Apple changed a lot with this version, the basic concepts are the same. Here's a tour of what you'll find once you launch the program—please keep your arms and legs in the vehicle at all times.

The Lay of the Land

If you've never used iMovie before, the program looks pretty barren when you first launch it—no raw footage, no movie-in-progress: You essentially have a blank canvas. But if you're upgrading iMovie, or if you spend a little time importing footage into the new version (page 13), you see a screen that looks like the one in Figure 1-3.

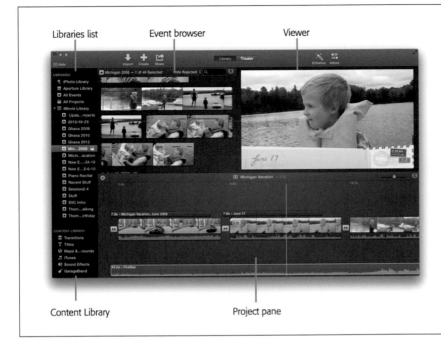

Libraries list   Event browser   Viewer

Content Library   Project pane

FIGURE 1-3

Once you import some video into iMovie (Chapter 2), you're ready to get to work. See the bullet points that follow for an explanation of the components labeled here.

An iMovie full of footage is a happy-looking iMovie. At first glance, it can also be a confusing iMovie. Here's a summary of the parts of the window shown in Figure 1-3. You'll learn about each of them in detail on the coming pages.

- **Libraries list.** iMovie stores all your imported footage here, organized by event (see page 27).

- **Event browser.** Here's where you review your imported footage and select the good bits for inclusion in your movie.

- **Viewer.** Review either your raw footage or your movie-in-progress here.

- **Content Library.** Here live the stock goodies that iMovie provides to jazz up your production.

- **Project pane.** This is where you build your movie, piece by piece, by dragging the footage you choose in the Event browser here.

Use Old Clips with the New iMovie

Upgrading iMovie from a prior version can take some time. Like, a *lot* of time. That's because the program makes a copy of your old iMovie clips so you can use the footage with the new version of the program.

The upside is that if you find yourself wanting to head back to the old iMovie to work on some prior projects in their original format, Apple thoughtfully held onto the clips for you.

The downside is that an iMovie library is usually really big, like dozens of gigabytes large. If you haven't got a lot of free hard drive space, you can kiss what free space you do have goodbye. Unfortunately, the only solution is to get rid of stuff. You can commit whole hog and delete your old iMovie library from the Finder, or you can delete footage from the old or new libraries. (See page 80 for help on deleting footage in the new iMovie.)

Events and Projects: The Core of Moviemaking

As Figure 1-3 shows, iMovie dedicates most of its screen real estate to two panes, the Event browser and the Project pane. The Event window displays all your raw footage, and the Project pane is where you assemble your clips into a movie. You'll do most of your work in these two windows.

> **NOTE** The Event browser is called that because, for most people, the things you film tend to be organized around events in your life, like vacations, weddings, and graduations. You'll learn all about events in Chapter 3.

The most basic edit you'll make in iMovie is highlighting some footage in the Event browser and sticking it into the Project pane. This simple process is described extensively in Chapter 5.

The new version of iMovie lets you display or hide the Project pane. (The old version dedicated permanent real estate to it.) In Figure 1-3, you can see a little ⊗ in the top-left corner of the Project pane. Click that and the Project pane disappears, leaving a usefully bigger Event browser, along with a bigger Viewer (see the next section). That's one of the many changes to how projects now work, covered in Chapter 4.

The Viewer

The Viewer sits in the top-right corner of the iMovie window. Its name is deceptive, though, because you can do a lot more than view your movie here. You can make quite a few cosmetic edits here, too, like correcting color and cropping frames (iMovie calls these edits "adjustments"). Take a look at Figure 1-4 to see some of the tools that call the Viewer home.

> **NOTE** In iMovies past, you used to be able to use a second monitor for the Viewer, giving you both a larger preview and more space for your project and event footage. This version of iMovie no longer sports that feature. Hopefully, Apple will reinstate it.

FIGURE 1-4

The Viewer's two states.

Top: This is the simple version, where you see the video clip you're working on.

Bottom: This is the "adjustments" version, where you can do things like change color, crop the frame, and add audio effects. (You call up these tools by clicking the Adjust button above the Viewer window; see Figure 1-3.)

The Content Library

Making movies takes a lot more than just piecing clips together. You'll also want to include professional elements like titles, music, transitions, and photographs. You'll turn to the Content Library for these sorts of things. Think of it as the place you'll find anything that's not a video clip. (In other words, the Content Library contains everything but "content.")

Figure 1-3 shows the Content Library in the lower-left corner. You'll learn about each of the items there in the chapters to follow. In the meantime, click around and explore the tools. You can waste a good hour entertaining yourself with the sound effects alone.

First Things First: Import Your Footage into iMovie

Before you can do any editing, you need some video to work with, and that's where this chapter comes in. In it, you'll learn how to import your raw footage, and, with a little help from iMovie, how to keep your clips in good order.

◼ Importing Video

When you import raw footage into iMovie, it winds up in a sort of folder known as an event. Why? Because Apple figures that most of what you record revolves around events in your life, like vacations, weddings, and graduations. And if, over time, you import hours of footage, you (and iMovie) need some way to organize all that material. That's why, when you import footage from, say, your iPhone, iMovie asks you to assign that video to an event (or to create an event to assign it to).

You'll learn all about events in the next chapter, but for now, it's time to import your clips to iMovie.

Importing Basics

You can get your raw footage from a lot of sources, only one of which is a camcorder (do they even make those anymore?). For example, iPhones, iPads, and iPod Touches shoot video, as do almost all digital still cameras. Most cameras store your footage as files, but some older cameras store it on tape or even on a DVD.

But no matter the source, any importing you do involves five initial steps:

1. **Connect the device to your Mac.**

   How you connect it depends on *what* you're connecting, but to do any import-ing, you have to connect a device to your Mac. That applies even if you want to import a movie that's on your Mac's hard drive—even your drive's connected.

2. **Click Import in the iMovie toolbar.**

   The Import button is a giant downward-pointing arrow at the top of the iMovie window. (Alternatively, you can press ⌘-I.) Once you do, iMovie opens the Import window.

3. **Choose the source of your raw footage.**

   iMovie lists all the possible sources of video on the left side of the Import window: cameras, hard drives, and memory cards. Select the device you're importing from.

4. **Select your movie file.**

   Once you select a source, iMovie shows all of the files in that source—the different scenes you've shot. Preview the specific clips you want to import by selecting each one and watching it in the Viewer.

5. **In the "Import to" drop-down menu, pick the event where you want to store your footage.**

   Once you select your movie file, your instinct might be to click the highlighted Import Selected button in the bottom-right corner of the window. Don't! You first need to tell iMovie in which event you want your footage stored. Otherwise, you might stash your movie in the wrong place.

   At the top of the Import window and smack-dab in the middle is the "Import to" menu. Use it to choose (or create) the destination event for your footage. Figure 2-1 shows this menu at work and explains what you need to do.

The following descriptions explain the details of importing from a particular source, picking up from where these five steps leave off.

From an iPhone/iPad/iPod Touch

Apple calls the iPhone the most popular camera on the planet, and, considering how convenient it is to capture those random moments with it, the claim certainly has merit. Whether you're shooting with an iPhone, iPad, or iPod Touch, iMovie can import its footage for you.

FIGURE 2-1

iMovie's Import window. Before you import a clip, be sure to choose the right destination event from the "Import to" menu. If you don't see an event you like, choose New Event to name and create one.

With your iDevice connected and the Import window open, iMovie displays your video clips using sample frames (Figure 2-2), and denotes the length of each clip with a little time indicator in the corner. You can preview a clip by moving your cursor over it without clicking: The viewer window above "plays" your footage as you skim. (See page 52 for more on skimming.) You can also play back a clip in full by selecting it and then clicking ▶ in the viewer window (the playback button appears only when you mouse over the window).

You can select and import *photos*, too. To see your source-material options, go to the drop-down menu in the top-right corner of the Import window and choose Videos, Photos, or Photos and Videos. To adjust your preview options, click the filmstrip icon beside the drop-down menu. There, you can change the size of the clips for easier previewing, show the audio waveforms (page 42) that go along with a clip, or tell iMovie to show or hide clips you've already imported.

FIGURE 2-2

Before you import video from an iPhone, iPad, or iPod Touch, iMovie shows you all the clips on the device. Choose the clip(s) you want to import, select a destination event, and then click Import Selected.

NOTE Once you import a clip from your iDevice, iMovie hides it from the list of available clips the next time you try to import video. This is convenient—unless you want to import a clip again. In that case, you can override the factory setting by clicking the filmstrip icon in the top-right of the import window and turning off Hide Imported Clips.

Once you're ready to start importing clips, follow these steps:

1. **Select the clips you want to import.**

   Select a clip by clicking it. A yellow border confirms your selection. (If you don't select *any* clips, then iMovie imports *all* the clips on your iDevice.)

2. **Click Import Selected (or Import All).**

   Once you do, iMovie displays the destination event you selected as it fills it up with your footage. It displays a little progress disc in the bottom-left corner (Figure 2-3, top).

Don't disconnect your iDevice right after you click the Import button—it takes some time to transfer the video files to your Mac. When iMovie finishes importing, it lets you know (Figure 2-3, bottom).

FIGURE 2-3

Top: As iMovie imports your clips, it displays a progress disc (lower-left corner).

Bottom: Once iMovie finishes the import, it lets you know that it's safe to disconnect your iDevice.

From a Camera or Camcorder

These days, pretty much all digital cameras shoot both photos *and* video. That means everything from a fancy digital SLR to the humble point-and-shoot can be a video camera. Video *quality* is another question entirely, because not all cameras are created equal.

Whatever camera you use, you probably connect it to your Mac with a USB cable, which comes with your camcorder (see Figure 2-4). (You can also pop out your camera's memory card, as described in the next section.)

Your camera may also need to be in a particular setting to talk to your Mac. The wording might vary and some cameras may sense the connection automatically, but every camera or camcorder has a mode for making PC or Mac connections (Figure 2-5).

Once you set up your Mac so it can see your camera, the camera shows up in the Import window's list of sources. From that point on, importing from your camera is identical to importing from an iPhone, iPad, or iPod Touch—follow steps 1 and 2 in the previous section.

TIP Every modern camera can talk to iMovie, but if you're considering a camera purchase and want to be sure, Apple offers a list of iMovie-compatible cameras at *http://help.apple.com/imovie/10/cameras/*.

FIGURE 2-4

Most cameras and camcorders come with a USB cable. The small end plugs into your camcorder (you may have to open some tiny plastic door on the camera to find the jack). The big end plugs into any of your Mac's USB jacks.

FIGURE 2-5

Camcorders and cameras generally have a switch or command that lets you connect it to a PC (or, in this case, to a Mac). It might be a dedicated position on the camera's "mode" dial, as shown here.

From an SD Card

Almost every recent Mac model comes with an SD card slot. (An SD card is the little postage-stamp-sized memory card most digital cameras use to store your photos.) Having a slot in your Mac means you can take the SD card out of your camera and plug it right into your computer, saving you the trouble of using a cable to connect.

NOTE If you're importing from a camera that uses tape, skip ahead to the next section.

Importing from an SD card works just like importing from a camera; the card shows up in iMovie the same way a connected camera does. If, instead of that, the card shows up as a drive, nestled in with the hard drives connected to your Mac, you probably don't actually have any videos or photos on the card.

NOTE Be sure you properly eject an SD card before pulling it out of your Mac. In iMovie, you do this from the Import window by clicking the Eject button next to the card's name.

From a Tape Camcorder or DV Deck

Browsing and picking individual clips from a camera is a relatively new convenience. Once upon a time, people recorded video onto tapes. The most popular of these was the MiniDV tape, and you may have a drawer full of them. The convenience of flash-based storage like SD cards put DV tapes out to pasture.

Luckily, as historical as this format has become, iMovie can still speak the ancient tape language. You'll need a few things to get this to work.

The first is a DV-based camera or deck. You may still have your old MiniDV camera around; as long as it still operates, it should work with your Mac. Alternatively, you can use a DV deck, which is a box dedicated to reading DV tapes. Either of these should have a Firewire connection on it, which brings you to the next thing you need.

Because pretty much every DV-tape-based camera and deck uses Firewire to connect to your Mac, you'll need a Firewire *cable*. Firewire connections come in two flavors: Firewire 400 and Firewire 800. This latest version of iMovie doesn't work on Macs with Firewire 400 connections (they're too old), so if you have a Firewire port on your Mac, it's probably the 800 variety (Figure 2-6).

The big end of the cable goes into the Firewire jack on the side or back of your Mac; it's marked by a radioactive-looking ⚡ symbol. The small end goes into your camera or deck.

If you have a Mac with no Firewire port of any kind, then you'll need an adapter. Apple sells one for current Macs (those that have Thunderbolt connections) for $30.

You'll also need to set your camcorder to playback mode, labeled Play, VCR, VTR, or just ▶ (Figure 2-7). Once you do that, follow steps 1–4 on page 14, and then follow the steps outlined next.

FIGURE 2-6

To connect a DV-tape camera to your Mac, you'll need a Firewire cable like the one pictured here. It has a Firewire 800 connector on the big end and a 4-pin connector in the little end.

FIGURE 2-7

Your camcorder's Play mode should be a fairly prominent knob or menu setting. If you can't find it, check the manual.

1. Cue the tape to the right spot.

This may be at a certain moment, like when everyone starts singing "Happy Birthday," or it may just be the beginning of the tape if you're importing the whole thing. You can use the playback controls on the camera, or the ones in the iMovie Import window (Figure 2-8).

FIGURE 2-8

When you import from a tape-based camera, use the Viewer's controls to cue the tape and preview what you're importing. Click Import to tell iMovie to start recording the footage to your Mac.

2. Click Import.

iMovie starts to play the tape, importing it as it goes. You can't import any faster than the tape can play back (one of the reasons people ditched tape-based camcorders), so if you're capturing 10 minutes of footage, it will take 10 minutes to import it. As iMovie captures your clip, it tells you how much it's taken in, measured in minutes and seconds.

3. Click Stop Import.

You can stop the import whenever you want. If you let iMovie import the rest of the tape, it stops on its own at the end of the tape. Most tapes can hold an hour (or more) of footage, so if you're importing an entire tape, don't bother hanging around until it's done. When you finish importing, close the Import window.

The footage you import shows up in your chosen event. You'll also notice a handy feature when iMovie finishes importing footage: The program automatically creates an individual filmstrip (clip) for each scene you shot. So an hour's worth of tape doesn't wind up as a single, mega-chunk of video—instead, you wind up with 30 or 40 individual clips, just the way you shot them.

That's because, behind the scenes, iMovie studies the *date and time stamp* that digital camcorders record on every frame of video. When iMovie detects a break in time, it assumes that you stopped recording, if only for a moment, and therefore considers the next piece of footage a new shot. It turns each new shot into a new clip.

NOTE DV tapes don't age well. If your imported video looks pixelated in strange ways, or if iMovie doesn't break clips apart correctly, an old tape is probably the culprit. Unfortunately, there's no way to fix this. Yet another reason tape-based camcorders lost to more modern ones. (And a reason to get those old DV tapes imported sooner rather than later.)

From a DVD Camcorder

DVD camcorders, like tape-based cameras, are also historic these days, but more like historical oddities. In general, DVD camcorders were a mess. They were fussy, took a long time to "initialize" and "finalize" a blank DVD, each disc didn't hold very much footage, and the recorded discs had a short lifespan.

This latest version of iMovie recognizes only two DVD camcorder models, the Sony HDR-UX20 and Sony HDR-UX20E. You can import from these two cameras the same way you do for an iPhone, iPad, or iPod Touch (see page 16). Any other DVD-based camera requires a prior version of iMovie.

From the Finder

If you have video clips on your Mac that you want to bring into iMovie for editing, you don't need a camera or anything. You just need to import the files.

The easiest way to do that is to drag them in from the Finder. Position the iMovie window so you can see your movie files in the Finder, and then drag the files directly onto an event in iMovie's Event list. iMovie then copies the clips to that event.

Alternatively, you can use the Import window to find and select your clips. In the window, you can see the hard drives connected to your Mac. Select one and you see a file browser just like the one in the Finder, except that it also lists how long your clips are (Figure 2-9). Select one or more clips and click Import Selected to copy them into the chosen event. (You can choose more than one clip by holding down the ⌘ key as you click each one.)

TIP The Import window offers a Favorites section for often-used folders. To add a folder to the Favorites list, drag it onto the Favorites label in the Import window's source list.

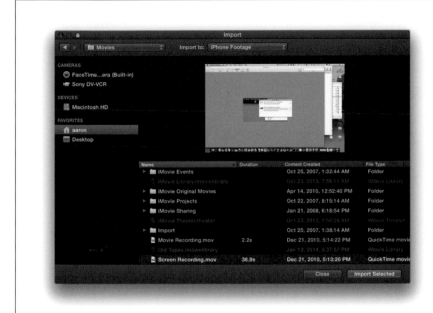

FIGURE 2-9

You can import files from the Finder, too. Navigate to the folder that holds your video clips, select them, and then click Import Selected.

Record Live with the iSight Camera

Every Mac laptop and iMac has a tiny video camera built in, just above the screen. This is your iSight camera, the one you use for things like Facetime chats or PhotoBooth shoots. iMovie can use this camera to capture video live, direct into your chosen event.

> **TIP** iMovie doesn't recognize external webcams, even if you can use them with other software on your Mac. For now, it's your built-in iSight or nothing.

Follow steps 1–4 on page 14, and then click the big, red button to start recording (Figure 2-10). Click it again to stop. You can do this repeatedly for multiple takes; iMovie sticks each recording in the event you chose. Close the Import window when you're done.

Importing Old Analog Tapes

We live in a new age, with digital everything, but millions of precious moments are trapped on VHS, VHS-C, or 8mm cassettes—that is, analog tapes instead of digital.

FIGURE 2-10

You can record live with an iSight camera. The big red button starts and stops the recording.

These days, people buy only digital camcorders. So how do you import and edit footage you shot before the digital era? Some local businesses might offer a digitizing service, but those cost money. Fortunately, it's fairly easy (and free) to digitize old footage if you have the right equipment. That equipment consists of a DV-tape camcorder that has analog inputs—in other words, older model video cameras that record to MiniDV tapes and that have red, white, and yellow input jacks (also known as RCA jacks). You'll also need a device capable of playing your old analog tapes, like a VCR or another old camcorder—and this unit has to have red, white, and yellow *output* jacks. Finally, you'll need an RCA cable (the kind that has red, white, and yellow plugs on both ends) to connect the recording and playback devices.

NOTE When you use the approach that follows, iMovie won't be able to chop the video into individual scenes automatically, as it does with digital video. That's because old analog camcorders didn't stamp every frame of every shot with an invisible time code, so iMovie doesn't know when you started or stopped your camcorder.

Then:

1. **If connected, unplug the FireWire cable from the DV-tape camcorder.**

   Most camcorders' analog inputs automatically switch off if you hook up a FireWire cable.

2. **Plug the RCA cable into the Audio Output and Video Output jacks on the side of the VCR or old camcorder. Connect the opposite ends of the cable to the Audio Input and Video Input jacks of your DV-tape camcorder.**

   Put a blank tape in your DV-tape camcorder.

TIP   If both your old camcorder and your DV camcorder have *S-video* connectors (round, dime-sized jacks), use them instead. S-video connections offer higher-quality video than RCA connections. (Note that an S-video cable doesn't conduct sound, however. You still have to connect the red and white RCA cables to carry the left and right stereo sound channels.)

---

3. **Switch both camcorders to VTR or VCR mode.**

   You're about to make a copy of the older tape by playing it into the DV-tape camcorder.

   By now, every fiber of your being may be screaming, "But analog copies make the quality deteriorate!" Relax. You're only making a first-generation copy. Actually, since you're making a *digital* copy, you lose only half as much quality as you would with a normal VCR-to-VCR duplicate. In other words, you probably won't be able to spot any deterioration. And you'll have the footage in digital format forever, ready to make as many copies as you want without further degradation.

4. **Press the Record button on the DV-tape camcorder, and press Play on the VCR or old camcorder.**

   You can monitor your progress by watching your DV-tape camcorder's LCD screen. Remember that a DV cassette generally holds only 60 minutes of video, compared with 2 hours on many previous-format tapes. You may have to change DV cassettes halfway through the process.

NOTE   Prior versions of iMovie support an *analog-to-digital converter*—a box that sits between your Mac and your VCR or older camcorder. This approach, and other analog-rescuing tricks, are covered thoroughly in past editions of this book.

After you record your old video onto your DV tape, import that tape by following the steps on page 21. It's not the most elegant solution to digitizing old videos, but you'll never have to do it again.

Events

In the last chapter, you learned that iMovie stores your raw footage in Event libraries, the repositories for the clips you'll use as you build your movie. Now that you've imported some footage, it's time to learn how you (and iMovie) work with events as you craft your film, and how you handle everyday housekeeping for events—to rename, merge, move, or delete them.

▉ How Events Work

iMovie stores two types of files in an event: source material and projects. Source material includes everything you need to create your movie, like the raw footage you imported earlier, along with any songs and photos you want to use (you'll learn how to import those in Chapters 11 and 12). A *project* is your movie-in-progress, described in Chapter 4.

Right now, your events include the individual clips you imported in the last chapter. To see what an event looks like, go to the iMovie Library (under Libraries on the left side of the iMovie window) and click an event name. iMovie displays all the clips inside that event in the *Event browser* on the right (see Figure 3-1).

iMovie starts out sorting your clips by date, oldest to newest. You can change that sort order by choosing View→Sort By and then selecting from the submenu (Figure 3-2). You can sort your footage by date, clip name, or clip duration. With any of these options, you can reverse the sort order (oldest to newest, reverse alphabetical, or longest to shortest) by choosing Descending from the same submenu.

FIGURE 3-1

When you click an event name (from the list on the left), iMovie shows you all the video clips in the event.

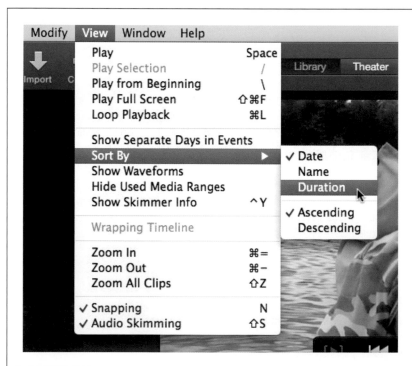

FIGURE 3-2

You can sort events or event footage by date, name (useful for events, but not for clips since most cameras automatically name them), and duration. Reverse the order by choosing Descending.

Review Event Footage

To see what's in a clip, iMovie gives you a couple of options. First, you can skim a clip to get a general idea of what it holds. To do that, drag your mouse cursor across the clip. As you do, iMovie shows you the clip in the Viewer, playing it back just as fast (or slowly) as you drag the mouse.

To play the clip at normal speed, click a spot and press the space bar. iMovie previews your clip in the Viewer. To watch a clip from the beginning, click anywhere in the clip and press the \ key. iMovie starts playing the clip from the beginning at normal speed.

UP TO SPEED

Organizing Your Events

Because you control how you organize your event footage, it's worth reviewing a little advice on keeping things tidy and easy to find.

The very idea of events is based on the idea that we tend to film our lives around important moments. Whether it's a birthday party, a vacation, or your kid's first steps, these are the things that get us to whip out the camera and press Record. You can even lump stuff that spans multiple days, like a soccer season, into a natural group of footage.

This idea is a powerful way to organize your iMovie events. Instead of having to worry about remembering *when* things happened, group footage by life events and you need to remember only *what* happened. It's easy to come up with names for events that tell you all you need to know, even if

you have more than one version of that event. For example, if you took the family to see Grandma and Grandpa in Michigan first in 2008 and then again in 2013, just name those events "Michigan 2008" and "Michigan 2013."

This idea works even if you're not using iMovie for personal footage. Let's say you use it for your real estate business, where you make YouTube videos showing off homes for sale. In that case, just organize your events by house. So you'd put the footage you shot of 123 Oak Lane into an event called "123 Oak Lane."

If you later change your mind about event names or how to split up footage, you can always rename them (read on). The most important point is that you're in charge, so keep things in an order that's easiest for you.

Rename an Event

To rename an event, click it once in the Libraries list to select it. Then, showing a bit of patience, click it again and wait a fraction of a second. When you do, iMovie highlights the old moniker, ready for you to type in a new one (Figure 3-3).

FIGURE 3-3

To change an event name, click it once to select it, wait a second, and then click it again. Movie highlights the text so you can change it. Then hit Return.

Merge Events

You can merge events, too. For example, if you filmed your kids during the month of May, and created a new event each time you imported a day's footage, you might want to group all those clips into a single event, called something like May Madness. To do that, grab an event and drop it onto another one (Figure 3-4). The grabbed event shows up in the event where you dropped it. If you like, rename the event to reflect the grouped footage.

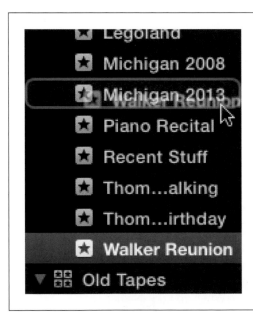

FIGURE 3-4

Merging events is just a matter of dragging one event and dropping it onto another.

Move Individual Clips to Another Event

To move a misplaced clip to its proper event, select the clip in the Event browser (using the techniques described on page 54) and drag it onto the name of the correct event.

TIP If, instead of *moving* a clip, you want to *copy* it from one event to another so that it lives in both events, hold down the Option key as you drag the clip to the new event. A green + sign appears along with your cursor, telling you that you'll be making a copy of the clip instead of moving it.

This works with multiple clips as well. Just remember that copying clips doubles the number of the files on your hard drive, taking up more space as a result.

Delete an Event or Event Footage

To delete an event (and regain some disk space in the process), select the event and then choose File→"Move Event to Trash" (or press ⌘-R). iMovie moves the event to a hidden trash folder (described on page 41) and deletes it for good when you quit iMovie.

To get the event back, choose Edit→Undo (⌘-Z). Just be sure to do that before you quit iMovie. (See page 72 to read up on the mighty Undo.)

To delete individual *clips* from an event, use the same technique.

■ iMovie Libraries

You know how you can put papers into folders, and then folders into a filing cabinet? In the same way, you keep your video clips in events, but you also have a larger container for all those events: libraries.

iMovie starts you out with just one library, called, fittingly enough, iMovie Library (that's where you reviewed your events at the beginning of this chapter). You can create more libraries (see the next section) or keep all your stuff in the iMovie Library, but the bottom line is that every scrap of footage you import goes into an event, and iMovie stores those events in a library.

iPhoto and Aperture Libraries

While iMovie includes just one stock library when you first use the program, you may see a few others as you start working. If you use either of Apple's photo-management programs, iPhoto for casual photographers and Aperture for pros, iMovie automatically detects these libraries and adds them to its Libraries list, making it simple to pull still images or clips from either program into your projects (see Chapter 12).

NOTE Did you know that the Apple programmer behind iMovie '08 onward is the same one who designed Aperture? (He led the first Final Cut team as well.)

The Content Library

In addition, once you start working on a film (Chapter 4), iMovie reveals a second library at the bottom of the Libraries list: the Content Library. It includes all the elements Apple gives you to enhance your movie: transitions, titles, maps, backgrounds, and audio tracks. (You'll find each of these components discussed in detail in the chapters to come.)

NOTE   To understand why iMovie needs these files handy, read how iMovie edits movies *by reference* on page 35.

■ Create Your Own Library

iMovie's iMovie Library may be all you need for a video project or two, but you might find additional storehouses helpful in keeping your projects organized. For example, you may have a bunch of home movies on your Mac, along with a collection of banjo lessons you posted to YouTube, and footage of your brother's wedding. You could create a library for each of these events, making it easy to pick up a project where you left off, or to send the library to, say, your brother.

Being able to share a library is one good reason to create one. For example, once your brother's wedding is over, you can copy the library from your Mac to your brother's, and he'll have all the elements that went onto his wedding movie: the raw footage, finished videos, photos, and music. When he opens the library in iMovie, he and his wife can enjoy the memories.

Fortunately, iMovie lets you create as many libraries as you want. To create a new one, choose File→Open Library→New. iMovie displays the Save window you see in Figure 3-5, where you name the library and choose a location for it on your hard drive (your Mac's Movies folder is the default).

Work with More Than One Library

You can work with more than one library at a time. To open a library, choose File→Open Library. If you've opened the library before, its name shows up in the drop-down menu; select it to go to that library. To open a library you've created but *haven't* worked with before, choose Other, and then click the Locate button (Figure 3-6). That brings up a file chooser where you specify the library (which can be somewhere on your Mac or on any other drive connected to it). Find and select the library you need and then click Open.

Once you open a library, it shows up in the Libraries list on the left-hand side of the iMovie window.

If you're done with a library and want it out of your way, select it in the Libraries list and choose File→Close Library.

FIGURE 3-5

*When you create
a new library by
selecting File→Open
Library→New, iMovie
prompts you to name it.*

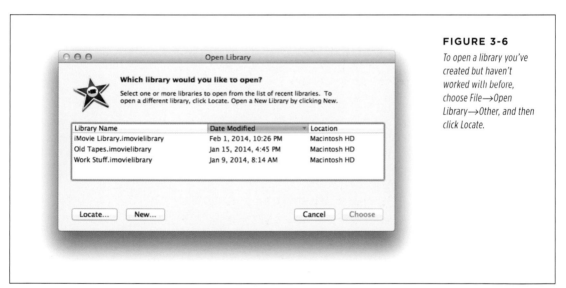

FIGURE 3-6

*To open a library you've
created but haven't
worked with before,
choose File→Open
Library→Other, and then
click Locate.*

NOTE In Chapter 5 (page 57), you'll learn how to use footage from different libraries in a single movie project. In the meantime, don't worry if you close a library that your current project uses—your movie plays back normally, just as though the library were still open.

Working with Movies in iPhoto

It's certainly convenient to have access to the iPhoto library from within iMovie, but for many reasons, you might prefer to work within iPhoto with movies as well. The problem is that iPhoto doesn't offer an immediately obvious way to see just those movies, and wading through thousands of photos to find your movies isn't exactly a fulfilling hobby.

Lucky for you, iPhoto Smart Albums can save you the trouble of digging through your iPhoto library. The trick is to make a Smart Album that collects all your movies.

In iPhoto, choose File→New Smart Album. In the window that appears, give your album a helpful name, like Movie Clips, and use these settings for the pull-down menus: "Photo" in the first menu, "Is" in the second menu, and "Movie" in the last menu.

Click OK and iPhoto saves your new Smart Album. Select it and iPhoto shows you every single movie file saved in your iPhoto library.

Projects

I n iMovie-speak, a *project* is a movie you're editing. You'll actually edit your movie beginning in Chapter 5, but this chapter reviews the basics of how projects work, how you manage them, and how you customize your workspace before you start editing. Think of this as learning how a car works before you learn how to drive it.

▓ The Concept of iMovie Projects

The way you build a video in iMovie is pretty neat, technically speaking: You select the footage you like from your raw material and then add it to your movie-in-progress.

While it may seem like you're copying video from an event library to your project, that's not the case. Behind the scenes, iMovie works much more efficiently—when you choose a clip, iMovie doesn't move the clip anywhere, it simply *points to* where it is on your hard drive. Then, when you play back your movie, iMovie instantly reads the clip from its place on your drive and displays it in the playback window, just as though the clip were physically embedded in your project. In effect, your project is a list of instructions telling iMovie what video to play when.

Historically speaking, this was a big leap forward from the old days of iMovie. In iMovie HD and older, projects showed up as icons on your desktop. In reality, they were cleverly disguised folders, and inside, you'd find all the gigantic movie clips you used in the movie. This was convenient in one way: It made projects fully self-contained, so you could, for example, easily back up a project or move the whole thing to another computer. But in another way, it wasn't ideal. If you wanted to use a clip in more than one project, you had to duplicate the clip (by pasting it into the second project), which ate up a lot of hard drive space.

The pointer-based approach has a number of implications:

- You can use the same clip in dozens of movie projects, without ever eating up more disk space (see Figure 4-1).

- You can create multiple versions of the same project—a director's cut and a short version, for example—without worrying about filling up your hard drive.

- Backing up or moving a single project is no longer simply a matter of copying a file. Instead, as you learned in Chapter 3, iMovie stores all your events—and everything in them—as a single file, in what iMovie calls a library. (Your first library is the iMovie Library, found in the Finder at Home→Movies. If you created any other libraries, you'll find them here, too.) This means you can't simply drag a small project file from one Mac to another. (There is, however, a way to move or copy a project to another folder or disk, together with all its event footage. Page 38 tells all.)

- Each project takes up disk space, but only an infinitesimal amount—about as much as a word processor document. It contains only a text list of *pointers* to bits of video on your hard drive.

FIGURE 4-1

An orange line along the bottom of a source clip lets you know which chunks of the clip you used in a project. When you work on a different project, where you use different parts of the same clip, you'll see the orange lines jump around.

But things change when you finish a project and you want to *send* it somewhere—to, say, YouTube, or a DVD, or a QuickTime movie. Only then does iMovie fetch the video stored in your event library, implement your edits, and stitch the footage together into a single, sharable file.

◼ Project Basics

You'll spend most of your time in iMovie editing clips from within a project, but as your projects grow in number, it helps to know how iMovie manages them.

Where Projects Live

If you're used to iMovie '11, you might be confused about where to find your projects in the new iMovie. That's because you're expecting a Project Library where iMovie keeps all your videos. But the new program stores projects inside events. Apple figures that most movies you create are based on events, so why not keep the raw footage and your working movie together? A Walker Reunion project, for example, will use clips from the Walker Reunion event, so iMovie stores the project in that event.

This is just iMovie's way of organizing things, and it doesn't—and shouldn't—stop you from using footage from one event in another. You can even use footage across *libraries* (though in that case, iMovie abandons the pointer system and actually copies the footage from Library 1 to Library 2).

If you can't remember which event holds the project you want, don't waste time hunting for it—choose All Projects in the Libraries list (Figure 4-2). iMovie displays every project in every event in every library. Double-click a project name to get working on it.

FIGURE 4-2

The easiest way to see every project in every event in every library in iMovie is to choose, well, All Projects in the Libraries list.

TIP If you open a project from the All Projects library, you don't go to the event where iMovie stores the project. To know where a project lives, look for a little film-clapper icon next to an event in your libraries (Figure 4-3). That's the event that stores your project.

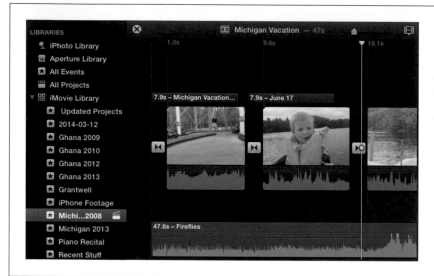

FIGURE 4-3

When you have a project open in iMovie, the event housing the project sprouts a little clapper icon. This is so you know where you can find the project.

Upgrading from iMovie '11

If you've used iMovie before, the new version of the program probably upgraded your old iMovie library when you installed it. That upgrade brought a few dramatic changes, like a single library file in the Finder instead of easy-to-navigate folders, as explained on page 41.

The new iMovie also changed where projects live: They now live inside events. As a result, iMovie had to put your old projects somewhere when it upgraded your iMovie library. Apple's solution was to create a new event for you called Updated Projects.

So now you have an event housing a bunch of old projects, but (most likely) no footage—remember, older versions of iMovie embedded your footage in your projects. (You probably will, however, see photos and audio clips in Updated Projects, because iMovie copies them there for safekeeping).

If you don't like this turn of events (ahem), you can move your old projects to more fitting event locations by following the advice on page 29.

Create a Project

To create a new project, you can do this:

- Click the + button in the toolbar, and then choose Movie from the drop-down menu.

- Choose File→New Movie.

- Press ⌘-N.

You click the + button to create *trailers* for your movies, too, but, sensibly enough, you select Trailer from the drop-down menu instead of Movie. Chapter 13 has the details.

Whichever method you choose, iMovie launches a Themes window (Figure 4-4). Themes, covered in detail on page 96, give your movie a common look and matching soundtrack. Fortunately for the creative minded, iMovie offers a No Theme option, giving you free reign over your creations.

Once you select a theme (or not), iMovie prompts you to name your project and choose (or create) an event as your video's home.

FIGURE 4-4

To create a new project, you first choose a theme and then click Create. Once you do, iMovie asks you to name your project and choose the event where iMovie should store it. Click OK and the project appears inside that event.

Duplicate a Project

It's often useful to create several versions of the same project. You could have several differently edited cuts so you can get feedback on which one works best, for example. The beauty of iMovie is that you can duplicate projects easily and simply, without filling up your hard drive with duplicate video files since each version of the project calls upon the *same* underlying clips.

To duplicate a project, click its name, and then choose Edit→Duplicate Movie. You'll see the new project appear in the same event, next to the original project, and complete with a temporary name (for example, if you called the original project "Baby Spaghetti on Head," iMovie calls the new one "Baby Spaghetti on Head 1." If you make a duplicate of the duplicate, iMovie is smart enough to call the newest copy "Baby Spaghetti on Head 2.") Feel free to rename your project using the method described in the next section.

Rename a Project

To rename a project, click its name in the Event browser. iMovie highlights the old name, ready for a new title.

Move Projects to Other Events

To move a project from one event to another (say you started the project in the wrong event), select the project and then drag it to the correct event.

> **TIP** You can copy a project to a new event this way, too, by holding down the Option key while you drag the project. iMovie displays a green + sign as you're about to drop the file into the new event, letting you know you're copying the project instead of just moving it.

Delete and Undelete a Project

To get rid of a project, click its name and then choose File→"Move to Trash," or press ⌘-Delete. Alternatively, right-click its thumbnail in the Event browser and then select "Move to Trash."

If you delete a project by mistake, you can get it back by selecting Edit→"Undo Move to Trash" or by pressing ⌘-Z immediately after deleting it. But if you do a bunch of stuff before you realize your mistake, you have to backtrack by repeatedly selecting the Undo command until your project is restored.

> **TIP** In prior versions of iMovie, you could salvage a deleted project from the Finder's Trash. Now, if you delete a project, the Edit→Undo command (⌘-Z) is the only reliable way to get it back. But even that option goes *Poof!* once you quit iMovie. That's because iMovie sticks trashed projects in a hidden, temporary folder where you can retrieve them—so long as the program's open. Once you quit iMovie, that deletion becomes permanent. (To learn more about this hidden folder, see the box on page 41.)

Consolidate Project Media

With how libraries work in iMovie (page 31), you can use footage from multiple libraries to piece a project together. To make sure all the footage is in the same library as your project, select the project and choose File→Consolidate Project Media (or "Library Media" if you select a library to do this for all projects in that library). iMovie will make copies of the wayward footage into the same library holding your project.

Project Properties

Every project you create in iMovie has some basic settings that dictate the way your movie plays back. These settings include things like the project theme (Chapter 7), transition timings (Chapter 7), and default photo treatment (Chapter 12). Future chapters will show you how to change these settings, but for now it's important to know how to find them.

Choose View→Movie Properties (⌘-J). iMovie displays basic information about your movie, including its name, quality, length, and whether you've shared it (Figure 4-5).

Behind the Scenes of iMovie

In this book, you'll occasionally read about some sneaky ways to go behind iMovie's back. For example, if you want to use a video clip that's in your iMovie library with another program, there's a way to get to the actual file on your computer instead of exporting it from iMovie.

These backdoor tricks work because iMovie is, in one way, just a front end for the files that actually sit on your hard drive. And knowing the relationship between what you see in iMovie and what you find in the Finder can be extremely useful.

It turns out that every project, event, and camera clip you see in iMovie corresponds to a file in the Finder. Want to see them? Open your Home folder (in the Finder, choose Go→Home), and then double-click the Movies folder. (Alternatively, click Movies in the sidebar at the left side of *any* Finder window.) Once there, you'll see a folder marked with a custom iMovie icon:

You can see the folders and files inside the iMovie folder by right-clicking it and choosing Show Package Contents. When you do, you see all the special folders iMovie creates. There's a folder for each of your events, and within that folder you'll find any projects you created in that event along with a set of subfolders that have all the actual QuickTime video clips you imported to the event. (Selecting a clip in an event library and choosing File→"Reveal in Finder" teleports you directly to one of these folders.)

You'll also see a few other folders, like Temp, which handles iMovie housekeeping chores, and a Trash folder, where iMovie stores your deleted projects until you quit iMovie. (If you don't see the Trash folder, you haven't deleted anything recently— iMovie spawns it only when necessary.)

So every time you open iMovie, what you see in each event library is mostly a mirror of what's in the corresponding folders in the Finder. (OK, you also see the videos you keep in iPhoto or Aperture, but that's another story.)

FIGURE 4-5

Top: iMovie displays the basic properties of your project in the playback window.

Bottom: Click Settings and you'll see the behavior for various elements of your movie: the standard clip length (Chapter 5), factory setting for transition length (Chapter 7), whether you trimmed the background music (Chapter 11),the photo treatment you applied (Chapter 12), the theme (Chapter 7), and whether you included Automatic content (Chapter 7).

■ Remodel Your Workspace

One of iMovie's strengths is how refreshingly respectful it is of your screen real estate. It offers a bunch of ways to maximize your work area without the hassle of buying a new monitor.

Hide the Libraries List

Once you start working on a movie, you probably don't need your Libraries list staring you in the face. Even without a project open, you might want to devote your whole screen to sorting through event footage. iMovie gets this and is happy to give you the extra room.

You hide the Libraries list by choosing Window→Hide Libraries, pressing Shift-⌘-1, or clicking the Show/Hide Libraries button (Figure 4-6). iMovie hides the list and expands the video-clip area.

To bring the list back, reverse any of these procedures.

Change the Size of Your Clips

iMovie represents your video clips as *filmstrips*—multiframe, horizontal strips whose lengths are proportional to the clip's duration. (You'll read more about filmstrips in Chapter 5.) You can make these filmstrips smaller, or show more of the frames for each one, by clicking the filmstrip icon in the upper-left corner of the Event browser (see Figure 4-7). Once there, adjust the Clip Size and Zoom settings to your liking.

NOTE   When you drag the Zoom slider to its extreme left, iMovie represents every video clip by only *one* frame; it no longer indicates the filmstrips' lengths relative to one another. That makes it easy to move and resequence clips (and it makes this version of iMovie more familiar to people used to working in iMovie HD and older).

Hide/Show Clip Audio

To see the audio waveforms for both event and project footage, turn on the Audio Waveforms checkbox in the same window (Figure 4-7). A graph of blue peaks and valleys sprouts under your clips (Figure 4-8). (You'll find waveforms discussed in detail on page 171.)

FIGURE 4-6

Top: The standard iMovie window.

Bottom: You can radically change the way iMovie looks. To swap the Project pane and Event browser, as has been done here, choose Window→"Swap Project and Event." To switch to a wrapping time-line, select View→Wrap-ping Timeline. You can also hide the Libraries list and adjust the size of your clips.

FIGURE 4-7

Click the filmstrip icon in the top-right corner of the Event browser to adjust the size of your clips.

FIGURE 4-8

Top: A clip without its audio waveform showing.

Bottom: Now you see the sound. (Yes, in this case, you can see sound.)

Adjust the Viewer

iMovie calls the movie playback window the *Viewer*. It sits in the upper-right corner
of the screen. You can't reposition it, but you can change its size by dragging the
top border of the Project pane.

The advantage of a large Viewer is, of course, that you get the best view of your
movie as you work. The disadvantage is that it eats up screen space. On smaller
screens, it squishes the Event browser so much that you have to do a lot more
scrolling to review your clips.

NOTE If you're pulling your hair out looking for a way to move the Viewer onto a second screen, like you
could in iMovie '11 or earlier, give your poor follicles a break. Apple removed this feature in this version of the
program. Here's hoping it makes a comeback.

Swap the Project Pane and Event Browser

When you first start editing a project, the Project pane, where you actually build
your movie, replaces your event footage. That's nice, because it gives you plenty of
room to work on your movie, but it comes at a cost. iMovie moves your event clips up,
wedged between the Project pane and the top of the Event browser (see Figure 4-9).

FIGURE 4-9

*When you start a project,
iMovie gives you plenty
of room to work on it, but
it reduces the size of the
Event browser.*

As you work on a movie, you may wish you could *swap* the two windows to make it
easier to review your footage. Good news: You can, by choosing Window→"Swap
Project and Event." Now you have a lot more room to work with your clips (see
Figure 4-6).

TIP It probably goes without saying, but you should make the iMovie window itself as big as you can. Do that by choosing Window→Zoom, or click the little round, green Zoom button in the upper-left corner of the iMovie window. Better yet, go full-screen, OS X style (without any Mac menu bar) by clicking ⬚ in the top-right corner of the iMovie window.

The Wrapping Timeline

If you've used a video-editing program other than iMovie, you've used a timeline before. It's a horizontally scrolling depiction of your movie-in-progress, showing the video and audio tracks you've assembled as long strips, punctuated by any transitions you added.

But if you've used iMovie '08, '09, or '11, you might have become accustomed to the *wrapping timeline*. In a somewhat controversial move (don't laugh—video-editing interfaces can get pretty controversial), iMovie '08 dumped the classic timeline and replaced it with one that worked more like a word processor. In that design, the "filmstrips" representing your project wrapped at the edge of the window, just like sentences wrap at the end of a line in a word processor. You had to scroll vertically instead of horizontally to review your project.

This got under the skin of people accustomed to the traditional timeline, so Apple restored that timeline to the new iMovie and made it the factory setting.

If you like the wrapping timeline better, choose View→Wrapping Timeline. While this removes the time codes that mark a clip's duration, everything else behaves pretty much the same way.

To go back to traditional timeline editing, choose View→Wrapping Timeline again.

Reset Your Workspace

If the kids (or you) monkey around with iMovie's layout and you want to revert to the stock design, choose Window→"Revert to Original Layout." The iMovie window disappears for a moment, and then, like magic, it reappears, resized and reordered to its original settings.

Build Your Movie

Create Your Movie

Whether you work with video on your Mac or on a multimillion-dollar Hollywood studio setup, film editing boils down to three tiny tasks: selecting, trimming, and rearranging *clips*. Of course, that's like saying that painting a portrait boils down to nothing more than mixing various amounts of red, yellow, and blue. The *art* of video editing lies in your decisions about the clips you select, how you trim them, and in what order you put them.

You work with clips in two place in iMovie. There's the *Event browser*, usually at the top half of your screen, where all your raw, unedited video lives. And there's the *Project pane*, also called the *storyboard*, which is usually at the bottom half of your screen—that's where you assemble and edit your masterpiece.

At its simplest, then, iMovie editing is all about this three-step process:

1. Reviewing your video in the Event browser and finding the good parts.

2. Adding those chunks to the storyboard, where iMovie plays them in one seamless pass, from left to right.

3. Adding crossfades, titles (a.k.a. credits), music, and effects.

This chapter shows you the mechanics of the first two tasks: selecting raw footage and adding it to your movie-in-progress. The following chapters cover the last step.

▉ Phase 1: Review Your Clips

Video editing always starts with a pile of raw, unedited footage. In iMovie's case, that's the bunch of clips you stored as events. Click an event's name to see what video lurks inside.

Working with Filmstrips

iMovie represents every imported clip as a *filmstrip*—a horizontal bar made up of sample frames from the clip and whose length reflects the clip's duration. You can adjust both how tall the filmstrip is and how many frames of your footage it displays. You make both adjustments in iMovie's "slider" window. Call it up by clicking the filmstrip icon at the top-right corner of the Event browser. The Clip Size slider adjusts the filmstrip's height, and the Zoom slider changes the number of frames you see (see Figure 5-1).

> **NOTE**   If you have iMovie's wrapping timeline turned on (page 46) and a filmstrip is too wide for the Event browser, it wraps around to the next line. A ragged filmstrip edge tells you that iMovie has wrapped your clip (think of that ragged edge as the video version of a hyphen). If you use iMovie's default timeline, your filmstrip is one long, uninterrupted filmstrip, and you have to scroll to the right to see it all.

FIGURE 5-1

When you click the filmstrip icon in the Event browser, iMovie opens a "slider" window.

Top: The Clip Size slider (left) changes the height of your filmstrip (right). (To see the audio that accompanies a clip, turn on the Show Waveforms checkbox.)

Bottom, left: Adjust the Zoom slider to see more frames of each strip. The highlighted clip (look for the yellow border) lasts about 22 seconds, and because you have the Zoom slider set to 30 seconds, you see just one frame of the clip.

Bottom, right: When you set the slider to display 1 second of video per frame, the clip becomes, sensibly enough, 22 frames wide.

You can make these same adjustments in the Project pane, but the controls differ slightly. To adjust the height of the filmstrip, click the filmstrip icon in the top-right corner of the storyboard (Figure 5-2). To change the number of frames iMovie displays, use the Zoom slider to the left of the filmstrip icon (Figure 5-2, circled).

FIGURE 5-2

The Clip Size and Zoom sliders as they appear in the project storyboard. Notice how the Zoom slider (circled, right) lives outside the filmstrip icon this time.

So what's the right setting for these sliders? That's up to you, but here are some suggestions:

- At the Zoom slider's extreme left position, iMovie represents every video clip as *one* frame. You can no longer tell the relative length of a clip. This arrangement makes clips easy to move around and resequence, and it makes a very long movie fit on your screen without scrolling. It also makes iMovie a lot more familiar if you're used to working in previous versions of the program.

- At the Zoom slider's extreme right position, each frame of the filmstrip represents a *half-second* of video, and you can edit your movie in the storyboard frame by frame, as explained in the box on page 56.

- As you work, you can fiddle with the Zoom slider, zooming in and out as necessary. For example, when you need to tweak the precise starting point of a piece of audio, you'll want to zoom in tight (by dragging the slider to the right); when you want to get a good overview of a long movie, you want to zoom out (drag the slider to the left).

- As for the Clip Size slider, the proper adjustment really depends on how well you want to be able to see what's going on in each clip. Make clips bigger and they're easier to see. On the downside, the bigger you make the clips, the less of your event footage or project you'll see at once. Of course, the Viewer is the best way to see what's going on in your footage, so get good at skimming, discussed next.

Skim Filmstrips

You're about to learn two iMovie skills that you'll use most often in editing your footage: *skimming* and *playing*. Practice them, commit them to memory, make them automatic, and you'll fly through the editing process.

Skimming means moving your cursor across a filmstrip. Do not *click* or *drag* the strip, which would mean pressing the mouse button. Just *point* with the mouse.

The *playhead*—an orange vertical line the height of the filmstrip—moves along with your cursor. And as you skim, the Viewer plays back the underlying video at high speed—or medium speed, or slow speed, depending on how fast you move the cursor. (You see the same video playing within the filmstrip itself, beneath your cursor.)

> **TIP** You can also play the *sound* of a clip as you skim—fast or slow, in forward or reverse. Sometimes, that's helpful. When it is, choose View→Audio Skimming (Shift-S) to turn the audio on. Then, when you skim, your clip will sound like you're fast-forwarding through a cassette tape. (Remember those?) But if the audio starts driving you crazy, turn it off by selecting View→Audio Skimming (Shift-S) again.

Skimming may take some getting used to, because it's such an unusual computer technique; it's probably the first time in history that moving the mouse without clicking does *anything* besides, well, moving the cursor to a new spot. But it means that you can control not only the speed of playback, but also the direction—forward or reverse—in real time, almost effortlessly.

Skimming works anywhere fine filmstrips are found—either in the Event browser or in the project storyboard (Figure 5-3).

> **TIP** You may sometimes wish you could use the cursor as, well, a *cursor*, instead of always making stuff play back. You may wish, for example, that you could freeze a frame as you skim—"Stay on this frame for just a sec"—while you go off to do something else with the mouse. You can. When you get to the spot you want to freeze, hold down the Control key. iMovie turns off skimming and leaves the video frame onscreen until you release the Control key. (This trick works only in the project storyboard, not in the Event browser.)

Play Clips

Skimming is great for quickly getting the gist of what's in your captured clips. But unless you're some kind of cyborg, you'll find it very difficult to skim at exactly the right speed for *real-time* playback.

Fortunately, iMovie can also play back clips all by itself, at the proper speed. To do that, use the space bar on your keyboard as the Start/Stop control. Hitting the space bar always begins playback at the position of your cursor, and hitting it again stops playback.

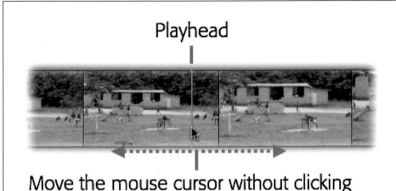

Playhead

Move the mouse cursor without clicking

FIGURE 5-3

When you skim, you move your cursor across the face of a filmstrip without clicking the mouse button. It's a fast, simple way to find out what's in a clip without having to sit through a full playback.

Once you master that difficult technique, you're ready for the real gem: using skimming and playback *together*. It works like this: Using your mouse, skim your footage, looking for the part you want to watch. When you get close to the right spot, tap the space bar. Playback begins from the precise position of your cursor.

Tap the space bar again to stop playback, move your cursor to another spot, and then tap the space bar once more. This way, you can jump around, spot-inspecting your clips (or even *within* a clip), without ever touching the mouse button—and without ever having to wait.

There are four other ways to play back a source clip or your movie-in-progress, complete with corresponding keyboard shortcuts. Page 62 has the details, but here are the CliffsNotes:

- Play the selected chunk (/ key).

- Play from the beginning (\ key).

- Play full-screen (Shift-⌘-F).

- Loop playback, so you don't have to keep replaying a clip that needs lots of rewatching (⌘-L).

◼ Phase 2: Select the Good Bits

The reason you're reviewing clips in the Event browser is, of course, to find the good parts—the highlights, the pieces you want to include in your finished movie. Once you select a chunk of video, you can drag it into the storyboard to make it part of your movie.

Selecting comes in handy for other purposes, too. As you'll read in the next chapter, you can designate part of a clip as either a Favorite (a snippet you know you'll want to use) or Reject (a worthless shot). These steps, too, require that you first *select* the piece of clip you want to tag.

Since selecting is such a critical step in iMovie moviemaking, Apple made sure you had all kinds of ways to do it. The following pages review them one by one.

Select by Dragging

The first selection method is the one you'll probably use most often: dragging. That is, slide the cursor across some footage while you press the mouse button, just the way you'd select a phrase of text in a word processor.

iMovie indicates which part of a clip you selected by surrounding it with a yellow border (Figure 5-4). A little bubble on the top edge of the filmstrip shows you how many seconds' or minutes' worth of video you highlighted. (If you select part of a clip, you can adjust it later; see page 55.)

FIGURE 5-4

You can highlight part of a clip by dragging across it. iMovie shows you what you selected by enclosing it in a yellow border.

Select an Entire Clip

In some cases, you may find that all this dragging business is just too much fussiness—you really want to select *entire clips* from the Event browser. To do that, either double-click the clip or *Option-click* it.

> **NOTE** This works only for selections in the Event browser. When you click a clip in the storyboard, you *always* select the entire clip.

Select Multiple Clips at Once

It's often useful to select *more* than one clip at a time. Imagine how much faster you could perform common tasks—deleting clips, dragging them, cutting and pasting them, and so on—if you could work on them all at once.

Selecting clips in the storyboard or Event browser works just like selecting file names in the Finder. For example, here's some of what you can do:

- **Highlight all the filmstrips.** Press ⌘-A (the equivalent of the Edit→Select All command).

- **Highlight random clips.** If you want to highlight, for example, only the first, third, and seventh clips in a storyboard, start by clicking clip No. 1, and then ⌘-click each of the others.

- **Remove a clip from the selection.** If you're highlighting a long string of clips and click one by mistake, you don't have to start over. Instead, just ⌘-click the errant clip again to deselect it. (If you *do* want to start over, you can deselect all the selected clips by clicking any empty part of the window.)

> **TIP**   The ⌘ key trick is especially handy if you want to select *almost* all the clips in a window. Press ⌘-A to select everything in the Event browser or storyboard, and then ⌘-click any unwanted clips to deselect them.

- **Highlight consecutive clips.** Click the first clip you want to highlight, and then Shift-click the last one. iMovie automatically selects all the clips in between, along with the two you clicked.

Adjust a Selection

Once you highlight a portion of a filmstrip, you're not stuck with that yellow boundary the way it is. You can adjust it in either of these two ways:

- Dragging the vertical ends of the yellow border to the right or left to select more or less of the clip.

- Shift-clicking another spot in the filmstrip. The nearest edge of the yellow border jumps to the location of your click, which makes the selection longer or shorter.

> **TIP**   These tips are great for making rough edits. For much finer control, get to know iMovie's Precision Editor (page 68).

Play a Selection

As you know, tapping the space bar begins playing back a clip *at the position of the cursor*. But when you're making a selection, fiddling with that yellow border, that's not always what you want to do. In fact, it's probably *not* what you want.

A much more useful keystroke would be one that means, "Play just what I've selected." And that's what the / key is for. (That's the forward-slash key, the one next to the period key.) Tap it once to play whatever you selected; tap it a second time to stop playback.

Frame-Accurate Editing

If you're accustomed to a traditional timeline, like the kind found in most other video-editing software, the storyboard in iMovie could make you feel fat-fingered. You might throw up your hands and decide that frame-precise editing is impossible. Happily, that isn't the case.

Modern digital video creates the illusion of motion by flashing about 30 frames of "film" onscreen per second. To edit down to a specific frame, you need to be able to zoom in close enough to see those 30 individual frames.

At first, it sure looks as though iMovie works in much larger chunks. But zoom way in, using the Zoom slider at the upper-right corner of the storyboard (see page 51). In fact, if you drag the slider all the way to the right, each frame of the filmstrip represents a *half second* of video.

Then, if you drag the end of the yellow selection boundary carefully and slowly, you can actually feel it snap against *individual frames* of the recording—15 times for every filmstrip frame, in fact.

Let's see—each frame of your filmstrip represents half a second, and there are 15 snaps per frame. Sure enough, that's true frame-accurate editing.

Deselect a Clip

To *deselect* whatever is selected—that is, to remove the yellow border entirely—use any of these three techniques:

- Click anywhere in the dark-gray background.
- Choose Edit→Deselect All.
- Press Shift-⌘-A.

Actually, there's another way, but it involves a little backstory; see the tip on page 55.

Select Specific Project Elements

By the time you finish building a project, it might be full of all kinds of stuff—video clips, transitions, maps, and so on. In iMovie, you can select all the stuff of one type—for example, all the background images—to make universal changes. For example, you could change all backgrounds from blue to black. To do that, choose Edit→"Select in Movie." iMovie lists all the elements you can isolate in a project: video clips, transitions, photos, maps, and backgrounds. Pretty handy.

NOTE Unfortunately, titles and audio tracks are conspicuously missing from the "Select in Movie" list. For some reason, iMovie doesn't let you select more than one of these components at a time.

■ Phase 3: Build the Storyboard

The project storyboard is the large work area that starts out at the bottom of the screen, as shown in Figure 5-5. The key to building a movie is moving your selected video bits from the Event browser to this storyboard.

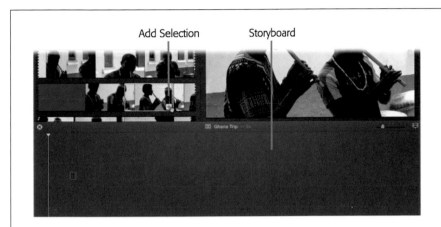

Add Selection   Storyboard

FIGURE 5-5

When the storyboard area is fresh and new, all you see are faint outlines representing what your project can become. Clicking the Add Selection button, dragging in a selection, or simply pressing the letter E key, starts to fill it up.

Add to the End of a Storyboard

Most people, most of the time, build a movie by reviewing a clip of raw footage from left to right—from beginning to end—and choosing bits, in sequence, to include in their final movie. In such cases, you add a selected clip or clips to the *end* of the storyboard.

iMovie offers two ways to do that automatically (that is, without selecting the clip and then dragging it to the end of the storyboard, which might be offscreen). Once you select some video in the Event browser, do one of these things:

- Press the letter E key.

- Click the Add Selection button (identified in Figure 5-5).

In either case, the selected chunk(s) of video flies from the Event browser to the *end* of your storyboard.

To check the result, point to the storyboard (without clicking) just before the spot where the new video has landed, and then press the space bar.

Add *X* Seconds of Footage

If you click a clip in your Event browser without selecting any of it, the Add Selection button still appears. But instead of adding a selection, it offers you the chance to add 4 seconds of footage to that clip, counted from the playhead forward.

The convenience this offers works this way: If you really just want random scenes for, say, a montage from your costume party (showing the different costumes, perhaps), just click into spots that look interesting and then click the Add button. You'll get nice, uniform clips added to your movie without the hassle of dragging little yellow borders every time.

The result is an evenly timed, easily made movie that you can get out to your friends right away. This feature shows off how iMovie was designed to be quick and simple.

Plus, if 4 seconds is too long or too short, you can change the default timing to anything from 1 to 10 seconds using the Clip slider in the Movie Properties window (Window→Movie Properties→Settings).

Insert Video in the Middle of Your Movie

You don't *have* to add a clip to the end of your storyboard. You can place it between clips or smack in the middle of a single, continuous clip.

To add a chunk of footage between clips, drag the selected chunk (by positioning your cursor inside the yellow border so that it becomes a handle) right into the storyboard. iMovie previews your insertion point with a blue shaded box. When you find the right spot, release the mouse (see Figure 5-6). The chunk of video slips right in between the surrounding clips.

FIGURE 5-6

Once you highlight some video, you can drag it to position it anywhere in the storyboard—in the gap between two existing clips, for example. iMovie previews your placement with a blue box.

What if you want to drop a clip *in the middle of another clip*, splitting it in two with your clip sandwiched in between? If you drop a chunk of video *on top* of a clip, iMovie launches a floating menu (see Figure 5-7). Its options include Insert, which splits the underlying clip into two pieces and drops your chunk between them (the other options are covered next).

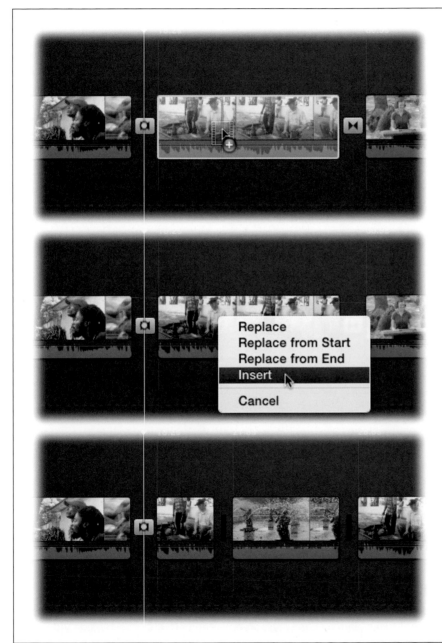

FIGURE 5-7

Top: To insert a clip in the middle of another clip, drop it on top.

Middle: Choose Insert from the menu that appears.

Bottom: iMovie splits the underlying clip in two and nestles the new clip in between.

Replace a Clip

Suppose you're editing a project that has music in it, and you worked hard to get the timing of the cuts to match up with the music. (Let's say you worked that hard because you haven't yet discovered the Beat Markers covered on page 182.) But as you preview your masterpiece, you realize that the video part of the clip is just plain dull. You have something much more interesting to replace it with, but you know that unless your replacement is exactly the same length as the original shot, it will mess up the timing of your entire project.

iMovie offers three ways to replace a clip with a better one of the *exact same length*. Select your replacement footage, drag it to your storyboard, and drop it onto the boring section. In the floating menu that appears (Figure 5-7), select from the following options:

- **Replace** replaces the entire underlying clip with the selection you're adding, no matter how long either one is. This option does *not* match lengths and will alter your project's timing (Figure 5-8, top).

- **Replace from Start** resizes the incoming clip to match the length of the replaced clip—by adding more footage to, or subtracting it from, the right end of the clip you selected (see Figure 5-8, middle).

  So if the soon-to-be-replaced clip is 8 seconds long and your incoming clip is only 4 seconds long, iMovie extends the incoming video by 4 seconds to the right end (assuming there's footage available). Alternatively, if the incoming selection is *longer* than 8 seconds, iMovie *cuts* from the right end of the clip so that it matches the duration of the original clip.

> **TIP** If the incoming clip isn't long enough to fully replace the original clip, iMovie warns you that the resulting edit will shorten your movie. (If you want to avoid this warning in the future, turn on the "Do not warn..." checkbox.)

- **Replace from End** is a lot like Replace from Start, except that it resizes the incoming footage by extending or reducing your selection to the *left* (Figure 5-8, bottom). So if you're replacing a clip that's 8 seconds long, but the replacement selection is only 4 seconds long, iMovie extends your selection by adding 4 seconds of footage to the *beginning* of the selection. If the incoming video is longer than the original, on the other hand, the first part of it gets lopped off.

> **TIP** If your resized footage doesn't display the moment just right, you can adjust it using the handy Clip Trimmer, covered on page 67.

Connect a Clip

iMovie offers one more way to add clips, by "connecting" them. Connected clips offer many cool tricks, namely cutaways, green-screen effects, side-by-side video, and picture-in-picture viewing. Each of these is explained in detail in Chapter 8 (page 112).

Replace

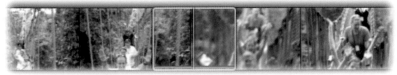

Only the selection is added.

Replace from start

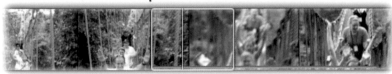

The selection, plus more from after it

Replace from end

The selection, plus more from before it

FIGURE 5-8

You can replace clips in your project without having to select exactly the right amount of video from a clip in the Event browser. In this example, you're replacing 10 seconds' worth of footage.

Top: If you selected only 4 seconds of video in the Event browser and choose "Replace," iMovie adds only that 4-second selection.

Middle: If you use "Replace from Start," iMovie adds 6 seconds of footage to the end of your replacement clip, so that it matches the clip it's replacing. (The orange line shows you how much event footage iMovie added.)

Bottom: If you select "Replace from End," then instead of extending your selection by adding 6 seconds at the end of the clip, iMovie adds 6 seconds to the beginning of it.

The Orange Stripe

Each time you add source video to your nascent movie, iMovie slaps an orange stripe across the bottom of the original clip in the Event browser, as shown in Figure 5-8. That's a reminder that you've *used* this segment of footage in your project. As your work proceeds, you'll be able to tell, with a glance at your Event browser, what portion of the original video you used in your finished opus.

Now, remember that all your edited movies—your *projects*—draw on the same well of source video on your computer. What's cool, therefore, is that iMovie memorizes the orange striping for every project. If you used a different set of Little League footage in each of three projects, you'll see the stripes jump around in the Event browser as you select each project in turn.

TIP An easy way to select a chunk of event footage already used in a project is to double-click the orange stripe. iMovie automatically selects *just* the striped footage.

Don't Remember to Save

You don't have to save your work. iMovie automatically saves as you go. (It doesn't even have a Save command.)

▩ Phase 4: Fine-Tune Edits

Once you've got a rough cut of your project, you may consider the Event browser a lot less necessary. Your focus will probably shift to the storyboard so you can fine-tune your edits. Now, in other words, might be a good time to hide the Libraries list and, if you swapped the storyboard and Event browser as explained on page 45, to move the whole storyboard back to the wider space at the *bottom* of the iMovie window.

The rest of this chapter explores a few ways to fine-tune your movie-in-progress.

Storyboard Playback

You can instantly play back your project to spot-check your work in the Viewer. Since you'll probably do this a lot, iMovie offers multiple techniques:

- **Anyplace playback.** Point (without clicking) to any spot in your project and then press the space bar to begin playback. Press the space bar again to stop.

TIP As you fine-tune your movie, you might want to make the Viewer bigger, so you see your work closer to full size. See page 45.

- **Selection playback.** Select some footage in the storyboard (click a clip or ⌘-click multiple clips). Then press the forward slash key (/, next to the period key) to play back *just the selected clips* from the beginning. Press / again to stop.

NOTE You can select part of a clip in the storyboard by clicking and holding a spot on a clip. The cursor changes to a little selection tool with a yellow handle and two arrows. Now, while you still hold down, drag the mouse to select a range of footage inside a clip.

- **Whole-storyboard playback.** Press the backslash key (\, above the Return key) to play the *entire* storyboard from the beginning. Press \ again (or the space bar) to stop.

NOTE There are menu equivalents for all three of these commands. In the View menu, select Play, Play Selection, or Play from Beginning. But it's far more efficient to use the keyboard shortcuts.

No matter how you start playback, you can always stop it by tapping the space bar.

Full-Screen Playback

You can make the Viewer window bigger to get a more detailed view of your video by dragging the top edge of the storyboard window. But, eventually, you'll want to treat yourself to iMovie's IMAX mode: *full-screen* playback. That's when all of iMovie's controls and menus disappear, and the Viewer fills your monitor.

No matter where you are in the storyboard, press Shift-⌘-F to begin full-screen playback of the selected video.

Once you have full-screen playback under way, moving your mouse makes the navigation tools shown in Figure 5-9 appear. They look a lot like the controls you see when you play a movie full screen in iTunes or QuickTime.

> **TIP** Don't miss the Play Selection button on the left-hand side. Click it to skip back to the beginning of the clip you selected instead of going back to the beginning of your project.

FIGURE 5-9
During full-screen playback, if you wiggle your mouse, you get the navigation tools shown here. Notice the handy Play Selection button on the left side.

Play selection   Play/Rewind/Fast forward   Exit full-screen

Here's how you navigate in full-screen mode:

- Press the space bar to start and stop playback without exiting full-screen mode. Or click ▶ in the middle of the navigation tools. (The button changes to **❚❚** as the video plays.)

- Use the diamond-shaped slider to move back and forth within your video. You can also click any spot in the slider track to jump straight to that point in the movie. During playback, if you move the slider, iMovie will continue playing the video from that spot on.

- Use the left and right arrow buttons to skip forward or backward to the beginning or end of clips.

- In a project with multiple clips, one click of the left arrow takes you to the start of the current clip; a second, quick click takes you to the start of the previous clip. Hitting the right arrow takes you to the next clip.

- To exit full-screen mode, click the diagonally opposing arrows in the upper-right corner of the playback controls, or press the Escape key.

TIP Depending on the size of your screen, your video might have lower resolution than your Mac. To fill your screen for playback, iMovie *stretches* the picture, which slightly lowers its quality. Don't get scared if it looks blurry. That's the result of having a really nice computer screen.

In a few other cases (for example, high-def video on a small laptop), the video may actually be too *big* for the screen. In that case, iMovie scrunches it *down* to fit.

Rearrange Clips

Unless your last name is Spielberg or Scorsese—and maybe even if it is—the first place you put a clip in the storyboard won't *always* be the best spot for it. Sooner or later, you'll wish you could move shots around in a film.

You can, if you know how.

1. **Select the clip or clips you want to move.**

   You can select just one clip or multiple clips by ⌘-clicking each.

   TIP At this point, consider adjusting the storyboard's zoom level (page 50) so you have an easier time finding where to place the moved video.

2. **Drag the selection to its new location.**

   Grab anywhere inside the yellow border, drag the selection to its new location, and then let go. Moving clips in a project works just like it does when you add footage from an event. That means you can add it to the end, replace a clip, insert it, or connect it. (See Figures 5-6 and 5-7 to remember what this looks like.)

Copy and Paste Clips

Dragging isn't the only way to move footage around in iMovie; the Copy, Cut, and Paste commands can feel more precise. These commands are also the *only* way to copy edited footage from one project to another. They're also a really easy way to insert clips into the middle of other clips.

> **NOTE** When you copy and paste clips, you're never duplicating files on your hard drive, so don't worry about eating up free space.

You already know how to indicate *what* you want to cut or copy; just use the selection techniques described on page 54.

Then use the Edit→Cut or Edit→Copy command (⌘-X or ⌘-C). Point to where you want to paste the copied material (do not click), and then choose Edit→Paste (⌘-V). Presto! The cut or copied material appears at the position of your cursor and shoves the rest of the movie to the right.

Resize Clips

Almost nobody hits the camcorder's Record button at the precise instant the action begins, or stops recording the instant an action stops. Life (not to mention animals, geysers, and children) is just too unpredictable.

Most of the time, of course, you'll leave the boring stuff (page 53) in the Event browser before you add a clip to the storyboard. Sometimes, though, you'll discover—only *after* you put the clip in the storyboard—that you didn't get the clip-editing process quite right. Maybe the shots are still *too* languorous and should be shorter. Or the shots are *too* quick, and it's going to be hard for your audience to figure out what's going on.

In both cases, it would be nice to shorten or lengthen a clip even after you place it in the storyboard.

> **NOTE** "Lengthen a clip?" That's right. iMovie is a *nondestructive* editing program. No matter how much editing you do, iMovie never, ever changes the original footage on your hard drive. For example, if you shorten a clip by hacking a piece off the right end, you can change your mind—even three presidential administrations later—and restore some or all of the missing footage, using the techniques described on these pages.

Fortunately, iMovie is crawling with ways to make these adjustments. They boil down to these approaches:

- Shorten or lengthen a clip-in-place by subtracting from or adding to the front or back.

- Trim (shorten) a clip to the position of the playhead.

- Shorten, lengthen, or reposition a clip with iMovie's Clip Trimmer.

- Shorten, lengthen, or reposition a clip using the Precision Editor.

The following pages cover all four methods.

> **NOTE** When you *shorten* a clip, all subsequent clips slide to the left to close the resulting gap. (That's called *ripple* editing.) On the other hand, when you lengthen a clip, exposing previously hidden footage, iMovie shoves all subsequent clips to the *right* to make room. Your movie, as a result, gets longer.

GEM IN THE ROUGH

Video Markers

While you do all this editing, you may find it helpful to mark the spots in your clips where important things happen, like the crack of a bat or the silly face your kid makes. iMovie offers a handy little tool, the video marker, to remember the spot for you.

To use it, position your playhead at the right moment in your movie and then hit the letter M key, or choose Mark→Add Marker. A tiny blue chip appears on the top edge of your clip. Now, when you go back to do something there, you have the precise moment preserved.

This trick is even more useful if you turn on snapping (View→Snapping or the letter-N key). With snapping on, the playhead magnetically jumps to the video marker as your cursor gets close to it, making it easier to ensure that your edit occurs at just the right spot.

You can add markers to songs as well, and, since snapping works with audio markers, too, it's easy to edit your movie to the beat of a soundtrack. You can learn the details on page 182.

To delete a marker, choose Mark→Delete Marker (Shift-Control-M), or just grab the marker and drag it off your clip. It disappears with a cute little puff of smoke.

■ RESIZE CLIPS IN PLACE

Perhaps the simplest way to resize clips is to drag the ends around. When you point without clicking to the beginning or end of a clip, your cursor changes to a couple of arrows with a line in the middle (Figure 5-10). You can now drag the end of the clip in either direction, making it longer or shorter.

As you drag, the Viewer shows the footage you're adding or subtracting from your movie. Also, a handy little bubble appears above the cursor telling you how many seconds of footage you're adding or subtracting.

If you see a red line at the end of a clip as you resize it, you've hit the end of the original footage: There's nothing more to add. In that case, you see just a single arrow at the end of the clip, telling you you can adjust it in only one direction (Figure 5-10).

■ TRIM TO THE PLAYHEAD

If all you want to do is shorten the end of a clip that's too long, you don't even need to drag. Just position the playhead where you want the clip to end and press Option-/. iMovie lops the end off the clip right at the playhead.

> **TIP** This command and many others are available in a floating menu you can call up by Control-clicking (right-clicking) in iMovie. (That's a two-finger click if you have a trackpad, like the one on a laptop, or a Magic Trackpad.)

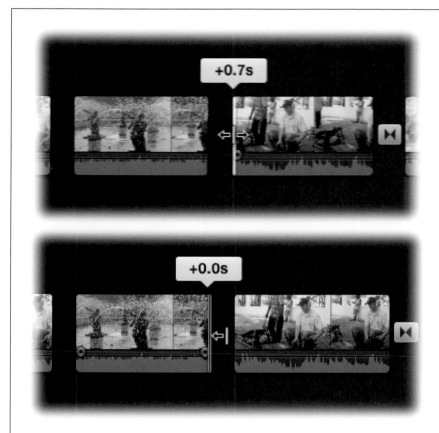

FIGURE 5-10

*Top: You're resizing this
clip in the storyboard; the
bubble tells you how many
seconds you're adding to
the movie.*

*Bottom: This clip has hit
the end of the road (or the
end of the original clip,
anyway), so there's no
more footage to add.*

■ USE THE CLIP TRIMMER

All right, resizing clips in place is a quick, efficient way to make basic changes. But you can't see what you're doing until you add or subtract it. What if you can't even grasp what you're looking at and wish you could see the entire original clip?

That's what the Clip Trimmer is all about. You open it by choosing Window→Show Clip Trimmer (⌘-\). iMovie displays the original footage in a strip just above the clip you're trimming. You can see it in Figure 5-11.

In essence, you're seeing the full-length clip, just as it originally appeared in the Event browser. The white borders indicate which part of the clip you're using in your movie. You can use the usual tricks to play back the footage, skimming the clip and hitting the space bar as necessary.

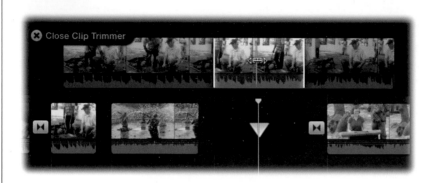

FIGURE 5-11

To open the Clip Trimmer, double-click any clip in the storyboard. In the Trim window, the white borders show which piece of the clip you're currently using in your movie. The dark-ened portions of the clip show the rest of that clip's raw footage. Drag either white line to lengthen or shorten the clip, or drag the clip itself to reposition it in your project.

Your main business here is to readjust your selection by dragging the white border. Make it longer if you want more of the clip in your project, shorter if you want less, just as if you were resizing the clip in place. Or grab any part of the clip, inside or outside the white boundaries, and slide the entire thing horizontally to include an earlier or later portion of the same duration.

When you finish reselecting, click the ✖ that says Close Clip Trimmer, or click the big blue down arrow on the clip in your storyboard.

■ THE PRECISION EDITOR

In editing jargon, a *cut* is the place where one clip ends and another begins—the crossroads where clips meet, in other words. A well-designed cut looks professional, even if it's subtle. For example, you might cut between two birthday parties that happened in the last year. To make the cut really cool, you could move from one birthday to the next using the exact moment when the candles are blown out. One of your kids would lean down to blow out the candles and, post-cut, the other would stand up smiling. The effect forges a connection between the two birthdays, even though they happened at different times.

The Precision Editor, an innovative tool that debuted in iMovie '09, makes cuts like these—cuts that would involve many steps in a professional editing tool—remarkably simple. Assuming you already have the clips in the storyboard, using the Precision Editor to create a refined cut goes like this:

1. **Call up the Precision Editor.**

   You can do this several ways. The easiest is to double-click the space between two clips. But if you already have a clip selected, you can choose Window→Show Precision Editor or press ⌘-/.

NOTE   If you placed a *transition* between two clips (page 83), double-clicking the transition's icon brings up the Adjustment Viewer for the transition. To get the Precision Editor instead, double-click the empty space just *above or below* the transition icon.

The Precision Editor and its controls overlay the storyboard and position the footage that comes before the cut above the footage that comes after the cut (see Figure 5-12).

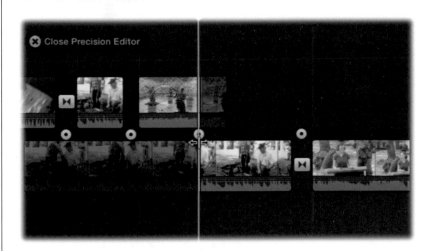

FIGURE 5-12

Behold the Precision Editor! The top layer holds the clips leading into a cut. The bottom layer contains the clips trailing the cut. You adjust the position of the cut by dragging the dot between the layers. Adjust the clips surrounding the cut by dragging the clips themselves. (The other dots running along the bar between the layers represent the different transitions and cuts in your project.)

2. **Adjust the cut point.**

   The gray vertical line with the dot in the middle is the cut line—think of it as the Precision Editor's playhead. It represents the position of the existing cut. You can drag the dot left or right to precisely position the cut. Dragging to the right extends the clip in front of the cut (called the *leading clip*) and shortens the clip that occurs after the cut (the *trailing clip*). Drag left for the opposite effect.

   If you added a transition, the dot looks more like a gray pill with two dots in it. Drag the middle part, between the two dots, to precision-cut here. (Dragging either of the dots increases the length of the transition, not the position of the cut.) Successfully grabbing the middle part may be hard to do if the dots are close together, so you may need to lengthen the transition (by moving the dots) to give yourself some room to work. You can then make the cut and shrink your transition back down to size.

3. **Adjust the clips surrounding the cut.**

   You may like where the leading clip cuts out, but not where the trailing clip comes in. To adjust the clip itself, drag it left or right (remember, the leading cut and trailing cut are on two separate lines, so you can move each independently of the other).

4. **Overlap the audio, if you like.**

   Say the leading clip has someone describing a fun memory in Grandma's backyard, while the trailing clip shows the next generation running out of Grandma's back door to play.

   Position the playhead where it crosses the audio track you want to edit (without clicking), and then move your cursor over only the *audio portion* of the playhead. You can then drag the cursor to "snap off" that audio portion from the Precision Editor's playhead and adjust the sound only (Figure 5-13). Drag the snapped-off part to specify where you want the audio to cut out. This means you can take the audio of the leading clip (memory of Grandma's backyard) and extend it into the video of the trailing clip (kids running out the back door) for a very nice effect. (Basically, this is another way to do the Cutaway audio trick explained on page 113.)

FIGURE 5-13

You can change the cut point for audio independently of the cut for your video. This kind of edit connects two clips in a way that a video cut can't. For example, if you shot an interview, you might want the person's voice to start before she actually shows up onscreen.

5. **Adjust the "extras."**

   Not everything involved in a cut is video. You may have titles, songs, or photo cutaways in your masterpiece. You can drag these elements left or right to adjust their timing, too, just as you do for audio or video.

6. **Preview your edit.**

   Previewing in the Precision Editor is just like previewing everywhere else. You can skim and play with the commands covered on page 52.

TIP When you skim in the Precision Editor, remember that skimming over the shaded area between clips shows you the cut. Skimming over the unshaded areas previews the clip. Don't skim a clip thinking you're seeing the cut!

7. **Go to the next cut.**

   Now that you have an Oscar-worthy cut, you can go to other cuts by clicking the gray dots that run along the middle bar. Each dot represents a different cut.

8. **Once you finish, click Done or hit the Esc key.**

Split a Clip

The techniques described in the previous section work well when you want to remove or add footage to a clip. Sometimes, however, you want to split a clip *without* removing or adding footage. For example, iMovie can only apply video effects to *entire clips*; if you want only *part* of your clip to get special treatment, you'll have to break that portion off into a standalone clip. (Don't worry; on playback, it still looks like part of the bigger clip.)

TIP If you were thinking of using Split Clip to insert something, maybe a picture, in the middle of a clip, save yourself the trouble and use the Insert feature discussed on page 59.

Or you may just want to break off one piece of a clip to use somewhere else in your movie. The Split Clip command is exactly what you need. Position your playhead where you want the split to occur, and then choose Modify→Split Clip (⌘-B).

TIP Because of the way skimming works, you'll probably misplace the playhead on your way to click a menu item. Remember that you can lock the playhead on a spot in a clip by holding down the Control key while you move your cursor out of the storyboard.

If you change your mind about a split immediately afterward, you can always use the Undo command to take back that step. If you split a clip and change your mind *much later*, after you've done a lot of other editing, iMovie can still accommodate you. Click either part of a split clip and choose Edit→Join Clip; iMovie plays marriage counselor and reunites the clip with its former soul mate, assuming it's still adjacent. (If something else is now between them, get it out of the way so iMovie can do its job.)

■ Aspect Ratios: The Missing Manual

You may find yourself editing new video clips together with old ones you imported from some DV tapes you had in a drawer. When that happens, you're combining video that has different aspect ratios. It's worth taking a moment to explain how iMovie handles this.

The Mighty Undo

As programs go, iMovie is forgiving. Its Edit→Undo (⌘-Z) command is an *unlimited* one, meaning that you can retrace (undo) your steps, one at a time, working backward all the way back to the moment you opened iMovie. (You can even unimport a clip from your camera!)

There's an Edit→Redo command, too (Shift-⌘-Z), so you can undo your undoing.

But be warned: Once you close iMovie, the program purges its Undo memory, so you can't reopen a movie and start back-tracking through your last session's commands.

Aspect ratio is an annoying geek term for the *shape of a movie frame*. Learning about aspect ratios is an unfortunate requirement of mastering video editing.

A history lesson is in order. As you may remember, the standard 1980 TV set's screen isn't the same shape as a movie screen. The TV is almost square, but the movie is wide and short. They have different aspect ratios (see Figure 5-14).

FIGURE 5-14

iMovie can accommodate any aspect ratio. Here you see two common ones: Standard (bottom), like the aspect ratio you see on old TVs, and Widescreen (top), like that of a high-def TV.

Old TVs have a 4:3 aspect ratio. Those are the horizontal:vertical proportions. So if your screen is 4 feet wide, it's 3 feet high.

NOTE   Weirdly, 16:9 is *not* the standard aspect ratio for Hollywood movies! Those are usually 1.85:1 or 2.35:1. (Don't ask why movie aspect ratios always have 1 in the denominator. Nobody ever accused the video industry of being consistent.)

Believe it or not, those aren't the only common aspect ratios. Consider the older iPhones (4s or prior)—their screens are 3:2.

Another common aspect ratio, the 9:16 format, is the opposite of HDTVs. This is the result of uninformed smartphone owners who hold their phones vertically when they shoot video. Read the sidebar below to find out why this is generally a bad thing.

iMovie doesn't bother wasting time with aspect ratios. Everything it edits comes out in the 16:9 format. That's an executive decision Apple made, based on the fact that HDTVs and the 16:9 format are the standard these days. But when you edit a movie that has footage shot at different aspect ratios, you have to choose how iMovie handles it, as explained in the next section.

UP TO SPEED

PSA: Hold your iPhone Sideways, Please!

This is the perfect moment for a brief public service announcement.

Almost everyone with a smartphone shoots video with it. This is pretty dang amazing, especially when you consider that these are high-definition movies! Shooting HD used to mean using a big ol' shoulder-mounted thing that cost thousands of dollars. Now HD smartphone cameras are standard. YouTube just wouldn't be the same without smartphone cameras. Vine wouldn't even exist.

But there's a rampant mistake people make when they whip out their phones and start shooting: They hold their phones vertically. All smartphones can record video this way, but that doesn't mean you *should*. If you do, you're wasting millions of perfectly good pixels.

Consider just about every TV and computer screen in the world. They're all oriented in landscape mode, meaning they're longer side to side than top to bottom (usually in a 16:9 aspect ratio). For any video to make full use of these screens, its aspect ratio needs to be the same.

When you shoot video with your phone held vertically, you're shooting in a 9:16 aspect ratio, not to mention at a *dramatically* lower video quality. (It has to do with how the light sensor in your phone captures video.) That means your footage played back on a typical TV or computer will be small and skinny, thanks to the gigantic black bars on either side. It's the only way the video will fit. (You could crop it to fit, but then you'd lose *over half* of it and it'd look terribly grainy.) Figure 5-15 illustrates the problem.

If you shoot video with your phone sideways, oriented just like a TV or computer screen, the camera shoots full-quality HD footage with the proper aspect ratio. Played back on another screen, it will look crisp and be free of the massive black bars.

In the end, we record stuff with our phones because we want to see it again. If you shoot with your phone sideways, you'll be sure to capture the moment in a quality and format that make it *worth* seeing again.

How iMovie Handles Mismatched Aspect Ratios

Whenever iMovie encounters source video that doesn't fit a frame, it can do one of two things:

- It can blow up the video large enough to fill the frame. In the process, of course, some of the picture gets chopped off the top and bottom of the frame. This is called cropping.

- It can add black letterbox bars on either side of the picture. This is called fitting.

Figure 5-15 shows what happens in both situations. By default, iMovie crops mismatched video. But you can change that.

FIGURE 5-15

You can tell iMovie how to handle non-16:9 aspect ratios.

Top: To make a clip shot with an iPhone held vertically (giving it a 2:3 aspect ratio) fill iMovie's 16:9 screen, choose Adjust→Cropping Tool→Crop from the iMovie toolbar (Figure 5-16).

Bottom: To see all of the 2:3 clip in iMovie, choose Fit instead of Crop. You'll see the entire iPhone shot, along with the requisite black bars.

Change How iMovie Handles Non-16:9 Footage

Yes, iMovie's factory setting is to crop mismatched video, but you don't have to play along. After all, this cropping could cut off the tops and bottoms of very important things, like Grandma and Grandpa.

To change the way iMovie displays non-16:9 footage, select the clip in your storyboard and then click the Adjust button in the iMovie toolbar. A set of editing tools appears in the Viewer. Choose the Cropping tool (Figure 5-16) and then click the Fit button. Now *all* of your clip appears in the frame, along with the necessary black bars on either side.

FIGURE 5-16

The cropping options in iMovie's Adjust tool. Choose Fit instead of Crop to see all of a clip shot with a non-16:9 aspect ratio. (The Ken Burns style is discussed on page 217.)

Video Chunks: Favorites and Rejects

I n iMovie, all your imported footage sits in your Event browser, like paints on a palette, ready to inspire your editorial brilliance. But that blessing is also a curse, because you likely have a huge pile of video to manage—and a lot of it's dreck.

Fortunately, iMovie comes with two tools to help you sort and manage these vast chunks of video. Working in the Event browser, you can do the following:

- Tag pieces of clips as Favorites, making them easy to find later.

- Flag pieces of clips as Rejects—bad footage you'll either *probably* or *definitely* not use in a project. The "probably" stuff you can just hide from view. The "definitely" stuff you can delete, freeing up space on your hard drive.

This chapter explores these clip-flagging tools and describes the proper way to get rid of bad shots forever.

■ Mark Clips as Favorites or Rejects

For iMovie's marking tools to actually save you time, they need to be easy to use. And they are. Marking footage as a Favorite or a Reject is just a two-step process:

1. **In the Event pane, select the video you like (or don't like).**

   You can select an entire clip (double-click it), multiple clips (⌘-click each one), or only part of a clip (drag your selection).

2. **Flag it.**

To flag the selection as a Favorite, press the letter F key on your keyboard, choose Mark→Favorite, or Control-click on the clip and choose Favorite.

To flag the footage as a Reject, press the Delete key, choose Mark→Reject, or Control-click the clip and choose Reject.

> **TIP** You don't have to follow step 1 if you're comfortable marking favorites or rejects in 4-second chunks. If you skim to any spot in your clip and then hit the F or Delete key, iMovie marks the 4 seconds of footage following the playhead as a Favorite or a Reject, respectively.
>
> Why 4 seconds? It's been a strange obsession ever since iMovie '08. For whatever reason, Apple thinks 4 seconds (and not 3 or 5) is the most useful length for video clips.

If you flag a selection as a Favorite, it sprouts a green line across the top. If you mark something as a Reject, you see a *red* line across the top (see Figure 6-1). (If you see a red line and the selection promptly disappears from view, you must have chosen Hide Rejected from the pop-up menu in the top-right corner of the Event browser—see "Hiding and Showing Favorites and Rejects.")

> **TIP** To mark an *entire* clip as a Favorite or a Reject, double-click it (or Option-click it). That's a lot faster than dragging through the whole clip.

Favorite footage   Rejected footage

Footage used in a project

FIGURE 6-1

Marking footage leaves green and red stripes on it. (The orange stripes point out clips you've used in one or more projects.) Green stripes denote favorite footage, while red stripes mark rejected bits.

Once you get the hang of these tools, you have an amazingly fast way to zoom through a freshly imported pile of footage, marking favorites and rejects as you go. And that, in turn, streamlines your editing, because you can work with just the good stuff.

TIP If you mark something as a Favorite or a Reject by mistake, you can unmark it quickly: Press ⌘-Z, or use the Unmarking tool (read on).

Selecting Marked Footage

In time, your event footage will twinkle with green, red, and even orange bars (orange means you used the clip in a project, as explained on page 61). But the stripes aren't just markers—they serve as turbo selection tools, too. Double-click a stripe, and *presto!*, iMovie neatly selects just that piece of film, ready for unmarking, cutting, deleting, or placing in a project.

TIP If you don't want to see the orange stripes, choose View→Hide Used Media Ranges. (Not the most obvious menu command, but there it is.)

Unmarking Clips

To unmark a clip, select it by double-clicking its stripe and then type the letter U key. The mysterious 4-second rule applies here, too. If you haven't selected anything, hitting the U key unmarks the 4 seconds that follow the playhead.

NOTE Of course, you can't unmark rejected footage unless you can *see* it on the screen. The following section shows you how to bring hidden footage back into view.

■ Hiding and Showing Favorites and Rejects

Marking clips won't save you any time if all it does is draw stripes on your footage. The payoff comes when you tell iMovie to *hide* everything except your Favorites or Rejects, making it easy to work with a big pool of extraordinary footage, or to review all your lousy footage before you delete it.

NOTE If you upgraded from iMovie '11, some of your event footage may show blue and purple stripes as well. These are holdovers from back when iMovie let you mark footage with keywords and face names. This new version of iMovie doesn't offer those tools, but Apple must have figured the markings might still be useful to you. Don't like them? Too bad: You can't *unmark* them in this version of iMovie, either.

You find the hide/show options in the Show pop-up menu in the top-right corner of the Event browser (Figure 6-2). These are your options:

- **All Clips.** iMovie displays everything: favorites, rejects, project-embedded footage, and unmarked footage. This view can work wonders when you know you have a certain shot but you can't find it using any of the other views.

- **Hide Rejected.** You'll probably use this option most of the time. It hides the dreck and shows your favorite clips, embedded footage, and unmarked footage.

- **Favorites.** Shows the cream of the crop.

- **Rejected.** You see only the bad stuff. Summon this view to review your rejected footage before deleting it for good (described next), or to hunt for a clip you can't seem to find among the good stuff (you may have rejected it by mistake).

FIGURE 6-2

Once you mark your footage, you can limit what you see in the Event browser to just Favorites, Rejects, or footage you could use anywhere ("Hide Rejected").

◼ Say Goodbye to Rejected Footage

When you mark a shot as a Reject, iMovie can hide it from view (see Figure 6-2) so you spend less time wading through mountains of bad video as you build your project. (Whether or not iMovie hides the rejected footage depends on your Show menu setting, as just explained.)

But marking shots as Rejects doesn't actually delete them from your computer. They're still there, gobbling up hard drive space. If you're sure you'll never need the footage again, you can permanently delete it from your Mac to reclaim that space.

A Warning Before You Delete Rejects

In previous versions of iMovie, when you deleted rejected footage from your Mac, iMovie did the magic of cutting just the bad bits out of the longer clip and sticking them in the Trash, leaving the rest of the footage available for you to work with. Things no longer work that way.

Now if you delete Rejects, iMovie sends the *entire* clip, not just the rejected part, to the Trash. That's a bummer, because the previous feature was a handy, hassle-free way to dump bad footage, reclaim disk space, and still have the rest of the footage to work with.

In the new version of iMovie, you need to be extra careful when you delete bad footage, because you could be throwing out good footage with the bad. You might want to take the extra step of selecting All Clips from the Show menu, looking for the red stripe of crud, and reviewing the entire clip before you move on to deleting rejected footage.

Delete Rejected Footage for Good

Once you're sure you don't need any part of a clip that contains rejected footage, you can purge the clips from your Mac:

1. **Choose Rejected from the Show menu.**

   TIP You don't actually have to reject a clip before you delete it. These steps work just fine with any clip you select in the Event browser. But rejecting clips beforehand is a nice way to set them all aside before you delete them.

   iMovie displays only the rejected parts of clips in the Event browser. This is your last chance to skim or play these clips to double-check their worthlessness.

   NOTE If you spot an *orange* stripe on any of these clips, you've used that footage in a project, though you might have marked part of it as rejected *afterward*. In this case, don't worry about deleting the clip, because iMovie made a copy of it in the project itself. Therefore, moving the event clip to the Trash won't remove it from your project.

   But it *will* remove the clip from your event footage, making it unavailable to use anywhere else once you delete it. So your current project isn't ruined, but future projects could be.

2. **Select the clip(s) you want to delete.**

   If you're in the Rejected clips view, iMovie automatically selects all of the clips for you. Otherwise, you need to manually select the clips you want to delete.

3. **Choose File→"Move to Trash" (or press ⌘-Delete).**

   If you're not using the clip in a project, iMovie warns you that this is the "last" version of the file, and you won't have it around for future projects. (See Figure 6-3 to learn why iMovie refers to this as your "last" clip. You get the same warning if you delete a clip from a project and the original clip isn't in your Event library anymore.)

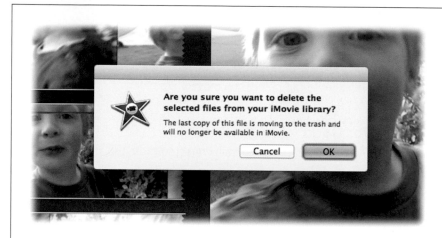

FIGURE 6-3

When you delete the last copy of a clip from the Event browser, iMovie makes sure you know that you won't be able to use that clip anymore. It also warns you when you delete a clip from a project if that clip isn't in the Event library anymore.

iMovie places all the rejected files in your Trash, and the filmstrips disappear from the Event browser.

NOTE At this point, the video isn't yet gone from your hard drive. If you accidentally moved a clip to the Trash, you can undo your mistake by choosing Edit→"Undo Move to Trash" (or pressing ⌘-Z).

Say, however, that you quit and restarted iMovie in the meantime. Then the Undo command won't work. You have one last, desperate chance to resurrect your deleted clip (assuming you haven't already followed step 4). Click 🗑 in your Dock. There you'll find the deleted clip.

To rescue the clip, drag it out of the Trash folder and import it into the event where you want to restore it. (Refresh your memory on how to import files by flipping back to page 13.)

4. **Empty your Trash.**

   In other words, switch to the Finder (click the Finder smiley face in the Dock), and choose Finder→Empty Trash. Or, if you can see 🗑 in your Dock, right-click it and then choose Empty Trash from the shortcut menu. Then enjoy the newly liberated space on your hard drive!

Transitions, Themes, and Travel Maps

Cutting and ordering clips into a coherent narrative makes them infinitely more entertaining than the hours of dreck you'd otherwise have. But why stop there? This is *computer* video editing, after all. The next two chapters cover what you can do *between* your clips (this chapter) and what you can do *to* your clips (video effects) to make your whole project more vivid.

■ About Transitions

What happens when one clip ends and the next one begins? In about 99.99 percent of all movies, music videos, and commercials—and in 100 percent of camcorder movies before the Macintosh era—you get a *cut*. That's the technical term for "nothing special happens at all." One scene ends, and the next one begins.

NOTE   Impressively enough, iMovie requires no *rendering time*—no delay while the program computes the video effect you're creating—as there is in most other video-editing programs. You see the effect instantly.

Professional film and video editors, however, have at their disposal a wide range of *transitions*—special effects that smooth the juncture between one clip and the next. For example, the world's most popular transition is the *crossfade* or *dissolve*, in which the end of one clip gradually fades away as the next one fades in (see Figure 7-1). The crossfade is popular because it's so effective. It gives the transition a feeling of softness and grace, and yet it's so subtle that you might not notice it.

FIGURE 7-1
The world's most popular and effective transition effect: what iMovie calls a Cross Dissolve.

Like all video-editing programs, iMovie offers a variety of transitions, of which crossfades are only the beginning. You'll find a catalog of them beginning on page 92. iMovie makes adding such effects easy, and the results look awesomely assured and professional.

When to Not Use Transitions

When the Macintosh debuted in 1984, one of its most exciting features was its *fonts*. Without having to buy those self-adhesive lettering sets from art stores, you could make posters, flyers, and newsletters using any typeface you wanted. In fact, if you weren't particularly concerned with taste, you could combine lots of typefaces on the same page—and thousands of first-time desktop publishers did exactly that. They thought it was exciting to harness the world of typography right on their computer screen.

You may even remember the result: a proliferation of homemade graphic design that rated very low on the artistic-taste scale. Instead of making documents look more professional, the wild explosion of mixed typefaces made them look amateurish in a whole new way.

In video, transitions present exactly the same temptation: If you use too many, you risk telegraphing that you're a beginner at work. So when you begin to polish your movie by adding transitions, consider these questions:

- **Does it really need a transition?** Sometimes a simple cut is the most effective transition from one shot to the next. Yes, the crossfade lends a feeling of softness and smoothness to the movie, but is that really what you want? If it's a sweet video of your kids growing up over time, absolutely yes. But if it's a hard-hitting "issue" documentary, then probably not, as those soft edges would dull the impact of your footage.

  Remember, too, that transitions often suggest the *passage of time*. In movies and commercials, consecutive shots in the same scene never include such effects. Plain old cuts tell the viewer that one shot is following the next in real time. But suppose one scene ends with the beleaguered hero saying, "Well, at least I still have my job at the law firm!" and the next shot shows him operating a lemonade stand. (Now *that's* comedy!) In this case, a transition would be especially effective, because it tells the audience we've just jumped ahead a couple of days. Learn taste in transitions. They should be done *for a reason*.

- **Is it consistent?** Once you choose a style of transition for your movie, stick with it for the entire film (unless, as always, you have an artistic reason to do otherwise). A consistent style gives your work unity. That's why interior designers choose only one dominant color for a room.

- **Which effect is most appropriate?** As noted earlier, the crossfade is almost always the least intrusive, most effective, and best-looking transition. But each of the other iMovie transitions can be appropriate in certain situations.

    The catalog on page 92 gives you an example of when each transition might be appropriate. Most are useful primarily in music videos and other situations when wild stylistic flights of fancy are more readily accepted by viewers.

> **TIP** iMovie's Fade to Black transition is exempt from this stern advice. Use it at the beginning of *every* movie, if you like, and at the end. Doing so adds a fade in and fade out, lending a professional feeling to your film. But it's so subtle, your audience will notice it only subconsciously, if at all.

■ Two Ways to "Transish"

You can insert iMovie's transition effects one by one, placing them between scenes only where appropriate, and hand-tailoring each one. That's the way you add transitions in most programs, including the old iMovie.

But lurking one millimeter beneath iMovie's surface at all times is its primary mission: letting you assemble edited video *fast*, automating *everything*. For that reason, iMovie also lets you turn on *automatic, global* transitions (great for slideshows!). The following sections cover both hand-crafted and automatic transitions.

■ Create Individual Transitions

To see the 20 transitions iMovie offers, click Transitions in the Content Library (identified in Figure 7-2), found in your Libraries list. (Or just press ⌘-1.)

> **NOTE** You see transitions and the other items in the Content Library only if you have a project open.

All the available transitions appear where your Event browser used to be. Skim over a transition's icon (like Cross Dissolve) without clicking to see an animated preview of it in the Viewer. (This behavior is a little buggy in the current version of iMovie after you skim the first transition. It helps if you skim something in the storyboard and then come back to skim a transition.)

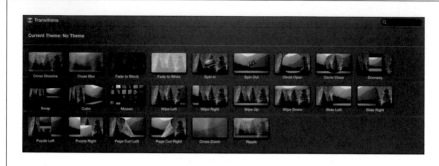

FIGURE 7-2

The Transitions library, where you can view, skim, and place all the transitions available in iMovie.

Once you find a good effect, drag its icon *out* of the Transitions panel and directly into the storyboard area, in the vertical gap between the two clips that you want transitioned. Figure 7-3 shows the technique. You can also insert a transition by double-clicking it. It appears in the gap closest to the storyboard playhead.

> **TIP** Most people think of putting transitions *between* two clips. But if you drag a transition to the *beginning* of your storyboard, the transition works just as well—except that it transitions out of blackness. Fade to Black and Circle Open work especially well at the start of a movie.
>
> The same happy surprise awaits if you drag a transition to the *end* of a movie. iMovie wipes, fades, or ripples from the final shot into blackness.

Once you drop a transition in place, you can review the result.

- To watch just the transition itself, click the transition's icon in the storyboard (it sprouts a yellow border to show you've selected it) and then press the / key. That's on the bottom row of the keyboard, and it always means "play the selection" in iMovie.

- It's a good idea to watch your transition by "rewinding" a few seconds into the preceding footage, to get a sense of the effect in the context of the existing footage. To watch the transition *and* the clips that it joins together, point to a spot just before the transition, and then hit the space bar.

- If you think the scene seam looked better without the transition, choose Edit→ Undo (⌘-Z).

You'll discover that the audio from the clips on either side of a transition still plays— you hear the sounds overlapping for a moment—but iMovie gradually crossfades the two.

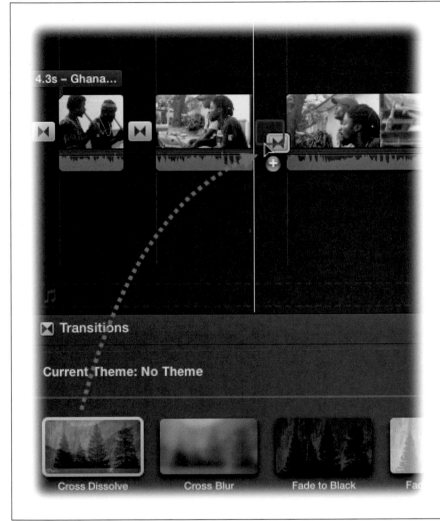

FIGURE 7-3

Insert a transition by dragging it out of the Transitions palette and in between two clips (or at either end of your movie). In the storyboard, a transition shows up as a tiny icon with arrows inside.

TIP If you want transitions on *most* of your scene seams, turn on the Automatic Transitions feature described on page 91. Then, using the Tip on that page, you can delete just the transitions you *don't* want.

Change or Delete a Transition

If you like the *idea* of a transition but you just don't like the one you put there, you can replace it in two ways:

- Drag a different effect out of the Transitions panel and drop it right on top of the old one.

- Highlight the transition in your storyboard and then, in the Transitions panel, double-click the replacement transition.

To get rid of a transition, even months or years later, highlight its icon and then press the Delete key. Your original clips return instantly, exactly as they were before you added the transition.

A Long Discussion of Transition Lengths

iMovie thinks that choosing a duration for each transition is a nuisance. Every transition you insert starts out at the same length—1 second for transitions found in the Content Library, 2 seconds for transitions added as part of a movie theme (see page 98). But iMovie isn't a complete tyrant; you can adjust the duration of transitions in three ways:

- **Change the duration of future transitions.** This option involves a visit to the Viewer. Go to Window→Movie Properties (⌘-J), and then click Settings in the Viewer window. That unearths the Transitions slider (Figure 7-4), where you can change the duration of *future* transitions, to anywhere from 0.5 seconds to 2 seconds. So what happens to the transitions you *already* added to your movie? They retain the duration they had when you inserted them, whether that was iMovie's default of 1 second or a custom duration you set using one of the methods discussed here. (If, for example, you set a custom duration using the Transitions slider, that duration remains in play until you select a new duration here, which will affect any transitions you add to the movie from this point forward.)

FIGURE 7-4

To set a transition duration, choose Window→Movie Properties, and then click Settings. In this window, drag the slider to indicate how long you want each transition to last. The setting applies to future transitions only.

- **Change individual transitions.** Fortunately for control freaks, you can change transition durations by simply double-clicking them. When you do, iMovie pops up a little balloon above your transition. Type in the new timing and click Apply. If you want more fine-grained control, you can also bring up the Precision Editor (page 68). It represents the current transition with a little pill-shaped icon and a dot at either end. Drag either dot sideways to make the transition longer or shorter. A balloon pops up with the durations as you make adjustments.

- **Change all transition durations at once.** If you want to change *all* of your transitions to be a specific length, double-click on any transition in your timeline so the transition bubble appears (Figure 7-5). Type in the desired length, but this time, click Apply to All. iMovie sets all your transitions to that duration. (Well, hopefully—see the next section for exceptions.)

NOTE   If you manually set the duration of individual transitions in the Precision Editor, be careful. Using "Apply to All Transitions" wipes out all your handiwork.

The transitions Viewer window, as you can see, is a way to change all transitions to a certain style, too. Just choose an existing transition for reference and then click the "Apply to All Transitions" button to make them all that way.

FIGURE 7-5

To set a universal duration, type in the number you want, formatted as seconds.tenths, and then click Apply to All.

Why You Don't Always Get What You Want

Even after you master transition durations, you may find yourself thwarted by iMovie itself. For example, you might tell iMovie to make all your transitions 3 seconds long, only to find that one of them is only 2 seconds long. The problem lies with either the leading or trailing clip. If either is too short to accommodate your requested duration, iMovie steps in and gets as close as it can. Thus, iMovie enforces its own Law of Reasonable Durations, which states that *no transition effect may consume more than an entire clip.* It doesn't take a genius to figure out why: A transition has to have enough video to transish.

NOTE You can't extend transitions into areas occupied by titles, either. You have to move or shorten the title (page 157) to put a transition there.

How Transitions Affect the Length of Your Movie

As you can see by the example in Figure 7-6, transitions generally make your movie *shorter*. To transition from the end of one clip to the beginning of the next, iMovie has to overlay the two clips—pull each one into the transition, in other words—which shortens your movie.

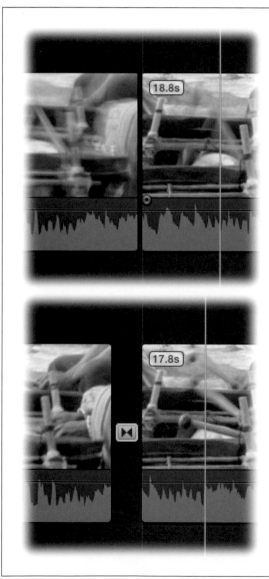

FIGURE 7-6

When you insert a 2-second transition between two clips, iMovie overlaps each clip by 1 second. Notice how the right-hand clip is now a second shorter? A transition shortens each clip, so the entire movie is now 2 seconds shorter.

Under most circumstances, there's nothing wrong with that. After all, that's why, when you insert your clips, you should avoid trimming off *all* the excess leader and trailer footage (known as *trim handles*) from the ends of your clips. By leaving trim handles on each clip—which you sacrifice to the transition—you give iMovie some fade-in and fade-out footage to play with.

Sometimes, however, having your overall project shortened is a serious problem, especially when you've been "cutting to sound," that is, synchronizing your footage to an existing music track. Even if you use the snapping feature to edit your movie to the beats in a song (covered on page 182), any transitions you add will throw off the timing.

In iMovie, there's no good solution to this problem if you opt for manual control over transitions. (The *automatic* transition feature, which puts a transition between every scene in the entire movie, offers a semi-solution; see the next section.) Your best strategy is to plan ahead. Don't fit your film to music until *after* you add all the transitions you want.

◼ Automatic Transitions

If you're really in a hurry to crank out your edited movie, like the now-legendary Apple programmer who wound up writing iMovie so he could whip out highlight reels without hand-tweaking everything, you're in luck. You don't have to bother placing transitions one at a time. Using the "Automatic content" feature, you can tell iMovie to put transitions between *all* your clips.

For themes (covered on page 96), this setting means iMovie will add transitions that match the theme—if you choose Neon, for example, iMovie's transitions will be flashy. (If you choose No Theme, iMovie simply adds a nice cross-dissolve between clips.)

This feature is OK *if* all of this is true:

- You want a transition between *every* clip in your movie (no simple cuts between scenes, in other words).

- You *want* cross-dissolves as your transitions.

- You set the duration to something short, like 1 second (because crossfades can get old fast).

- You're creating a highlight reel—a sequence of shots that aren't intended to tell a story (simple cuts move a narrative along).

If you're not careful, these frequent transitions can get annoying or cloying, and they'll lose their impact in a hurry.

If you want all the transitions to be something else, you can change them all at once using the instructions on page 89. Just remember that this *removes* any customizing you did to individual transitions; all your adjustments get wiped away.

TIP There is, however, a way to turn all of these automatic transitions into *individual* transitions that you can edit separately; see the section below.

Still interested? Then proceed like this:

1. **Choose View→Movie Properties.**

   Alternatively, press ⌘-J. Either way, the Movie Information screen appears in the Viewer.

2. **Click Settings.**

3. **Turn on "Automatic content." From the pop-up menu, choose the transition you want.**

   Remember, this works only if you chose No Theme for your movie. (You can change that in the movie settings, too.) You also don't get to choose the transition style, but the only one you'd ever use this much anyway is the Cross Dissolve. (Right?)

Now, if you add any new clips to your movie, iMovie adds your chosen transition to the end of them automatically.

Adjust Automatic Transitions

To make changes to all of these automatic transitions, use the steps described on page 89.

NOTE When you try to change automatically inserted transitions, iMovie warns you that you still have "Automatic content" turned on, and you can't make changes until you turn it off. Click Turn Off Automatic Content, and iMovie dutifully makes the changes you request.

Turn Off Automatic Transitions

If you're sick of the automatic transitions, just go back into your movie settings and uncheck the "Automatic content" box.

▪ Transitions: The iMovie Catalog

iMovie gives you a choice of 20 transitions. Here's a description of each, along with what editing circumstances might call for it. They're listed in the same order they appear in iMovie.

Cross-Dissolve

The crossfade, or dissolve, is the world's most popular transition. iMovie superimposes the end of the first clip over the beginning of the second one, making the image in the leading clip gradually disappear while the image in the trailing clip gradually fades in. If you must use a transition, you can't go wrong with this one.

Cross Blur

Like an autofocus adjustment gone awry, the first clip gets blurry, only to have the focus return with the second clip now onscreen.

Fade to Black, Fade to White

Use Fade to Black at the beginning and end of every movie, for a handsome, professional fade in/fade out. (While Fade to Black at the beginning of a movie may seem like a contradiction, here's where it works: Once the opening titles roll, insert a Fade to Black transition to signal the end of the credits and the start of the movie.) Or use Fade to Black at the start of any scene that begins in a new place or time. In that situation, the first scene fades to black momentarily, and then the next scene fades in (Figure 7-7).

FIGURE 7-7
Fade to Black.

Fade To White works the same way, with one big difference, of course: It fades out to, and then in from, *white* instead of black. Fading in and out to white lends a very specific feel to a movie: It indicates something ethereal, ghostly, or nostalgic. In today's Hollywood movies (including *The Sixth Sense*), a fade to white often indicates that the character you've been watching has just died.

Fade to White is a popular technique in today's TV commercials, when the advertiser wants to show you a series of charming, brightly colored images. By fading out to white between shots, the editor inserts the video equivalent of an ellipsis (... like this...) and keeps the mood happy and bright. (A fade-out to black would stop the flow with finality.)

Spin In, Spin Out

Did you see *Superman 3*? Where General Zod ends up in a floating jail cell that looks like a playing card flipping through space? Now you, too, can create that effect. Amaze your friends!

With Spin In, the second clip looks like a tilted card that straightens up and zooms into the middle of the screen, eventually filling the frame. Spin Out looks similar, but the first clip looks like a card zooming off, while the second one serves as a backdrop. Spin In trains your focus on the clip coming in, while Spin Out dwells on the departing clip.

Circle Open, Circle Close

This effect, called *iris open, iris close* or *iris in, iris out* in professional editing pro-grams, is a holdover from the silent film era, when, in the days before zoom lenses, directors used the effect to highlight a detail in a scene.

It creates an ever-enlarging or narrowing porthole. In Circle Open, the second clip sits inside the expanding porthole, and it eventually takes over the frame. With Circle Close, the first clip dwindles to nothing, leaving the second clip full-frame (Figure 7-8). The effect is useful at the beginning or end of a movie, when the subject of the first clip is centered in the frame and the second clip is solid black. In that setup, the movie begins or ends with a picture that grows or shrinks. (If the subject in the center waves goodbye just before being blinked out of view, the trick is especially effective.)

FIGURE 7-8
Circle Open.

Doorway

Here's an effect that takes full advantage of the three-dimensional powers built into your Mac. The first clip splits in half, and the two halves swing open like double doors. The second clip then charges through the doors, filling the screen.

Swap

This transition leaves no doubt that you're changing clips. Again harnessing your Mac's ability to animate in 3D, the first clip slides backward and to the left, as the incoming clip slides in from the right, eventually filling the screen. Several of these transitions in a row would leave the impression of some sort of assembly line.

Cube

Another 3D effect, this one makes it look like your first clip is playing on the side of a box that suddenly makes a quarter-turn, revealing the second clip. The effect conveys a sense of different scenes from the same event.

Mosaic

Like an impatient game of Memory, iMovie breaks your first clip into a bunch of little cards, and then flips them all over to reveal the second clip. The flipped cards blend together to finish the effect.

Wipe Left, Wipe Right, Wipe Up, Wipe Down

In this transition, the outgoing clip slides offscreen to the left, right, or up or down, trailed by the second clip (Figure 7-9). The transition gives you the feeling of a change in time and place. If you're a *Star Wars* fan, the Wipe will look familiar—George Lucas used it so much you'd think he owned the patent on it.

FIGURE 7-9
Wipe.

Slide Left, Slide Right

Just in case you want to make a convincing recreation of a vacation slideshow (back when people used manual slide projectors), this effect slides the new clip in on the heels of the old one—it's basically the Wipe, but with sharper edges. You could use the Slide in a clever, self-aware documentary, where the host, who appears in the second clip, pushes his way onto the screen.

Puzzle Left, Puzzle Right

This transition is a mix of the Mosaic and Slide transitions. Your incoming clip slides on top of the outgoing one as three separate "puzzle" pieces coming from different directions. It's fun and lighthearted, something you might use for a montage.

Page Curl Left, Page Curl Right

This slightly tacky transition makes the upper corner of the video frame appear to curl inward and toward you from the left or right, as though you were peeling a giant Post-it note off of a pad (Figure 7-10). The second clip is revealed underneath.

FIGURE 7-10
Page Curl.

Cross Zoom

If you've ever jumped into hyperspace—and hey, who hasn't?—this transition will look familiar. The first clip turns into a streaky tunnel, giving you the illusion of speeding through space, only to come out on the other end with the second clip showing. This transition emphasizes what's at the end of the wormhole.

Ripple

The Ripple effect is gorgeous, poetic, beautiful—and hard to justify. It invokes the "drop of water on the surface of a pond" metaphor (Figure 7-11). As the ripple expands outward, it pushes the first clip (the pond surface) off the screen to make way for the second one (the expanding circular ripple). It's a soothing, beautiful effect, but unless you're making mascara commercials, it calls a little too much attention to itself for everyday home movies.

FIGURE 7-11
Ripple.

■ Themes

Themes are like fancy wrapping for your videos. They add professionally designed and animated transitions, titles, and soundtracks that run throughout your movie, usually including an opening-credit sequence, some special transition styles, and a closing-credit sequence. Best of all, iMovie sews them right into your movie, with all the cool artwork and animations included.

iMovie gives you a choice of 15 themes. They have names like Travel, Comic Book, Photo Album, and Scrapbook. Each one includes unique transitions, titles, and soundtracks, adding serious production value to your movies. The iReport, News, and Sports themes also offer some fun customizability.

Choose a Theme

When you create a new project, iMovie asks you to apply a theme (happily for Type A's, one option is No Theme). Choosing one opens the Themes window (Figure 7-12), where you can preview your choices with sample footage. That way, you get an idea of what your stuff will look like—or at least, what it would look like if your family and friends were professional models. Still, iMovie themes can make your footage look pretty great.

FIGURE 7-12

Each of these themes has its own character and style. Click the Play arrow in any of them for a montage preview of what your themed project will look like.

Once you select a theme, iMovie automatically adds transitions, titles, and a soundtrack to your project, and turns on the "Automatic content" checkbox in the Viewer (page 91). From that point on, iMovie applies its theme magic to each new clip or picture you add to your storyboard. It mixes things up to avoid too many similar transitions in a row. Sometimes, for example, it uses stock transitions, like a simple cross-dissolve, while at others, it adds theme-specific transitions, like an animated photo album.

You can always override iMovie and add your own transitions, but the moment you do, iMovie warns you that you'll be turning off automatic content (Figure 7-13). Then you're back in manual mode. All the transitions already inserted will stay, but iMovie won't add anything automatically anymore.

NOTE You can avoid having to insert transitions individually by first letting iMovie do the work for you. Then, once all the transitions are in place, you can change them to your heart's content.

FIGURE 7-13

When it comes to themes and transitions, iMovie insists on being in charge if you accept its help. Once you try to do things your way, iMovie withdraws due to creative differences.

If you turned off automatic content and then decide that you really were better off with iMovie in charge, go to Window→Movie Properties (⌘-J) and click Settings, where you can turn automatic content back on (just turn on the checkbox). iMovie begins anew, adding the custom elements for the theme you initially chose, with one exception: It preserves any custom transitions you added to your project.

Custom Theme Transitions and Titles

If you choose a theme for your project, iMovie offers you transitions (and titles and soundtracks) available to that theme only, as shown in Figure 7-14. (If you chose No Theme, you don't see these options at all.)

> **TIP** If you like having options but don't want your movie dominated by a theme, go ahead and pick a theme—but turn off "Automatic content." You can still add theme elements manually.

On the other hand, if you choose a theme, you're locked out from the custom stuff available in the *other* 14 themes. (Maybe that's for the best. Mixing themes could look pretty ugly anyway.)

Change a Theme

iMovie is very generous to the wishy-washy. Each theme has title, transition, and soundtrack elements that correspond precisely to those in the other themes. When you change to a different theme, iMovie just replaces elements from the old theme with the matching elements from the new one.

To change a theme, choose Window→Movie Properties (⌘-J) and click Settings. Then use the Theme drop-down menu to choose a new theme. Once you do, iMovie takes a moment to update all the corresponding elements. Everything else, like timing and the clips in the project, stays the same.

FIGURE 7-14

When you choose a theme for your project, iMovie offers up to four custom transitions; choose one, and the program includes it in the mix of stock transitions it adds to your project. If you don't like the theme itself, go to Window→Movie Properties→Settings (page 41) to change it.

Adjust Theme Transitions

You can adjust a theme transition's length the same way you adjust a regular transition's length in the Precision Editor. Read more about that on page 68.

But one of the coolest things about themes is that they incorporate your pictures and video *into* the neat animations that go between clips. The animated photo album, for example, displays your video and photos as though they were actual photos in the album (Figure 7-15).

FIGURE 7-15

Your movie looks professionally designed thanks to the way iMovie inserts your photos and videos into theme transitions and titles, like this transition from the Photo Album theme.

iMovie automatically chooses what clips go where in the animation, but you can have some influence on the outcome. (This may be especially useful if iMovie happened to choose the part of a clip where you're shoveling birthday cake into your mouth.) To make a more dignified appearance in theme animations:

1. **Click the animated transition you want to adjust.**

   When you click the theme transition that needs changing, orange numbers hover above various points in your storyboard. The numbers represent different frames in the animation (see Figure 7-16).

> **NOTE** If you don't see the orange numbers, one of two things may be going on. First, some transitions just aren't editable. Second, there are often canned *portions* of editable transitions.

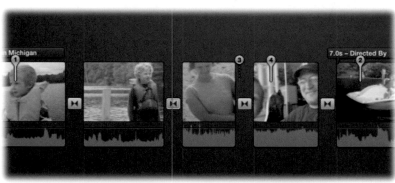

FIGURE 7-16

You can adjust some theme transitions so that the images in the animation show the part of the project you choose. Dragging the orange numbers around in your project changes a corresponding frame in the transition.

2. **Drag the numbers where you want them.**

   As you drag the numbers to different points in your storyboard, iMovie updates the transition frames, displaying whatever image is under the corresponding number. This is how you change focus from *your* cake-stuffed face to your *brother's* cake-stuffed face.

3. **Preview your changes.**

   As with most editable iMovie elements, such as titles and photos, you can preview your changes by clicking ▶ in the Viewer.

4. **Click away from the transition.**

   Your changes stick as you make them, so once you're done, just carry on with editing the rest of your movie. iMovie displays the transition with the updated images.

NOTE If you used themes way back in iMovie HD or iDVD, you know that those theme elements could use *any* photos and videos, even if they didn't show up anywhere else in your project. Now iMovie isn't so generous. Its themes point only to parts of photos or clips that actually appear in your storyboard. Anything that isn't going to be shown full screen isn't going into the theme transitions, either.

Customize Transitions That Are Maps

The CNN iReport, News, and Travel themes offer opening titles that show a map pinpointing a location on the globe. Obviously, this is meant to convey where the movie is taking place. That's why you can customize it.

But first, in a typical example of Apple brilliance, the opening map may already be updated for you. If your footage was shot with a GPS-enabled device—like an iPhone—your clip may already be *geotagged*, or embedded with information about where the footage was taken. iMovie reads this data and updates the map, even with the name of the particular place (like Cascade Golf Course) instead of just the city. Pretty neat.

If you're not lucky enough to have a geotagged clip, you can customize the map by double-clicking the title banner in your storyboard. The Viewer displays tools that help you make title changes (covered in Chapter 10), one of which is a little globe. That opens a window with a list of locations in it. Pick a location or, if it's not listed, type one in. Now the map in your theme shows the right locale.

Customize the Sports Theme

If you're using the Sports theme, you can take it a lot further than just a few neato transitions and titles. Apple devised a slick, professional theme for presenting your team to the world. It works by pulling players' names and stats from a roster you build using the Sports Team Editor. Then, when you want to show a cool graphic highlighting a player during your movie, you just drag a title into your project and choose the player from the roster. Voilà! You're making a highlight reel worthy of ESPN.

To build your team and put the Sports theme through its paces, follow these steps:

1. **Open the Sports Team Editor by choosing Window→Sports Team Editor.**

   The handy window that appears prompts you for all the information you need to enter (Figure 7-17).

2. **Create your team.**

   The top third of the Editor window lists all the teams you've created. iMovie already has one there to get you started. You can make changes to that one or create a new one by clicking the + button at the bottom of the list.

> **TIP** If your assistant coach has created a team roster in her copy of iMovie, she can export it using the Export Teams button under the teams list. This produces a file that she can email to you. Once you have it, import it using the Import Teams button. Now you have everything she's already typed in. That's what you call teamwork.

3. **Customize your stats.**

   At the bottom of the Sports Team Editor window, click ▼ next to Sports, and you'll see a list of sports already entered into iMovie. You can customize the list of sports, as well as the stats you see for each player. Notice that you can set the stat categories to whatever you want, and even specify your players' favorite colors (Figure 7-17).

4. **Add players to your roster.**

   In the middle of the Editor, start adding players by clicking the + button. iMovie creates a new player form so you can fill in the details. iMovie fills out the number field automatically, but be sure to change it to the player's jersey number.

5. **Add the Sports theme graphics to your project.**

   All your work in the Editor pays off when you start adding player graphics to your project. These come in the form of titles, which you can read about in detail on page 149. A customized player graphic/title looks like the one you see in Figure 7-17.

> **NOTE** You can customize some of the Sports theme elements with things like a game score or two teams facing off. If you find you can't edit them with the titles tool (page 149), click the ❶ tool instead. Then, when you click the scores or the team names in the Viewer, you can change them.

A movie with these awesome Sports theme graphics will get the other players/parents wondering how much you paid to have it professionally edited. You can just tell them you know a guy at ESPN and they won't have any reason to doubt you.

FIGURE 7-17

Top: The Sports Team Editor is where you keep track of all the teams you want to make movies about. You can make team rosters, add player pictures and stats, and even drop in your team's logo.

Bottom: Once you complete your roster, add one of the custom Sports titles to your movie and you can choose from the player list to make a broadcast-worthy graphic highlighting that player.

Remove a Theme

You may come to realize that a particular project is worse off with a theme applied to it. If so, choose Window→Movie Properties (⌘-J), click Settings, and then click the Theme drop-down menu, which opens the Themes window, where you choose No Theme. iMovie sweeps away all the theme-related titles and transitions, leaving you with a decidedly less theme-y project. (Non-theme transitions, like cross dissolves, survive iMovie's sweep.)

◼ Travel Maps

Just in case you didn't get the memo, here's some big news: iMovie loves travel footage. Maybe Apple did some rigorous focus-group research, or maybe the Apple programmer behind iMovie just loves to tour the world. (He does.) Whatever the reason, if you travel, iMovie has a special place in its heart for you.

Travel Maps are the grandest token of iMovie's travel-love. These are animated maps that take viewers from Point A to Point B with a snaking, animated red line across a map or a globe, à la the Indiana Jones movies. They're great for conveying your itinerary in a quick, visually compelling way. Although you might think of them as transitions—after all, they fill the space between things (in this case, places), much as transitions do—iMovie doesn't think of them that way. To iMovie, they're specialized video clips.

Add a Travel Map

In the Content Library list, click Maps & Backgrounds (or press ⌘-3) to show the pane with all the maps (see Figure 7-18). You see eight animated map options at the top of the list: a globe version and a flat version of four different map styles. You also see non-animated versions of each map that you can stick in your project as images. Scrolling down, you find a bunch of images that look nothing like maps (hence the "Backgrounds" part). Backgrounds are just pictures that you can use as backgrounds for titles, for example.

Adding an animated travel map to your project is a matter of dragging one of the eight icons into your project, just as you would a transition or a video clip. iMovie generates a specialized video clip you can now customize.

Change Travel Points

After you drag a map icon into your project, you'll probably need to make changes to it. Highlight the map clip and then click the Adjust tool. The Viewer reveals a custom tool for editing maps.

That's fortunate, because your first order of business is to change the endpoints of your new animated map. After all, showing your dramatic flight from Topeka to Tangiers is why you're putting this thing into your movie to begin with. You can choose your departure and destination points from a list of hundreds of preset locations (Figure 7-19).

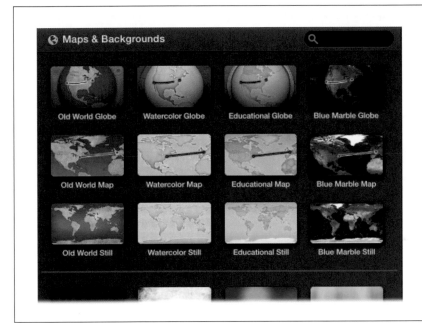

FIGURE 7-18

At the top of the Maps & Backgrounds pane are eight animated map options—four globes and four flat maps—to choose from. To add one to your project, just drag it in.

FIGURE 7-19

iMovie offers hundreds of destinations for your travel map. If you don't see the place you need, choose a nearby location, and then change the display name of that spot.

To change a location, click the San Francisco button (or whatever it says next to Start Location). iMovie reveals a huge list of cities and airports. You can winnow the list down by typing a destination's name into the box at the top of the window. Click to highlight the desired location, and then click Done.

Repeat the process for the End Location so the red line knows where to go.

If the location you need isn't in the list, choose the one closest by and then type a custom name in the text box at the bottom of the little location chooser.

> **TIP** If the list doesn't offer the location you want, you can type in the decimal coordinates (for example, *44.768056, −85.622222* points to Traverse City, MI). You can get these coordinates at *www.itouchmap.com/latlong.html*. Then just edit the "Name to display" text at the bottom of the Inspector window.

Change a Map's Style

If you started with a globe map and decide you prefer a flat one, or if you started with the Educational Map and like the Watercolor Map better, you can easily change it. Just drag a new map from the Maps & Backgrounds pane onto the map you want to replace. iMovie preserves locations and the length of the animation.

> **TIP** Because iMovie treats travel maps like clips, you can apply most video effects to a map as well. You might do this to match a map's style to the rest of your video, for example. Read all about video effects in Chapter 8.

If you chose a Globe map, you can find extra options in the Viewer; click the map and then the Adjust tool in the toolbar. By clicking the Style button you can change between the four map styles and even zoom in on the globe by checking the Zoom In box. You can also hide the destination names or the red travel line connecting the points, just by turning off the corresponding checkbox.

Change a Map's Timing

If a map's animation is too slow or too fast, you can adjust it by simply dragging the ends of it in the storyboard, or by dragging it around in the Precision Editor. iMovie helpfully shows you how much time you're adding to or subtracting from it.

Remove a Map

To remove a map, just select its clip icon in the storyboard and hit the Delete key.

Video Effects

t's a funny thing that we'll take pristine HD video and make it look old and grainy. On purpose. But video effects, like the popular Aged Film effect, create a mood that you can't really communicate in any other way.

Apple has put a lot of work into juicing iMovie's video effects. They include not only classic old tricks like Slo-Mo, Picture-in-Picture, and filters, but also some very cool new ones, like a one-step Instant Replay. Moreover, the new iMovie simplifies how most of the effects work. Now more than ever you can edit stuff in place, rather than having to fiddle with settings in a separate Inspector window.

NOTE Still no plug-ins, though, just in case you've been holding out for them. Don't expect that set of third-party plug-ins you bought for iMovie HD to *ever* work in the new iMovie.

Maybe best of all is that you don't have to wait for iMovie to *render* (process) an effect. Your project immediately reflects any effect you select.

◼ Video Effects

What iMovie calls video effects may be better described as video filters. They generally change only the color and definition of the underlying video. (The one notable exception is the Flipped effect, which displays a mirror image of your clip.)

The Effects

A rundown of iMovie's video effects is in order (Figure 8-1).

FIGURE 8-1

Most of iMovie's video effects are really video filters, each of which adds a unique style to a clip. This image demonstrates some of the effects. Clockwise from top-left: The original clip, Cartoon, Vignette, X-Ray, Heat Wave, and the much-adored Aged Film.

- **Flipped.** Turns your clip into a mirror image of itself.

- **Raster.** Covers your clip with horizontal scan lines, like you'd see on an old TV.

- **Cartoon.** Smooths the different colors in your clip to make it look like the clip was taken from a comic book.

- **Aged Film.** One of the most popular effects, Aged Film applies a sepia tone and film noise to make your clip look like an old, worn-out filmstrip.

- **Film Grain.** Applies a mild sepia tone and adds tiny speckles that look like grainy film.

- **Hard Light.** Overexposes the light colors and darkens the dark colors.

- **Day into Night.** Darkens the whole clip with a bluish hue, as though it were shot at night.

- **Glow.** Overexposes the light colors *without* darkening the dark colors.

- **Dream.** Blurs the clip and washes out its colors, to convey the idea of dreaming.

- **Romantic.** Blurs just the edges of the clip, so your focus rests on whatever's in the center (presumably the object of your desire).

- **Vignette.** Instead of blurring the edges, this effect fades the edges to black, not unlike what you'd see in studio photography from the 1980s.

- **Bleach Bypass.** Washes out colors, just like bleach.

- **Old World.** A sepia tone and a glow combined. Yet another way to make that high-tech footage look low-tech.

- **Heat Wave.** This is what your clip would look like under the punishing desert sun, yellow and overexposed.

- **Sci-Fi.** If you've seen the *Matrix* movies, you know exactly what Sci-Fi looks like. It applies a green hue to everything.

- **Black & White.** The old classic.

- **Sepia Tone.** The other old classic. Applies a brownish hue to everything, making it look like ancient photographs or films from the turn of the century (the turn of the *previous* century).

- **Negative.** Inverts all the colors in your clip by replacing them with their color-wheel opposites.

- **X-Ray.** Turns everything into shades of greenish-gray, with lights and darks inverted. Presumably, this is what your movie would look like if you filmed the whole thing with an X-ray machine.

Apply a Video Effect

You can apply video effects to any clip or photo in your project, even cutaways and travel maps. Start by selecting the clip, and then click the Adjust button in the toolbar. The Effects icon (shown highlighted in Figure 8-2) offers both video and audio effects.

Clicking the Effects button reveals a bunch of thumbnails that show what your clip would look like with the various video effect applied (Figure 8-2). Click an effect and iMovie skims across it, previewing it in the Viewer. To apply an effect, click the thumbnail itself.

iMovie doesn't update filmstrip thumbnails on the fly, so the filmstrip in the storyboard doesn't reflect the change. But the effect will show up when you preview the clip.

> **TIP** You can also play the clip (with the effect applied) by tapping the space bar while you preview the video effects. iMovie plays the clip repeatedly while you make up your mind. As your clip plays back, you can point to other effect thumbnails in the preview window (without clicking) to see what *they'd* look like if you applied them to your looping video.

Adjust a Video Effect

You can't make any adjustments to iMovie's video effects. If you don't like the way an effect that comes from Apple looks, you're out of luck.

Remove a Video Effect

To remove an effect, pull up the Effects chooser again, and then click the None thumbnail. Your clip is back to normal.

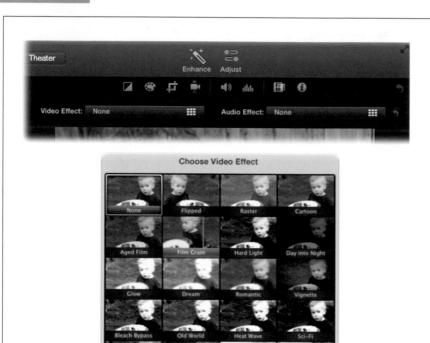

FIGURE 8-2

Top: To find iMovie's video effects, select Adjust in the toolbar.

Bottom: The effects generally affect the color and clarity of your clips. You can preview them by selecting an effect. To implement one, click the effect's thumbnail.

■ Fast/Slow/Reverse

Whether you want to mimic the race in *Chariots of Fire* or a Benny Hill chase scene, you can add a lot to your movie by changing the speed of your footage. Slowing a clip down emphasizes the drama of a moment. Speeding it up conveys urgency, depicts the passage of time, or just makes it funny. Throw in a good Reverse effect and you could pretend your protagonist has a remote control that rewinds time.

Change a Clip's Speed

iMovie offers two principal ways to make a clip play back faster or slower:

- **Speed changes from the menu bar.** In the Modify menu, iMovie gives you options for Slow Motion, Fast Forward, Instant Replay, Rewind, and Reset Speed. The first two options are simple clip speed changes. The next three are cool, complex effects you can apply with just one click.

The value of these menu options is that they're easy. They may not give you the precision you want, but you can't find a simpler way to make these edits. Plus, you can fine-tune them later using the next method.

- **Speed changes with the Speed Editor (⌘-R).** A huge improvement in this new version of iMovie, the Speed Editor is a very simple way to adjust the speed and direction of clips right in the storyboard.

The Speed Editor comes in two flavors. One lets you make rough speed changes; the other gives you finer control (Figure 8-3 shows both of these parts at work).

For quick-and-dirty speed changes, press ⌘-R or Control-click your clip; choose Show Speed Editor from the shortcut menu. A dot appears in the top-right corner of your footage. Drag the dot to change your clip's playback speed. When you do, you see either a bunny or tortoise button on the clip. Click either to launch the Speed Editor tool in the Viewer, where you can control speed by the numbers. To go directly to the Speed Editor window, call up the speed dot and then click the speed line once, no dot adjustment necessary.

FIGURE 8-3

Top: Drag the Speed Editor dot to change the playback speed of a clip.

Bottom: You can also use the Speed Editor in the Adjust tools to choose or type in a new speed (and to reverse a clip and preserve its audio pitch). Once you make an adjustment using the speed dot, you'll see a bunny or tortoise button on the clip. Click that to go straight to the Speed Editor. If you don't see a button, click the speed line once to use the tool in the Viewer.

TIP Normally, when you speed up or slow down a clip, the pitch of the clip changes, making it sound low, like Barry White, or high, like everyone in the clip sucked on helium. Check the Preserve Pitch box in the Speed Editor to stop this from happening.

Reverse a Clip's Playback Direction

Playing a clip backward has been a comedic staple since film was born. To do that in iMovie, just check the Reverse box, shown in Figure 8-2.

With the Speed Editor turned on, your reversed clip appears with a ◄ button on it.

Remove Speed and Direction Changes

If you *just* finished fooling with a clip's speed or playback direction, you can undo your changes with the Mighty Undo (Edit→Undo or ⌘-Z). But if you meddle with your clip in the meantime, or quit iMovie and then restart it, you can undo changes (or set a new speed) through the Speed Editor tool. But an even easier option is to select Modify→Reset Speed (Shift-Option-R). That removes any speed or direction changes.

■ Connected Clips

Some video effects mingle two clips together in various ways, like the video box that hovers over a news anchor's shoulder or the ubiquitous green-screen effects that Hollywood uses. iMovie handles these marriages through a feature called "connected clips." The idea is that you join two clips so that they interact in one of these special ways.

Specifically, iMovie can do cutaway, green-screen, side-by-side, and picture-in-picture effects. Each is discussed in the following sections.

Connect a Clip

To get any of these effects, you first need to connect two clips, and there are many ways to do so. With a clip in the storyboard, select the second clip in your Event browser. The slow way is to choose Edit→Connect. The super fast way is to press the letter Q key. In either case, iMovie connects the second clip starting at the playhead. You can also drag a selection from the Event browser (or even drag a clip in your project, so long as it includes no titles) and drop it just above the first clip.

Once connected, the second clip hovers above the first, with a little blue flag denoting the arrangement (Figure 8-4). You can move a connected clip wherever you want; you can even change your mind and drag it into the main row of clips to have it behave as a normal clip.

FIGURE 8-4

Once you connect a clip, you can drag it around so that it makes its entrance at any point in your movie. Also notice the little blue and gray adjustment handles. They change how quickly the clip (upper) and its audio (lower) fades in and out in relation to the clip below it. (The video cues work only in tandem, while the audio cues work independently.) A blue handle means there's no fade; a gray one means there is some fade.

Adjust the Fade-In and -Out

You can't add a special transition to a connected clip—iMovie uses a basic cross-dissolve on all of them. But you can adjust the timing of the transition to a connected clip using the little gray and blue handles shown in Figure 8-4.

Drag these handles inward to increase the video and audio fade. Drag them out to the ends to have your clip and/or audio appear immediately, without any fade.

Trim. Edit. Go Nuts.

You can adjust connected clips in pretty much all the same ways you work with normal clips. You can trim or edit them with the Clip Trimmer or Precision Editor, apply video or audio effects, and use them with titles. You can even make speed and direction changes. Don't hold back just because it's not a normal clip.

Cutaways

The first, most basic kind of connected clip is the *cutaway*. A cutaway is an important, basic editing technique. That's when someone on-camera begins talking...and you hear her *keep* talking, even as the video switches to something different (like something that illustrates what she's saying, for example). You see cutaways all the time on the nightly news, and in every documentary you've ever seen.

iMovie makes cutaways ridiculously easy. Just add a selection as a connected clip. iMovie chooses the cutaway automatically. But doing it like the professionals takes a little bit of planning.

In the following discussion, you'll work with what the pros call *A-roll* (the beginning video, usually of the person talking) and *B-roll* (the soundless footage that illustrates what she's talking about). Then, to make a cutaway:

1. **Start with the A-roll footage in your project.**

   Make sure that the footage has audio that's useful while showing the B-roll, like someone describing what the audience is going to see.

2. **Select your B-roll footage from the Event browser.**

   This is whatever footage you want to cut away *to* while the audio of the A-roll plays underneath.

3. **Drag and drop the B-roll selection onto your A-roll filmstrip in the project.**

   When you do, iMovie inserts the clip as a cutaway.

4. **Select your cutaway clip, and then press Shift-⌘-M to mute it.**

   You've just silenced any audio that came along with the B-roll clip, so it doesn't compete with the sound of the person talking.

Adjust a Cutaway

As mentioned, you can use all the standard editing tools with your cutaways, but two additional tools are specially designed for cutaways, and they're very cool. You find them by selecting the cutaway and then clicking the Adjust tool. Once there, click the Video Overlay tool (Figure 8-5) to see two other options:

- **Fade in/Fade out.** You don't have to cut abruptly to the cutaway; you can use a graceful crossfade into or out of it using the Fade slider.

NOTE If you made adjustments using the little blue and gray fader handles described on page 113, then your adjustments will be lost once you move the Fade slider.

- **Opacity.** Your cutaway doesn't have to completely *replace* the talking-person video, either; you can make it appear *superimposed* on the talking-head video, as though it's translucent. It's a special effect you won't use often, but it's good to know it's there. Drag the Opacity slider to control *how* see-through the superimposed video looks.

Remove a Cutaway

To get rid of a cutaway, select it in your project and then press the Delete key.

Video Overlay tool

FIGURE 8-5

Using the Video Overlay tool, you can adjust the fade and opacity of your cutaway clip.

Green Screen/Blue Screen

iMovie has opened the door to all kinds of fun with this effect. Why film your kids playing in the backyard, when you can film them playing on the *moon*? Or wherever.

iMovie's Green Screen and Blue Screen effects let you superimpose your subjects on whatever background you can think up, just as Hollywood has been doing for decades. With a little preparation, you could film things that would otherwise be impossible to shoot (Figure 8-6).

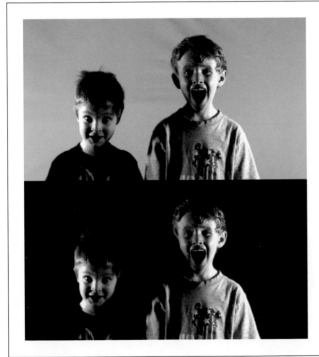

FIGURE 8-6

Top: This is what your kids look like in front of a green screen.

Bottom: This is what your kids look like hurtling through space. Pretty cool.

■ PREPARE A GREEN SCREEN

Professional green screens can cost hundreds or thousands of dollars, which is *way* too much for something you're editing in iMovie. The brains behind iMovie get this, so they designed the Green Screen effect to work with some pretty common, inexpensive materials.

You can try almost any kind of green background, as long as it's a bright, pure green (no limes, turquoises, or pines) and isn't too shiny (read on). To get a good idea of the right shade of green, use the color chooser you can find in most applications on your Mac, like TextEdit. (Pressing Shift-⌘-C usually brings it up.) Click the crayons tab and choose the Spring crayon. This is the color you need for your background. Fabric stores are a good bet, as are hardware stores that carry broad paint selections. Figure 8-7 shows how you can fake it.

> **NOTE** The instructions here describe making a green screen, but if you have your heart set on blue, don't let these instructions stop you. Just use the purest blue you can find, like what you'd see if you used the color chooser in OS X and picked the Blueberry crayon. Then follow the instructions in this section.

A popular, low-budget approach to green screens is to buy some green fabric and attach it to a frame you make from plastic pipes or wood slats. If you don't glue the pipe joints, you can even make it collapsible. Use green paint only if you have a stiff, smooth surface that you can paint green, like the wall in your basement or garage. Keep in mind that surfaces like this are probably less mobile.

FIGURE 8-7

This poor man's green screen cost $20, and is made with four yards of fabric from a fabric store, 24 feet of plastic pipe, and four "L" joints.

■ GET THE SHOT

Besides having the right color green, here's a short list of other tips that will make a world of difference in your green screenshots:

- **Good lighting.** The last thing you want are shadows on your green background, because shadows change the color that your computer sees and ruin the seamless effect. Shadows cast by the actors themselves are particularly frustrating. Your best bet is to light the background and the actors with separate light sources.

- **Lots of space.** Whether or not you have great lighting (but especially if you don't), keep lots of space between your actors and the green background. Four feet is a decent minimum. This reduces the likelihood that shadows will mess up the effect your computer will apply.

> **TIP** Good lighting and lots of space also help you avoid the dreaded halo. When the lighting is poor or the actors are too close to the green screen, green light can reflect off your subjects. The outcome is a strange halo effect that makes it easier to tell that the subject isn't *really* flying through outer space.

UP TO SPEED

How Green Screens Work

Green screen (like its predecessor, *blue screen*) is another term for an editing technique that the Hollywood pros call chroma key. The idea is that you tell your computer to replace every pixel of a certain color (like vibrant green) with new footage. In other words, anything that's *not* green (like an actor) gets superimposed onto the background stuff.

This is how Superman flew, how Neo dodged bullets in *The Matrix*, how *The Daily Show* correspondents seem to be in Paris or Iraq or Washington, and how TV actors never seem to hit anyone when they're in driving scenes and paying no attention to the road. The actors performed their scenes with smooth green fabric filling the car windows; later, editors (and their computers) replaced all patches of green with passing scenery. Watching actors in front of a green screen can be quite funny. They have to pretend they're being chased through the jungle by a dinosaur, when in fact they're sitting in a nondescript studio with its walls painted green, without so much as a vine in sight.

Green replaced blue as the most popular color for this technique because digital cameras are most sensitive to green. (Blue remains the runner-up, which is why it's sometimes used in place of green. iMovie works with either.) Of course, this also means you can't wear green clothes in the shot, unless you're intentionally going for the floating-disembodied-head thing.

- **No shine.** Some green materials, like poster board, come in the right color but if they're shiny, they reflect white light in addition to green. Green fabric is preferable, because it diffuses light and minimizes reflections. If you use poster board, just make sure you don't see any glare.

- **No bumps or wrinkles.** We're not talking about your actors here. To eliminate shadows, the green surface has to be smooth. Wrinkles and bumps make the computer-added background look wrinkled and bumpy, too.

- **No other greens.** Don't let your actors, or anything else you want in the shot, wear green.

■ INSERT A GREEN-SCREEN EFFECT

Now that you've shot your green-screen footage and imported it into iMovie, the rest is refreshingly easy.

1. **Choose your background footage and add it to your project.**

   You can choose a still image or video footage, but avoid using backgrounds that distract from the subjects in the foreground. Be especially aware of scale; for example, closeup footage of garden flowers will make your actors look unnaturally small. (Of course, you may be going for that *Honey, I Shrunk the Kids* look on purpose.)

   If you use moving footage as the background, consider two things. First, because you lit your subjects a certain way, try to shoot the background with similar lighting. (Or try to shoot your actors with similar lighting, like daylight for daylight.)

   Second, make sure you filmed *enough* background footage to cover the duration of your actors' scene. Or just repeat the background footage—loop it—by adding it to your project several times over.

2. **Select your green-screen footage. Drop it onto your background clip.**

   When you drag and drop it onto your background, it first appears as a regular cutaway clip.

3. **Click Adjust in the Viewer toolbar, select the Video Overlay tool, and then choose Green/Blue Screen from the drop-down menu (Figure 8-8).**

   iMovie superimposes your green-screen clip onto the underlying background. In the storyboard, the green-screen clip has a green border and floats on top of the background clip.

4. **Crop and clean up your green-screen background.**

   With your green-screen clip selected, use the dots in the corners of the Viewer to tighten the green-screen replacement area around your subject (Figure 8-8). Everything outside the points will show your background, whether it was green or not, so you don't have to worry about shadows, lighting, or wrinkles there. When you drag the boundaries, be careful not to eliminate an area where your actors will be at some point or they'll wind up losing body parts in a most unnatural way. (To check, play the entire clip by clicking the |▶| button in the Viewer.)

   Use the eraser tool (shown in Figure 8-8) to clean up parts that need to disappear into the background. For example, if a wrinkle shows up in your video, erase it with this tool.

   Once you finish, click the checkmark to apply your settings.

FIGURE 8-8

The Green/Blue Screen options let you "soften" (blur the edges of) the superimposed clip using a slider.

Top: The "Clean-up" tool lets you crop out part of the background, in case it isn't all green.

Bottom: The eraser tool lets you clean up trouble areas caused by bad lighting, wrinkles, or other inconsistencies in your background.

5. **Adjust the timing.**

   You can drag the green-screen clip (the upper one in the storyboard) left or right to adjust its playback relationship to the background clip. You can also drag its ends to make it longer or shorter. To get really specific about the clip's timing, use the Clip Trimmer (page 67).

6. **Adjust the sound.**

Use the ducking tool, the volume slider, or any of the other volume-adjustment tricks described in Chapter 11.

■ ADDING EFFECTS TO THE GREEN-SCREEN EFFECT

You can stabilize a green-screen clip and change its speed or direction. In fact, you can do anything to it that you can do to a regular clip, *even* add a video effect.

That's awesome, too. Imagine how fun it would be to have the green screen actors look like X-rays of themselves while talking to other actors you put in the background shot. The possibilities are endless.

You can add video effects to the *background*, too. That dramatically increases the potential for amazingness.

■ REMOVE A GREEN-SCREEN EFFECT

To remove a green screen, select the green-screen clip and press the Delete key.

Side by Side

The Side by Side effect displays your additional clip by filling up half the screen with it. This is a common effect in movies when you want to show two events taking place at the same time, like a house being broken into while the family is having a great time on vacation.

You add Side by Side clips to a project as connected clips, though you will need to change it from a cutaway to a side-by-side in the Video Overlay tool (Figure 8-9).

NOTE Use this effect only with clips that have the subject *smack dab in the middle* of your shot. When two clips share the screen, iMovie cuts off the left and right ends of the clips. Widescreen footage, in particular, gets severely trimmed on either side. If you're not careful, one of your clips might show a shot of a talking tree instead of the person you filmed.

■ CHANGE THE SIDE BY SIDE APPEARANCE

There isn't a whole lot to adjust in terms of how the Side by Side effect looks on-screen. You can only change its location (Left or Right) and its entry/departure timing (Slide). You make both of these adjustments in the Video Overlay tool (Figure 8-9).

TIP The Slide setting makes your Side by Side clip slip onto the screen with a slick animation. Little touches like this really make your movie look professionally edited. But notice that the little fade handles discussed on page 113 don't work for the video part of Side by Side clips. The Slide setting is fully in charge here.

Picture in Picture (PiP)

Picture in Picture is the effect that lets TV junkies watch two channels at once. The football game fills the big screen, but *60 Minutes* plays in a small inset window in the corner.

In its heyday, PiP was a boon to those who hated commercials. When the ads came on, you could switch to another show, all the while keeping your eye on the channel carrying the game. The moment the commercials ended, click, you were back.

Commercials are obviously not why you'd use the Picture in Picture effect in your movie. It's more likely that you'll use it to recreate the effect on the nightly news (or *The Daily Show*), where a magic box floats over the anchorperson's shoulder to display some corny graphic to go along with the story. The PiP box in this case is *supplemental*.

iMovie's PiP effect lets you do the same kinds of things. It might be a family member narrating that great hit from the reunion softball game. It might be a shot of the crowd as your kid takes her bows at a recital. Whatever the reason, the primary footage stays primary, while the PiP box helps it along.

■ INSERT A PIP

Add some event footage to the storyboard as a connected clip. Select that clip and use the Video Overlay tool to change it to a Picture in Picture shot (Figure 8-10).

Add a keyframe

FIGURE 8-10

Here's the same shot as the one in Figure 8-9 but now used as a Picture in Picture effect. You can adjust the size, borders, and location of the PiP box. You can even animate its location and size by adding keyframes and then moving and/or resizing the box.

◼ ADJUST THE PIP SIZE AND POSITION

On a TV, PiP boxes are relegated to one corner of the screen and usually have a fixed size. If iMovie insisted on such behavior, a PiP box might cover up Aunt Bertie's face the entire time. (Of course, that might not be such a bad thing.) The point is that when it comes to PiP placement, iMovie is much more flexible than your TV.

When you select the PiP clip in your storyboard, look at the preview window to see the effect. Notice the inset picture? You can drag that box anywhere in the frame. You can also resize it by dragging one of the corners inward or outward. In fact, you can, if you want, make the box big enough to cover *all* of Aunt Bertie. (Of course, if you're going to make the PiP box fill the whole screen, it may make more sense to use a cutaway [page 113].)

NOTE Although you can change the size and position of a PiP box, you can't change its *dimensions*. The box will always have the same proportion of height to width, usually 16:9. (See page 71 for a primer on aspect ratios.)

■ **ANIMATE A PIP**

Maybe the first thing you thought when you read about this feature was, "Boy! Wouldn't it be great if I could make the PiP box fly around the screen?" Well, if you thought that, you're in luck (and maybe a little too "creative" for your own good).

It's hard to imagine a situation when this would be useful, but don't let that stop you. (Or maybe *do* let that stop you, for your audience's sake.) You can use iMovie to shift the position of the PiP clip while your movie plays. It could start out in one corner, move to the middle, and then do a big loop in the screen, if you really want it to.

In Figure 8-10, you can see how the Viewer offers keyframe tools just below the PiP tools. You'll use keyframes to animate your PiP.

> **NOTE** A *keyframe* is an animator's tool for determining how an animation should behave. Basically, you give the video-editing software point A and point B using keyframes, and it figures out how to move the object between the two.

To animate a PiP effect, follow these steps.

1. **Have your PiP effect added to your movie and ready to go.**

   Position and resize your PiP box the way you want it to look.

2. **Move the project playhead to the moment when you want your PiP box to move. This spot will be the "point A" from which iMovie knows to start the animation.**

3. **Click the Add Keyframe button.**

   That's the button between the two arrows.

4. **Move and/or resize your PiP box.**

   Once you move/resize the box, iMovie knows how to process the necessary animation for making it change from point A to point B. You don't get to control how long it takes the box to change, but that also saves you the hassle of managing such details.

> **NOTE** When iMovie animates your changes, it does the resizing first, followed by the moving. That means that if you both resize and move the PiP box in one keyframe, it will *not* do both in one fluid motion. In fact, it doesn't look very good.

5. **Repeat steps 4 and 5 as needed.**

   You can move the box around as much as you want. In fact, you can create smoother motions by adding a lot of keyframes.

6. **Preview your work.**

   Click the checkbox to finish.

If at any point you place a mistaken keyframe, you can always delete it. Just use the arrow keys to page through each keyframe. As you do, the Add Keyframe button changes to a Delete Keyframe button. Page to the errant one and delete it with a simple click.

■ CHANGE THE PIP APPEARANCE

There's more to a PiP box than just size and position. You can actually change quite a few other aspects of its appearance. Each of these appear in the Video Overlay tool (Figure 8-10).

- **Change the PiP effect.** Using the PiP Effect pop-up menu, you can control how the smaller, inset video makes its appearance. "None" means it simply blinks onto the screen. "Dissolve" makes the inset fade in and out. "Zoom" makes the PiP box zoom forward to its spot, and then, at the end, zoom back to its original location. "Swap" makes the two clips trade places, so that the underlying footage becomes the PiP. Type a time (in seconds.tenths format) in the timing box to adjust how long it takes the PiP to appear and disappear.

> **TIP** You can also use the fade handles on the clip itself (page 113) to change the timing of how your PiP appears.

- **Change the box border.** The Border Width and Border Color options control the outline that appears around the inset video. Your width options are None, Thin, or Thick. Choose any color you like for the border color, from a nearly infinite number of options, thanks to the color picker that appears (more on the color picker on page 163).
- **Add a drop shadow.** Turn on Drop Shadow to make the inset cast a subtle shadow on the underlying video, as though it's floating just above it.

And remember, even though it's a PiP clip, you can still manipulate it every which way—stabilize it, add a video effect, or speed it up and slow it down. In fact, you may need to make these adjustments to get the clip to look more like the rest of your project.

■ MIX PIP AUDIO

There are a lot of reasons to use a PiP effect, and *none* of them involve having the audio from both clips on full volume. You want either the underlying clip *or* the PiP clip to be heard.

Fortunately, you can control their relative volume levels just as you would any other clip, using the Volume slider, rubber-band editing, or the ducking feature. You'll find all three described in Chapter 11.

■ **MOVE AND TRIM A PIP CLIP**

Odds are, you didn't get your PiP clip into *exactly* the right place you wanted when you dropped it into your storyboard. You can fix its position by grabbing anywhere inside the clip and dragging it to the correct spot.

TIP Even if your PiP clip covers a transition, the transition will still work. iMovie carries out the transition *underneath* the PiP clip.

You may also have to adjust the *length* of your PiP clip. You don't want too much or too little of the clip to play. Grab either end of the clip and drag it to make the clip longer or shorter.

TIP To get *really* precise with the length and content of your PiP clip, use the Clip Trimmer (page 67) instead.

■ **REMOVE A PIP CLIP**

Change your mind? Select the PiP clip and hit the Delete key.

■ One-Step Effects

Having read this chapter on video effects, your mind is probably cranking away on all the possibilities. For example, you could use the Slo-Mo effect to create an instant replay of your nephew's home run. To do this, you'd find the footage in your project that you want to replay, select that footage in the event and insert it into the middle of your clip, use the Slo-Mo setting (Modify→Slow Motion) to slow down the replay, and then add a title to the replay clip saying "Instant Replay." It might take you 5 minutes to get this all to look right, but now all your relatives can enjoy the crack of the bat replayed like it would be in any Major League game.

Or you could just select your clip and choose Modify→Instant Replay to have iMovie do all that work for you, instantly and automatically.

This example shows you the sheer coolness of iMovie's new One-Step Effects: Select any of the effects in the Clip menu of the menu bar, and iMovie executes all the same steps you'd take to create the effect.

Now that you know how One-Step Effects work, all that's left to do is run through the list of what each one does.

Choose a clip in your project, and then click the spot where you want the effect to start. (If you don't do this first, your effect will appear in the wrong place.) Then, in the Modify menu, choose a One-Step Effect to do any of the following:

- **Fade to Black and White/Sepia/Dream.** To enhance a particular moment in a clip, this effect takes the part of a clip you select and fades it to the Black and White, Sepia, or the Dream filter you read about on page 108.

- **Flash and Hold Frame.** This effect turns the last frame of your selection into a still frame (page 219). There's also a flash-like transition before the frozen frame and a zoom effect to make it look like someone just took a photograph.

- **Add Freeze Frame.** Just like the Flash and Hold effect, but it doesn't insert the flashbulb or the zoom. Instead, it looks just like someone hit the pause button for a moment.

- **Slow Motion.** Slows your clip down to 50%, 25%, or 10% of normal speed, without your having to fiddle with the Speed Editor.

- **Fast Forward.** Speeds up your clip by 2x, 4x, 8x, or 20x the normal speed, again saving you the minor inconvenience of fiddling with the Speed Editor.

- **Instant Replay.** This effect takes either the current position of your playhead or the selected part of a clip and then creates and inserts a Slo-Mo version. It even includes a cool-looking "Instant Replay" title. Once the Slo-Mo clip ends, your movie picks right up where it left off. (Figure 8-11 shows what this looks like and how to adjust it.) Choose 100%, 50%, 25%, or 10% to dictate how slowly the clip replays.

TIP When you use one of these effects that changes your clip's speed, the Speed Editor offers a Smooth checkbox to make the speed change less abrupt.

NOTE The Instant Replay and Rewind effects do a special trick in the Speed Editor. They add something like keyframes in the speed line. These are basically extra (and draggable!) handles that tell iMovie to do something different with the speed and direction.

You can adjust the speed of either of these effects by dragging these handles around. You can even reposition where the keyframes occur by dragging the filmstrip icons around (Figure 8-11).

Remember that you can choose part of a storyboard clip by clicking and holding on a spot and dragging the mouse once your cursor turns into the special selection tool.

- **Rewind.** Takes part of the clip and plays it quickly backward, as if you rewound an old VCR tape for just a moment. It's basically the Instant Replay effect but without the title, and with a fast rewind instead of a slow replay.

- **Reset Speed.** To undo an effect that changes a clip's speed or direction, choose Modify→Reset Speed (Shift-Option-R).

TIP   Even if a One-Step Effect doesn't get you exactly where you're going, it might still save you time. You can tweak all these effects to your liking, since they're all fully editable after the fact.

If, after you apply an effect, you don't like the results, press ⌘-Z to undo it.

FIGURE 8-11

Here's how you create an instant replay.

Top: Either select part of a clip or position your playhead on the spot you want to replay and then choose Instant Replay from the Modify menu.

Bottom: iMovie automatically creates a slo-mo instant replay that you can adjust to your liking.

Stabilization, Color Fixes, Cropping, and Rotating

Not every piece of video needs fancy effects. In fact, most video is probably better off without a Dream filter or a Picture-in-Picture overlay. The unadulterated stuff straight from your camera usually looks best.

If your footage needs any help at all, it's probably in the camera operator department. Don't take this personally. Handheld shots, the most common kind of home video, are notoriously unstable, and that's an instant giveaway that you're an amateur. You can have the hands of a surgeon and still end up with shaky footage. This is true even with all the newfangled image-stabilization technology that comes in the latest cameras.

Don't give up (and don't resort to carrying a tripod everywhere). iMovie can stabilize your video *after the fact*—one of its most amazing features.

And stabilization isn't the only way iMovie can fix your footage, either. The Adjust tool lets you make slight or gigantic changes to the white balance, skin-tone balance, brightness, saturation, and other image qualities of any clip.

For example, if a shot looks too dark and murky, you can bring details out of the shadows without blowing out the highlights. If the snow in a skiing shot looks too bluish, you can de-blue it. If the colors don't pop quite enough in the shot of a winning soccer goal, you can boost their saturation levels.

In addition, iMovie offers two other features that make up for human error:

- **Cropping.** If you're just not close enough to your subject, cropping video lets you home in on just a portion of the frame; it's like an artificial zoom.

- **Rotation.** If you shot video with a vertical orientation (see page 73 for all the reasons you shouldn't do this), you can turn the entire image 90 degrees. You can even turn it upside-down if you're going for a cool effect.

Best of all, iMovie does most of this—color fixes, cropping, and rotating—*instantaneously and nondestructively*. That is, you don't have to wait around while iMovie renders (processes) your edits, which makes joyous, real-time experimentation possible. (Stabilization is the major exception to the instantaneous thing, but that doesn't make the results any less impressive.) Furthermore, you're never actually making changes to your original clips—you can restore the original video anytime you like.

This chapter introduces you to all of iMovie's more subtle video effects.

■ Video Stabilization

Say what you will about iMovie, one thing's for sure: It has powers that leave other "beginner" video-editing programs panting with envy. It's filled with tools you'd historically find only in professional editing programs. iMovie inherited its stabilization feature, for example, from Apple's $1,000 Final Cut Pro software. Its rolling shutter fix was built for Final Cut, too—but only as a separately sold plug-in. (That's right, you're getting a feature that Final Cut users had to *pay* for, for *free*. How's that for a deal?)

Video stabilization works by analyzing every frame in a clip, recognizing the changes in both camera position (movement up, down, left, or right) and camera rotation. Once it figures that bit out, it knows how to slide and rotate your clips to iron out the shakes.

You need to know three things about how iMovie does all this:

First, iMovie won't let you stabilize clips in your Event browser. It saves the analysis work for clips added to a project.

Secondly, and unfortunately, this sort of analysis takes a long time—roughly 1–2 minutes for every minute of video (more or less, depending on your Mac's speed). The results, however, are worth it. The stabilization feature works absolute magic on most jerky, bumpy handheld footage. It works so well, in fact, that it can look positively creepy, as though you were floating along on a magic carpet.

Finally, iMovie fixes two kinds of stabilization problems: normal shaky footage and "jellyroll" footage (see page 133). But for iMovie to fix these two problems, it has to analyze the clip through two separate processes. (You can tell iMovie to do both at once, however.)

So to summarize, when you add a clip to a project and turn on either of these two settings—fixing shake and fixing jellyroll—iMovie gets to work in the background, analyzing each frame. Lucky for you, in the meantime you can keep editing your movie. Eventually, iMovie finishes its analysis, and your footage no longer looks like you shot it during an earthquake.

Unstable Stabilization

The iMovie stabilizing feature is impressive, but it isn't magic. In fact, iMovie can't fix a common distortion caused by camera shake, called *motion blur*. iMovie actually makes this distortion look *worse* because it removes the shake that motion blur likes to hide in.

So just what is motion blur? Unless you have a camera that shoots at really high frame rates, like an iPhone 5s, it's possible to swing your camera around so fast that the pixels actually become *blurred*. Although iMovie can stabilize the frames rela-

tive to one another, it can't sharpen the blurriness of individual frames. When you play back stabilized footage with blurry frames, it looks like the camera is moving in and out of focus.

When faced with this unfixable shake, it's up to you to decide which looks better: shaky footage or blurry footage. In general, you're probably best off leaving the footage in its natural, unbalanced state rather than fixing it, since people are more accustomed to seeing shaky home footage than weird, blurry footage. The best alternative? Get a better shot.

Fix Shaky Footage

If you need to stabilize a clip in your project, select the clip and then click the Adjust button in the iMovie toolbar. Click the Stabilization tool (Figure 9-1) and you'll see two checkboxes: Stabilize Shaky Video and Fix Rolling Shutter.

FIGURE 9-1

The Stabilization tool in the Adjust toolbar offers two choices. The first stabilizes camera shake, and the second fixes rolling shutter problems (a.k.a. "jellyroll"). Turn on either checkbox (not shown) and you see these little spinners instead of the checkboxes—which let you know iMovie's analyzing your clip so it can apply fixes.

Turn on the Stabilize Shaky Video checkbox and iMovie replaces the checkbox with a little spinny-thing to tell you it's thinking, analyzing the clip's frames so it knows how to stabilize them. If you're stabilizing a long clip, don't bother waiting for iMovie to finish. Carry on editing, and iMovie will eventually fully analyze and stabilize the clip.

NOTE If you later decide to lengthen the clip you stabilized by more than a second, iMovie needs to do more analyzing. It'll automatically analyze the clip to cover what was added, without your needing to check the box again.

■ DEGREES OF STABILIZATION

Once you stabilize some video, you may be delighted and amazed at how professional and smooth it looks. You might ask yourself, "Was I wearing a Steadicam?" (those gyro-mounted camera harnesses the Hollywood pros wear for stability). Or not.

You may be a little alarmed by how fake it looks. You were running down a flight of stairs, for crying out loud—it should look a *little* like you were on foot, not like you were gliding down a sheet of ice.

For that reason, you can *throttle back* the amount of stabilizing that iMovie does. Select the clip in your storyboard and go back into the Stabilization tool shown in Figure 9-1. Next to the checkbox, you see a percentage slider.

What does the percentage slider do? It changes the amount of zoom in your stabilized clip. iMovie does the stabilizing trick by rotating and shifting the whole picture around in the frame, counteracting your hand shakes pixel by pixel. This means, however, that you would see momentary glimpses of black emptiness between the video and the frame around it, which would be even more distracting than the shaky video. So iMovie conceals those slivers of blackness by zooming the video just enough to fill the frame and eliminate the exposed black emptiness. See Figure 9-2 to see the difference between a 10% zoom and a 100% zoom.

Of course, magnifying a photo (or a video frame) also reduces its resolution, and therefore its quality. It's very unlikely you'll actually notice the degradation, but if you think you do, here's another reason for the stabilizing zoom slider: It can reduce the degree of zooming-in. In other words, the slider limits both the stabilizing effect *and* the zooming that goes along with it.

Two more stabilization notes:

- The more shake in your footage, the more zoom iMovie offers. 100% zoom for a really shaky clip will zoom in on your shot far more than 100% zoom for a relatively tranquil clip.

- If you crop away the shakiest part of a clip, iMovie may do a better job of stabilizing the rest. That's because iMovie figures out exactly how far it needs to zoom in to fix the *shakiest part* of a project clip, and then applies that zoom to the whole clip.

■ REMOVE STABILIZATION

You may change your mind and decide that a clip looks better without stabilization. It can happen (see page 131). Just select the clip and uncheck Stabilize Shaky Video in the Stabilization tool. The shake comes back.

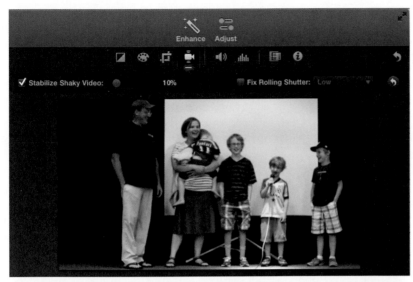

FIGURE 9-2

Top: This clip has the stabilizing zoom set to 10%, so the video will be shakier, but you can see everyone.

Bottom: This clip is zoomed 100% for the full stabilizing effect, but you've lost half a head and almost an entire 10-year-old.

And don't worry about having to reanalyze footage if you change your mind yet again. Once analyzed, always analyzed.

Fix Jellyroll Footage

There's a second type of distortion you should know about, called *jellyroll footage*. It arises when you shoot with a camera that contains a so-called CMOS light-sensor chip. Most cameras these days, including iPhone and iPad cameras, contain this sort of chip. (In fact, fewer and fewer cameras use the alternative technology, called CCD, so odds are this section on jellyroll footage will apply to you.)

Unfortunately, CMOS cameras use a rolling shutter, which means that the sensor records an image starting at the top and working its way down to the bottom, really fast. If the camera moves too much as you film, the subject gradually shifts left or right as the sensor records the image.

The resulting image makes the world look like it's suddenly made of jelly—a source of endless frustration and bewilderment to amateurs and pros alike. "Dang it!" they say, "what's wrong with my camera?"

Unfortunately, iMovie's stabilization feature tends to exaggerate this bizarre jelly effect.

■ ROLLING SHUTTER ADJUSTMENTS

To reduce the jellyroll effect, select the clip in your project and click the Adjust button in the toolbar. Under the Stabilization tool shown in Figure 9-2, check the Fix Rolling Shutter box. iMovie immediately gets to work analyzing the clip and will show a successfully checked box when it's done.

The jelly effect is the product of how fast your camera's rolling shutter works. Slower shutters need the High or Extra High settings in the Amount menu (Figure 9-3). Faster shutters can use the Low or Medium settings.

Less expensive cameras, like point-and-shoots, need the High or Extra High setting (they have slower shutters). Midrange cameras, like most consumer camcorders, typically need the Medium setting. Expensive cameras, such as DSLRs, generally get by with the Medium or Low setting because they have very fast shutters.

TIP Of course, if you want to get precise adjustments, test things out with your own camera. Find a vertical, linear object like a telephone pole. Film it while you pan side to side. (Use a tripod if you want to be really exact.) Pan quickly enough to get the jellyroll effect going. Now just import and analyze the footage, add the clip to your project, and try different Amount settings until you get a nice, straight telephone pole.

FIGURE 9-3

The Fix Rolling Shutter setting helps reduce the jellyroll effect you get in footage shot by certain cameras. Once iMovie analyzes your footage, turn on the rolling shutter fix with this checkbox in the Stabilization tool. Set the level of adjustment ("Amount") to best compensate for your camera.

■ **REMOVE SHUTTER ADJUSTMENTS**

Uncheck the Rolling Shutter box in the Stabilization tool to turn off adjustment for a clip. You can always turn it back on later. And don't worry about iMovie analyzing your footage again if you do. Once analyzed, always analyzed.

■ Auto Enhance

Before digging into the color adjustment tools that follow, you may decide it's worth skipping all of this thanks to iMovie's magical Enhance button. (The magic wand tells you it's magical.) Found in the iMovie toolbar, Enhance instructs iMovie to automatically assess a clip and fix its color and sound to, well, look and sound the best it can.

What really happens when you click Enhance is that iMovie uses built-in tools to adjust color balance, exposure, temperature, and even background noise. Once you click Enhance, the tools in the Adjust menu light up to show you that iMovie made changes to the clip's color and sound (Figure 9-4).

FIGURE 9-4

When you click the Enhance tool, iMovie applies changes to the color balance, exposure, color temperature, and audio noise of a clip so that it looks and sounds its very best.

Top: Before you click Enhance, none of the tools in the Adjust menu show any changes.

Bottom: Once you turn on Enhance, iMovie automatically lights up all the relevant Adjust tools to show you that it applied changes to your footage.

You can take these adjustments exactly as iMovie makes them, or you can go in and tweak them to your liking using the instructions that follow. If you change your mind completely, just click the Enhance button again to turn off all the adjustments.

Color Balance

iMovie can apply some technologically advanced color-balance effects to your video, and no matter what camera you're using, you'll probably need them. That's because digital cameras work by capturing light that then gets processed by what are basically little computers that manipulate light according to their settings. Depending on the combination of the camera settings with the lighting of the room, things will look very different to the camera than they do to the human eye. (For example, fluorescent lighting can sometimes make everything look greenish.)

Most cameras have an automatic feature that tries to balance the colors back to where they belong, but these features don't always work out. If your camera gets the balance wrong, iMovie gives you the chance to make it right.

iMovie offers four ways to balance color, and for all of them, you'll need the Color Balance tool that appears when you select a clip and click the Adjust button in the toolbar (selected in Figure 9-4).

iMovie can apply color fixes only to an entire clip at once. You can't make the effect fade in or out, you can't apply it to just a portion of a clip, and you can't apply it to multiple clips at once (although you *can* copy and paste the adjustments you make).

Before you apply an effect, therefore, you may want to start by isolating the piece you want. You can always chop up a clip into smaller pieces (page 71).

But, unlike stabilization effects, you can correct color balance for clips in your Event browser, not just clips in your project. Select any clip anywhere in iMovie, and these tools let you make color changes. (Of course, the truth is, you're never *really* changing anything at all. You can remove all your changes and revert to the original camcorder-captured clip at any time, even months or years from now.)

iMovie offers four color-balancing options.

Auto Balance

The easiest of the Color Balance tools is the automatic one. When you click this to turn it on, iMovie will decide what balance it thinks looks best, using complex algorithms devised by very smart Apple engineers. Auto gets it right more often than not, so this should be your go-to tool.

Color Matching

Colors often change as you shoot, especially if you shoot outdoors. (A cloud passing in front of the sun can dramatically change how everything looks to your camera.) The Match Color tool gives you the chance to make up for this.

Once you click this tool (shown in Figure 9-5), iMovie previews the clip you're editing on the right, next to the preview of a clip from somewhere else in your storyboard or the Event browser. Skimming around in your other clips will change the left-hand preview (Figure 9-5). Notice how your cursor turns into a dropper tool.

The idea is to pick a clip from a similar setting where the colors are just right. Once you find it, click with the dropper tool and iMovie shows what your edited clip will look like with the matched colors. Use the On/Off switch to see the before and after. Click the ✓ button to save your changes and the ✕ button to cancel.

White Balance

Color balance is easiest when you have an anchor color to rely on. That color is good ol' white. White light, scientifically speaking, contains all the colors in the spectrum, so a perfectly white object will reflect all those colors at once. With this knowledge in hand, iMovie can do really nice color balancing as long as you tell it what should look white.

When you click the White Balance tool, iMovie changes your cursor to a little dropper tool (Figure 9-6). Use it to click anything in your frame that should look white. Once you click, iMovie changes all the colors based on this reference point.

NOTE Of course, if you click something that isn't really white and actually a little beige, iMovie doesn't know that. The adjusted colors will be off accordingly. In fact, if you want to have some fun, pick a most-definitely-not-white part of your clip and see how iMovie reacts.

FIGURE 9-5

The Match Color tool shows the clip you're editing on the right next to a reference clip from somewhere else in your movie. Skim around the clip to find the spot with the right color balance, and then click the clip. Click the ✓ button to close the Match Color tool.

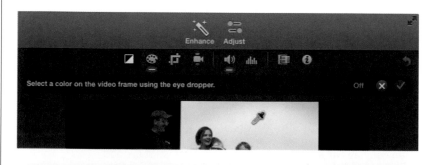

FIGURE 9-6

Top: With the White Balance tool open, pick a spot in your clip that should look white (like the projector screen shown in this image) and then use the dropper to select it.

Bottom: iMovie adjusts the clip's colors so that the white part looks white and every other color matches as it should.

Skin Tone Balance

This tool works the same way as the White Balance tool, but instead of choosing something that should look white, you choose a spot on someone's skin that should look like skin, like his face or arm. Of course, shading and natural skin color can alter what changes iMovie applies, but overall it does a pretty nice job for all skin types.

◾ Color Correction

Color balance is only half of what iMovie can do to change the colors of your footage. As impressive as the balance tools are, they're quite limited in terms of the control they offer. If you want to be pickier about how your clips look, the Color Correction tools hand you a lot more power.

There are basically three correction sliders available to you, all from the Color Correction tool in the Adjust toolbar. The first slider gives you control over the light and dark (or contrast) aspects of your video. The second changes how vivid the clip's colors appear (also called saturation). The last one makes your clip look warmer or cooler (the clip's temperature).

Contrast

Sometimes your colors are fine, but the problem is too much or too little light. It can be a problem for all of a shot or different parts within a shot. In any case, making adjustments to the clip's lighting can fix these problems.

The contrast tool can't fix all lighting problems, however. Whenever you shoot video, your camera has to decide how much light to let in, based on the amount of available light in the room. Too much light can overwhelm your camera. It also can't make up for too little light, like in a dark room.

In some cases, it can have too much light in one part and too little in another. If you video someone standing in front of a daytime window, for example, your camera has to make a choice. Does it let in lots of light to better see the person's face, but in the process overexpose everything coming in from the window? Or does it dial down the sensitivity, making the window look normal but the person just a dark shadow?

iMovie's contrast tool can do its best with problems like these, but ultimately it can only draw on whatever light your camera captured. Avoid these problems by making sure you film with adequate lighting. Preview your camera's light sensitivity before you start filming.

Assuming your clip's lighting is within iMovie's reach, follow these steps to make contrast adjustments:

1. **Select the clip in your storyboard or Event browser that you want to edit.**

2. **Click the Adjust button and then the Color Correction tool (shown in Figure 9-7).**

    The Viewer displays three sliders above the preview of your clip.

3. **Adjust the contrast slider (Figure 9-7).**

That's the leftmost tool here. Apple calls this curious thing a *multislider*. That means it has more than just one point to drag around. In fact, this one has *five*.

The center point changes the clip's overall brightness. Drag it left and everything gets darker. Drag it right and everything gets lighter.

The far left and far right points change the lowlights and highlights. The left one makes just the dark parts darker or lighter. The right one makes just the bright parts darker or lighter.

Finally, the remaining two points adjust the contrast, reducing or increasing the difference between the light and dark parts. (Drag either one of these points and the other one comes along for the ride.)

FIGURE 9-7

Top: Sometimes you shoot stuff that's too dark or too bright—or both within the same shot. Use the leftmost slider in the Color Correction tool to make changes to the brightness and contrast of your clip. The middle point of the slider adjusts overall brightness. The left and right ends adjust lowlights and highlights, respectively. The half-moon buttons together change the contrast between light and dark.

Bottom: Just a few changes can bring out details hidden in the shadows.

You can always come back and make more changes to a clip later; iMovie doesn't do anything permanent to a clip's contrast. To return a clip to its original appearance, click the undo button (the swirling arrow whose tooltip says "Remove color adjustments") to the far right of the color sliders.

Saturation

Sometimes what you've shot looks dull. Not because the clip isn't interesting, but because the lighting washed out the colors. (Hazy weather or a lens flare can have this effect.) iMovie's saturation slider can make up for this.

Click the Adjust button and then the Color Correction tool to show the middle of the three sliders (Figure 9-8). Dragging the slider to the left will strip a clip's color, all the way down to black and white. Drag it to the left and the colors become much more vibrant.

FIGURE 9-8

Top: The wrong lighting or weather can make your footage appear washed out.

Bottom: Dragging the saturation slider (the one in the middle) a bit to the right makes the blue sky and ocean in this clip far more vibrant.

You can undo any of these changes after the fact with the slider itself or the undo button on the far right.

Warmth

Most light that hits your subjects isn't pure white. It's either on the cool side (bluer) or on the warm side (oranger). This difference is called color temperature. The warmth slider is a way to compensate for shots that are too cool or warm.

This slider basically works like the saturation slider, but instead of making footage bland as you drag it left, this makes everything more blue. Dragging it to the right turns everything yellowish-orange.

As always, you can make these changes and undo them later with the slider or the undo button to the far right of your color sliders.

TIP   Although iMovie comes with a Sepia effect built-in (page 109), you can use the warmth and saturation sliders to create your own. Drag the warmth slider a bit to the right and the saturation slider a little bit left. Voilà! Homemade Sepia.

■ Copy and Paste Adjustments

While you can make color adjustments on more than one clip at a time (see page 54 on selecting multiple clips), this is helpful only if you had the foresight to select multiple clips while you were making changes. Instead of going back to try to figure out the exact changes you made, you can copy and paste *just* the color adjustments. Once you get the blue cast worked out of the first skiing shot, for example, you can wipe it out of each additional shot with a single command. Figure 9-9 shows the drill.

TIP   If you're the kind of person who plans ahead, consider this: If you intend to excerpt several clips from a single, long, master clip in the Event browser, you'll save time by fixing *the original clip* before you start adding the clips to your storyboard.

The reason: If you make color adjustments to the master clip *before* you grab chunks of it, the pieces inherit the fixes. If you adjust the master clip *after* you add pieces of it to the storyboard, the pieces themselves won't change. (You can always use the Paste Adjustments command at that point, of course, but that's still more steps.)

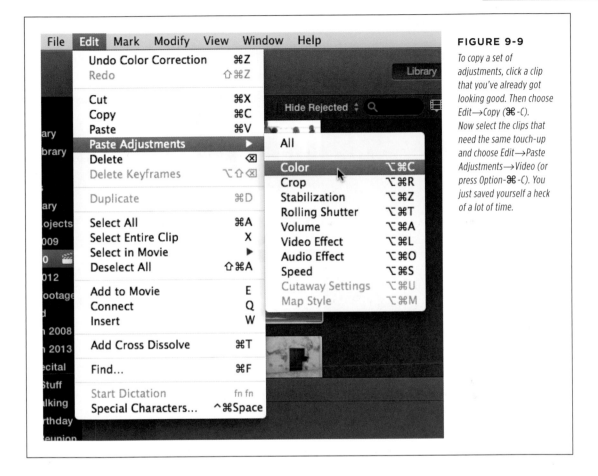

FIGURE 9-9

To copy a set of adjustments, click a clip that you've already got looking good. Then choose Edit→Copy (⌘-C). Now select the clips that need the same touch-up and choose Edit→Paste Adjustments→Video (or press Option-⌘-C). You just saved yourself a heck of a lot of time.

Crop Video

Something as sophisticated as cropping video was previously relegated to the stratosphere of professional video-editing programs like Final Cut Pro. This tool lets you crop a video clip the same way you crop a photo; that is, you chop off the edges of the video frame.

Figure 9-10 gives you the idea.

FIGURE 9-10

Top: Suppose you were too far from your subject, or your zoom wasn't powerful enough to catch the action.

Middle: Use the Cropping tool to adjust the white rectangle so that it encloses the portion of the video you want to keep.

Bottom: After you crop, the smaller portion of the frame expands to fill the entire frame. You lose some resolution, but you won't notice any graininess unless you crop out a lot of the original image.

Cropping isn't something you'll do every day, but it can be handy in situations like these:

- **You add a clip to a project that's got the wrong aspect ratio (page 72).** For example, say you're creating a regular widescreen movie, but you want to put an older, squarish, standard-definition clip into it. The Cropping tool lets you lop off the top and bottom of the standard-def clip so it fits perfectly into the widescreen frame without using any black bars.

- **There's something at the margins of the picture that you want to get rid of.** Maybe your finger was on the lens. Maybe there's some ugly pipe or wire that you didn't notice. Maybe a telephone pole appears to be sticking out of your interviewee's head. Or maybe you just want to crop out the bonehead who kept trying to get on camera.

- **The scene is off-center.** Maybe the camera was on a tripod, self-running, when you and a buddy did your comedy shtick, but you didn't frame the scene right. By cropping away the empty part of the frame, you can recenter the whole thing.

- **The subject of the shot isn't prominent enough.** This happens often with accidental footage: That is, you were filming Uncle Ned reminiscing about his days working for the National Guard when, *bam!*, there's a three-car collision in the intersection behind him. By cropping away Uncle Ned, you can isolate the car-crash portion of the frame. It now fills the screen; in effect, you created an artificial zoom.

Whenever you crop video, you leave fewer pixels behind. You therefore lose resolution and create a less-sharp picture. If you crop away a *huge* amount of video info—more than half of the frame—you may wind up with noticeable pixelation and graininess.

If that happens, you can either live with it or use Undo.

In any case, here's how you crop a shot in iMovie:

1. **Select the clip in your event or storyboard that you want to edit.**

   By skimming, find a good representative frame of the clip to work with in the Viewer. Remember, you're working with video here, so things do tend to move around on the screen, but the iMovie cropping area *doesn't* move. You don't want to crop the clip in a way that centers your subject nicely in frame 50 but cuts it out completely in frame 100.

2. **Click the Adjust button and then the Cropping tool (shown in Figure 9-10).**

   Now the Viewer window sprouts a few new controls at the top, with Fit, Crop, and Ken Burns. Select the Crop control. A white selection rectangle appears over the Viewer.

3. **Adjust the white rectangle in the Viewer window to select what you want to keep.**

   As you work, you can drag inside the rectangle to move it around the frame. And you can drag any of the four corners to make the rectangle bigger or smaller. (You can crop away almost all of your clip, but the result will look terribly pixelated.)

   Drag the playhead in the storyboard to spot-check the video, to make sure you don't crop out anything important somewhere else in the clip. Or just click the Play button (or press your space bar) to play the clip as a preview.

4. **Click the ✓ button.**

   This completes the crop.

Adjust or Remove a Crop

Cropping, like any iMovie edit, is nondestructive. That is, you haven't done anything permanent to the source video on your hard drive, and you can adjust or remove the cropping anytime you like.

To do that, just follow steps 1–4 on the previous page, resizing the white rectangle to the better size and position.

To remove the cropping altogether, click the Fit button in the Viewer.

The Ken Burns Effect, Now for Video!

If you've ever filmed a sporting event, like a kid's football game, the biggest problem is framing the action just right. If you zoom in too close, you're sure to miss something. But if you're too far away, there's no amazing detail to enjoy because you're basically watching ants. And even if you are zoomed out, there's no guarantee that the amazing play will happen in the middle of the screen, where it belongs.

Since you don't have the Monday Night Football crew at your disposal, you might be excited to know that you can dynamically zoom and pan your video with the once-limited-to-photos Ken Burns Effect. Read more about it on page 217. Once you know how it works, applying the effect is pretty easy.

Choose a video clip in your project and open the Cropping tool. Now, instead of cropping, click the Ken Burns button and you'll see the exact same interface you get for using Ken Burns on photos. You control the effect the same way. The speed of the pan and zoom depends on the length of your clip.

Just as with photos, the effect pans and zooms in only one direction for each clip, so if you want to zoom in, hang for a few moments, and then zoom back out, you need to split your clip into corresponding pieces, applying the correct Ken Burns Effect for each one. (Read page 71 for instructions on splitting clips.)

There's one caveat. When you zoom in on a photo, it's usually of high enough quality that you won't notice any graininess (unless you zoom in *a lot*). Not so with video, even HD video. There simply aren't as many pixels to go around, so you'll notice some quality degradation if you use the Ken Burns Effect to zoom in on your clips.

Knowing that you have this tool at your fingertips means you don't have to chase the action all the time. Instead, you can keep everything in frame and then come back later to make the good stuff fill the screen.

◼ Rotate Video

If there's any iMovie feature you'll use even less often than cropping, it's rotating. But sure enough, iMovie lets you rotate a clip by 90 degrees, or even upside-down.

When would you use this? Well, here are a couple of possibilities:

- Somebody actually filmed the scene with the camera turned 90 degrees. (This often happens when people record video with a smartphone, which they're used to holding vertically. People forget that they shouldn't hold it that way when they *shoot video*. See page 73 for all the reasons why.)

- You shot a kid crawling along the rocks and want to make it look like he's mountain-climbing, vertically, straight up a cliff.

- You're making some strange, avant-garde film, and you're hoping to intentionally disorient your audience.

Anyway, if you're reading this, you must have your reasons, so here's how you rotate video:

1. **Select the clip in your storyboard.**

2. **Click the Adjust button and then the Cropping tool.**

3. **Click one of the Rotate buttons at the top of the Viewer (Figure 9-11).**

   With each click, the entire video image rotates 90 degrees in the corresponding direction. If you click twice, you flip the whole picture upside-down.

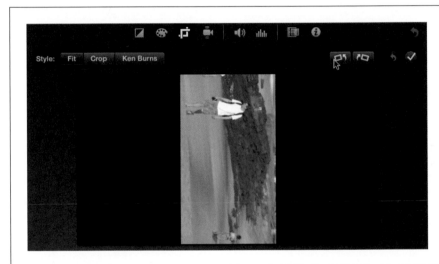

FIGURE 9-11

With each click of the rotation arrows, you rotate the image 90 degrees. Use for special effects, or just for fun.

   If you rotate the image only 90 degrees, of course, the video no longer fits in the frame and black bars appear on either side. At this point, you have two options: You can either leave it as is, or you can crop it so that it fills the frame.

   To do the latter, click the Crop button in the Viewer, and then drag the white rectangle exactly as described in the previous section.

4. **Click the ✓ button.**

   This finishes rotating the image.

Adjust or Remove the Rotation

When you rotate your video, you're not changing the underlying footage. You can adjust or remove the rotation anytime. Click those rotation arrow buttons again until the video looks the way you want it to.

Titles, Subtitles, and Credits

Text superimposed over film footage is incredibly common in the film and video worlds. You'd be hard-pressed to find a single movie, TV show, or commercial that doesn't have titles, captions, or credits. In fact, one telltale sign that you're watching an amateur video is the *absence* of superimposed text.

In iMovie, the term *title* refers to any kind of text effect: titles, credits, subtitles, copyright notices, and so on. You don't need to be nearly as economical in your use of titles as you are with, say, transitions. Transitional effects interfere with something that stands perfectly well on its own—your footage. When you superimpose text on video, on the other hand, the audience is much more likely to accept your intrusion. You're introducing this new element for their benefit, to convey information you couldn't transmit otherwise.

Moreover, as you'll see, most of iMovie's text effects are far more focused in purpose than its transition selections, so you'll have little trouble choosing the optimum text effect for a particular editing situation. For example, the Scrolling Credits effect rolls a list of names slowly up the screen—an obvious candidate for the close of your movie.

■ Add Titles

Adding text to your movie involves choosing a style for your title, positioning it, adding the text, and then choosing the type style. Here are the steps in detail.

Choose a Title Style

With your project open, start by choosing Window→Content Library→Titles (⌘-2), or by clicking Titles in the Content Library (found under your Event list). iMovie launches the Titles panel in place of your Event browser (Figure 10-1). You can preview the titles by skimming them.

FIGURE 10-1

The icons here represent iMovie's various title styles. Apple gives you more than 50 to choose from.

Figuring out the idea behind each title style isn't rocket science, but here's a rundown, listed in the order they appear in iMovie:

- **Standard.** The Standard title style may be the most useful of all iMovie text effects. It produces centered lines of text that fade in and then zoom in, stay onscreen for a moment, and then fade out, making this style ideal for the title of your movie. This is a tasteful, professional, and powerful effect.

- **Standard Lower Third.** The name "Lower Third" comes from the TV business—it refers to the lower third of a TV screen. This one basically does the same thing as the Standard title, but in the lower part of your screen.

- **Expand and Expand Lower Third.** These titles work like the Standard ones, but the letters drift apart from the center to the sides of the screen.

- **Reveal and Reveal Lower Third.** The words look like a spotlight is shining across them from the bottom up.

- **Focus and Focus Lower Third.** The letters drop in individually and go from blurry to clear. They drop out again with a blur, as though losing focus.

- **Line and Line Lower Third.** An elegant title, this one has a thin line expand from the center, followed by words above and below the line.

- **Pop-up and Pop-up Lower Third.** This is the first whimsical effect in the list. The letters appear and disappear in a way that looks like a stadium full of people doing the wave.

- **Gravity and Gravity Lower Third.** Back to serious again, these words blur in, except for the first letter of each word, which descends gracefully into place.

- **Prism and Prism Lower Third.** This title looks as though you're turning a prism, where the letters shift in and out in geometric shapes.

- **Centered.** The old iMovie classic. Plain old letters (Gill Sans font, of course, but you can change that, as explained on page 160) fade in and out without any other style or effect. Of course, this title has become so recognizable, it basically screams to people that you're using iMovie.

> **TIP** You can always string together several consecutive Centered titles to imitate the way a movie's major stars' names appear at the beginning of a typical Hollywood movie.

- **Lower Third.** This most closely resembles the lower-third titles you see on TV, like when a show identifies a talking head ("Harold P. Higgenbottom, GrooviTunes CEO"). You can use it that way, or use it to identify the location of a scene, or as a subtitle to translate what a person (like a baby) is saying.

- **Lower.** This title hovers in the bottom-right corner of the screen, as in an MTV music video, but on the wrong side.

- **Upper.** This one gives you Lower's exact opposite: The text appears in the upper-left corner.

- **Echo.** This unusual style features a title, a subtitle, and an *echo* of the main title. An enormous, semitransparent, all-caps version of the main title appears *behind* your text, almost as a graphic element.

- **Overlap.** Two bits of text, one red and one white, meet briefly in the middle at the bottom of the frame, and then keep going their merry way. If you place several Overlap titles consecutively, they alternate colors.

- **Four Corners.** A very colorful series of titles, where the text swoops in from different sides to meet in the middle before swooping out again. Each time you add one of these titles, the entry points and colors of the text change, with up to four variations.

- **Scrolling Credits.** This effect produces a line of text with two columns, for credits like *Director...Steven Spielberg* and *Writer...Robert Towne*, or *character name...actor name* (Figure 10-2).

  Be careful when you use this effect, for two reasons. First, iMovie automatically adjusts the speed of the scroll to make sure the effect displays all the names you specify within the duration you specify. If you make the title effect too short, the credits will scroll by too fast for anyone to read.

> **TIP** Setting up this title style requires special instructions, which appear on page 159.

Second, the type is fairly small, which could be a problem if you intend your movie to be viewed on something like an iPhone.

FIGURE 10-2

You control the duration of titles, like Scrolling Credits, by adjusting the length of the title strip in your storyboard.

- **Drifting, Sideways Drift, Vertical Drift.** These are three variations on the same basic idea: The text zooms onto the screen, decelerates as it gets to the middle, and then speeds up to leave the frame, never really coming to a full stop. If your clip were a stop sign, these titles would probably get a ticket.

- **Zoom.** Like a centered title, but one that subtly grows (slightly) bigger over time.

- **Horizontal Blur.** This effect simulates your eyes coming into focus to see the title, then going out of focus again.

- **Soft Edge.** Another very subtle effect. The text drifts slightly right, and then a magic eraser wipes it into existence and promptly erases it again.

- **Lens Flare, Boogie Lights, Pixie Dust.** These titles all use something shiny to announce themselves to the world (Figure 10-3). Definitely useful when you want something flashy.

- **Pull Focus.** If you play around much with the manual focus on a camera, this one will look familiar. As the text comes into focus, the background goes blurry. At the end of the title, the background comes back into focus, only to have the title get blurry and disappear.

- **Organic Main and Organic Lower.** These are both very elegant titles, the kind you'd love to have in a wedding video. Both involve delicate, viny animated plants that grow along with the title before fading away.

- **Ticker.** You know how cable-news channels run breaking news headlines across the bottom of the screen? In the same way, the Ticker title runs text, right to left, across the screen. It's much more plain, however, than what you see on CNN.

FIGURE 10-3

The Boogie Lights title exemplifies iMovie's cool, animated titles.

- **Date/Time.** The only entirely uneditable title. When you select it, the preview window denies you access. It just sits there, impervious to clicking. This title's only job is to display the date and time of the underlying clip, which can come in handy if you want to remind viewers of when an event (like a vacation) took place. It appears in the bottom-left corner of the screen.

TIP OK, this style isn't *totally* uneditable. You can change the date and time of your footage, as described on page 367.

- **Clouds.** This is a whimsical, animated, lower-third title. Two clouds, one blue and one pink, bounce up into the frame, carrying some equally whimsical text.

- **Far Far Away.** For all the budding George Lucases out there, this title displays text in the iconic, scrolling *Star Wars* style.

TIP For added fun, you can display this title on top of the starscape image that comes with iMovie. See the next section for details.

- **Gradient (White or Black), Soft Bar (White or Black), Paper, Formal, Torn Edge (Black or Tan).** These are all variations on the Lower Third style. The only difference is what's *behind* the text. You have a choice of semi-opaque backgrounds to make the text more readable and to make it stand out more from the video playing behind it.

■ THEME-BASED TITLES

If you added a theme to your project (page 96), iMovie lists three to eight additional title styles (depending on your theme) at the top of the Titles pane (Figure 10-4). Some of them are heavily animated, embedding your clip into a shot of a photo album, for example. The other titles are simpler, but stylistically designed to match your theme.

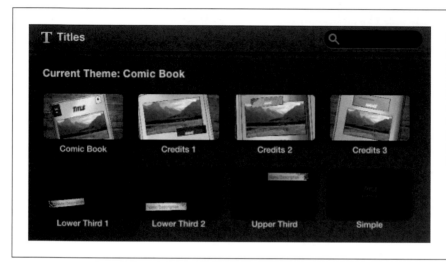

FIGURE 10-4

If you added a theme to your project (page 96), you'll see customized theme titles to go along with iMovie's stock offerings. Each is designed around the theme's style. This movie uses the Comic Book theme, for example.

You can use theme titles only if you applied a theme to your project. This also means you can't use titles from multiple themes in a single project.

TIP   Want a particular theme title, but not the entire theme itself? Just make sure that when you add a theme, you *turn off* the "Automatic content" checkbox, which tells iMovie to automatically add transitions and titles (see page 91). That way, your movie uses only the theme elements *you* choose, even if you end up using just one theme-based title in your entire project.

Drag the Title into Position

Once you choose a title style, drag its icon directly into the storyboard. As you do, iMovie highlights part of the underlying filmstrip in white (Figure 10-5)—that's iMovie's way of helping you position your title.

As you'll soon see, knowing when to release the mouse button is extremely important. As you helicopter over a clip, you'll find that you can drop it at any of four places; at each one, iMovie snaps the title into place. Here's what happens when you have the cursor at various positions over a clip:

- **At the beginning of the clip.** As the white highlighting in Figure 10-5 illustrates, iMovie proposes covering the *first 8 seconds* of your clip with the title. When you play back the clip, placeholder text appears over the video.

NOTE When you place a title at the beginning or end of a clip, iMovie automatically makes it 8 seconds long. You can change that duration by dragging the end or beginning of the purple title bar.)

FIGURE 10-5

As you drag a title onto a clip, iMovie previews its position and duration with white highlighting. The title snaps into three positions relative to the clip, shown in these examples.

Top: If you drag toward the beginning of the clip, the title covers the first 8 seconds of it.

Middle: If you drag over the middle, the title covers the entire clip.

Bottom: If you drag toward the end of the clip, the title covers the final 8 seconds of it. Of course, you can adjust any of these durations later.

- **Over the middle of the clip.** If your cursor winds up here, the title covers *the entire clip*, beginning to end.

- **At the end of the clip.** If your cursor falls here, the title stretches over the *final 8 seconds* of the clip.

- **Between clips.** Under normal circumstances, iMovie text gets superimposed over video. But you might want the title to appear on a nice, black background for a striking and professional-looking effect.

  In those cases, drag the title to the gap *between* filmstrips. iMovie drops a 4-second version of the title into place with a black background. In your storyboard, the title looks like a clip, but one that's a solid purple rectangle (see Figure 10-6).

NOTE If you're upgrading from an old version of iMovie, you no longer see a checkbox for "Over black," nor is there a background selector that automatically pops up, as in previous iMovie versions; you simply drag the title between two clips, or to the very beginning or end of the storyboard. See Figure 10-6.

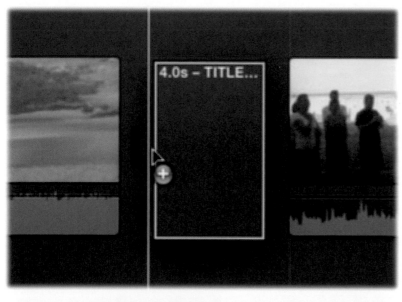

FIGURE 10-6

Top: If you drag a title between two clips, iMovie creates a title-clip hybrid and displays the title over a basic black background.

Bottom: You can adjust the title's time onscreen by dragging its ends.

You may prefer a title background other than black. In the Content Library, under Maps & Backgrounds, iMovie offers 20 animated or still backgrounds (see page 209). You insert one of them by dragging it into your timeline. Then just drag and drop a title onto the background you inserted.

In professional movie editing, a black background is by far the most common. More often than not, this is the one you want to choose, for three reasons. First, it looks professional. Second, the high contrast of white against black makes the text very legible. Third, the audience will *read* it, instead of being distracted by the video behind it.

NOTE   When you create a title over a background or between clips, you *add* to the total length of your movie. You force the clips to the right of your title to slide further rightward to accommodate the credit you just inserted. That's just a reminder in case you're editing a video in sync with music. (When you insert text over video, by contrast, you don't change the overall length of your movie.)

Add by Double-Clicking

Instead of dragging and dropping a title into your storyboard, you can always just double-click it in the titles panel. When you do, iMovie drops in a 4-second title right where the playhead is in your storyboard.

Adjust the Timing

Once you drop a title into place, it turns into a purple stripe over the filmstrip. The stripe indicates how long the text appears onscreen. As you can see in Figure 10-7, the stripe can straddle part of a clip, a whole clip, or many clips, which gives you a huge amount of flexibility.

FIGURE 10-7

When your cursor approaches either end of a title stripe, it changes to a double-headed arrow. That's your cue that it's OK to start dragging the stripe's endpoint to make it longer or shorter. You can drag the stripe so that it spans multiple clips.

NOTE iMovie doesn't let you overlap titles. You can, however, have more than one title in the same clip. Drag one onto the front third and another onto the back third of the clip, for example. Then move the titles away from the ends of the clip and add even more titles, always using the clip ends as landing spots. The only rule is that titles can't overlap.

You can adjust this stripe three ways:

- **Adjust the starting point** by dragging the *left* end of the stripe.
- **Adjust the ending point** by dragging the *right* end of the stripe.

TIP Adjusting either end of the stripe also changes its duration.

- **Move the entire title in time** by grabbing it *anywhere else* and dragging it horizontally.

As you make adjustments, take into account your viewers' reading speed. There's only one thing more frustrating than titles that fly by too quickly to read, and that's titles that sit onscreen forever, boring the audience silly. Many video editors use this guideline: Leave the words onscreen long enough for somebody to read them aloud twice.

Also consider the location of your title carefully. If you superimpose it on a solid-color background or a still image, no problem. But if you plan to superimpose it on moving video, choose a scene that's relatively still, so the video doesn't distract the audience from the text.

Be particularly careful not to superimpose your titles on an unsteady shot; the contrast between the jiggling picture and the rock-steady lettering will make your audience uncomfortable.

NOTE The beauty of titles in iMovie is that there's no rendering (computing) time. They appear instantly, so you can freely adjust their placement and timing as often as you like.

Type the Text

Unless the name of your movie is, in fact, "Title Text Here," you probably want to edit the dummy text of your newly born title.

To do so, double-click the purple stripe in the storyboard. That opens the Adjust menu in the Viewer and automatically selects the Title tool. In the Viewer, the title's text boxes change from static placeholders to text boxes ready for an edit.

For most styles, you actually see *two* text boxes: a main title and a subtitle. Click inside one of the boxes to edit the dummy text.

> **NOTE** You don't have to type text into both boxes. The subtitle box is there solely for your convenience, for those occasions when you need a second, smaller line of type underneath the larger credit. If you don't need text there, just delete the placeholder text. When you play back your movie, both the text and its editing box are gone.

All the usual OS X text-editing tricks apply to the text boxes. For example:

- Double-click a word to highlight it.

- Triple-click inside the text box to select the entire title.

- Press Option-arrow key (left or right) to jump one word at a time.

- Press ⌘-arrow key (left or right) to jump to the beginning or end of the text box.

- Add Shift to the above two keystrokes to jump *and* select the intervening text simultaneously. For example, Shift-Option-right arrow highlights the word to the right of your insertion point.

- Cut, Copy, and Paste work just as you'd expect.

- Press Tab to jump between text boxes.

When you finish editing, click ✓ in the Viewer, or style the text using the instructions that follow.

Special Notes on Scrolling Credits

When you click the purple stripe representing a Scrolling Credits title, you see placeholder text snippets like the one shown in Figure 10-8.

FIGURE 10-8

Using the Scrolling Credits title and a combination of the Enter and Tab keys, you can create a sophisticated list of scrolling credits of any length.

To replace the dummy text with the names of your actors and characters, heed these notes:

- First, double-click where it says "Title." Now you can type something new in its place, like "Featuring" or "Cast."

- Next, drag diagonally through the scrolling list of placeholder names. Once you highlight them, you can begin typing your own cast list: Type in the character name ("Raymond," for example), press Tab, and then type in the actor's name ("Dustin Hoffman," for example). Press Tab to go to the next row. Type the next character name, press Tab, and then add that actor's name. And so on.

- As you go, you can create headings like the ones shown in Figure 10-8 by pressing the Enter key at the end of a row. iMovie places the insertion point at the *left* side of the frame, so you can type the heading (like "CREW" or "SECOND UNIT").

- You create a blank line in the credits by pressing Enter, Enter, Tab.

> **TIP** Using the Font panel, you can control the spacing between the lines of credits. See the Tip on page 162.

If you have too many names to fit on one screen, don't worry; the list scrolls automatically when you reach the bottom of the frame. You can keep typing until you credit every last gaffer, best boy, and caterer. (You can scroll back up again by holding down the up arrow key.)

■ Font, Size, and Style

iMovie's creators are rather fond of Gill Sans; that's a typeface, not a renowned video editor. iMovie uses the Gill Sans Serif font in most of its title styles. It looks great, but it also looks like everyone *else's* iMovie videos.

> **NOTE** Unfortunately, you can't change many of the fonts that iMovie uses in its titles, thanks to the way the software animates them. If you can't click the font drop-down menu as you edit your title, sadly, your title is a one-font pony.

Fortunately, you have a surprising amount of typographic flexibility with many titles. That may come as a surprise, considering that you can't see *any* font, size, style, or justification controls when you create a title.

Start by double-clicking the purple stripe of a title you've already placed. The Title settings tool appears in the Viewer. Then drag through some of the text in the Viewer.

TIP For most titles, iMovie doesn't limit you to a single font and size. You can use different fonts within a single text block, if you must. You can even use a different font for *every letter*, if you so desire (or if you're making a ransom-note video).

If the font tools in the Viewer are editable, you're in luck. Your options (shown in Figure 10-9) include these:

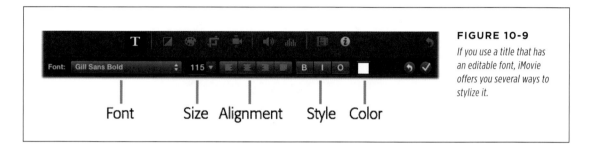

Font Size Alignment Style Color

FIGURE 10-9

If you use a title that has an editable font, iMovie offers you several ways to stylize it.

NOTE Some title styles are only partially editable. For example, you might be able to change the font but not the alignment. When that's the case, the non-functioning tools either disappear or are grayed out.

- **Font.** iMovie recommends a set of 14 fonts of different styles and weights. If you'd like to customize a bit more liberally, choose Show Fonts at the bottom of the Font drop-down menu to use your Mac system fonts instead.

- **Size.** You can choose one of the recommended sizes from the drop-down menu, or just type in a value, like 120.

- **Align.** These buttons adjust the horizontal alignment of the text within its text block. You can choose Left (against the left side), Center (centered), or Right (against the right side). (The final choice, Justified, does nothing in iMovie unless you have big long paragraphs for titles, which you probably shouldn't. If you must, Justified makes your text line up straight on both the left and right sides by adding space between words.)

- **Bold/Italic/Outline.** These three buttons change the style of your letters, to be either bolded, italicized, or surrounded by a black outline.

- **Color.** If white is not your thing, you can change the font color by clicking this box. The color picker offers millions of colors. (See page 163 for how to use the color picker.)

Figure 10-10 shows examples of many of these styles in use at once in a single, truly hideous opening credit.

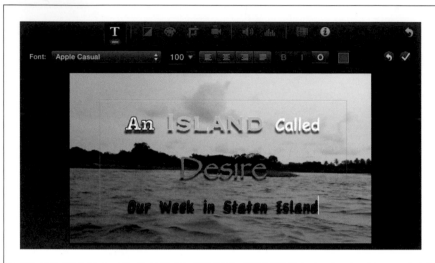

FIGURE 10-10

*You would never use all
of iMovie's typography
variations in a single title,
but you could.*

The System Font Panel

Handy as it is to have iMovie recommend fonts, it offers only a tiny slate of options, just 14. What is this, graphic-designer preschool?

Fortunately for control freaks, iMovie also gives you full access to the System Fonts Panel, a standard OS X feature that puts all typographic controls in a single place.

Suppose you just highlighted a title block, and now you want to choose an appropriate typeface. At the end of the Font drop-down menu, choose Show Fonts.

Here's what you'll find there (Figure 10-11):

- **Collection.** The first column lists your *collections*, which are canned sets of fonts. Apple starts you off with collections called things like "PDF" (a set of standard fonts used in PDF files) and "Web" (fonts you're safe using on web pages—that is, fonts likely installed on all Macs and Windows PCs).

> **TIP**   You can create your own collection of fonts called, for example, Headline or Sans Serif, organized by font type. Then you can switch these groups on or off at will, just as though you'd bought a program like Suitcase. You use OS X's Font Book program to do this.

- **Family, Typeface.** The second column shows the names of the actual fonts in your system. The third, Typeface, shows the different style variations—Bold, Italic, Condensed, and so on—available in that type family. (Oblique and Italic are roughly the same thing; Bold, Black, and Ultra are varying degrees of boldface.) Just click the font you want.

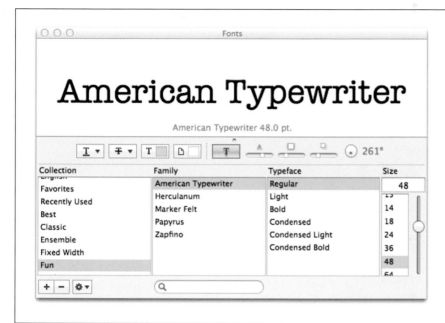

FIGURE 10-11

The OS X system fonts offer elaborate control over the color, shadow, and underline style of a title's text. If all you see is the font preview, grab the tiny bubble on the line below the preview and drag it upward. What if all you can see is the font list, but no preview? To get that, choose Show Preview from the ✿ drop-down menu at the bottom-left of the panel. Or use the mousy way: Place your cursor just above the headings (Collection, Family, and so on) and then drag downward.

- **Size.** The last column lists a sampling of point sizes. You can use the Size slider, choose from the point-size pop-up menu, or type any number into the box at the top of the Size list.

■ **UNDERLINE, STRIKETHROUGH, COLOR, SHADOW**

You'll see five rectangular buttons at the top of the Font Panel. Each is a pop-up menu that gives you an even more ridiculous amount of typography control:

- **Underline.** You can choose how you want iMovie to underline the selected text: with one underline, two, or none. If you choose Color, then the OS X Color Picker appears (Figure 10-12), so you can specify what *color* you want the underlines to be.

- **Strikethrough.** This option draws a line through your text, as though you crossed it out. These days, there's really only one situation when you might find it useful: the way bloggers indicate a correction, either a real one or a fake one done for humorous purposes. You know: "Cellphone Companies Are ~~Greedy Slimebags~~ Profitable."

- **Text color.** The third pop-up rectangle opens the Color Picker dialog box. Here you can specify the *color* of the highlighted text. (See the box on page 164.) The important thing is to choose a color that *contrasts* with the footage behind the lettering. Use white against black, black against white, yellow against blue, and so on.

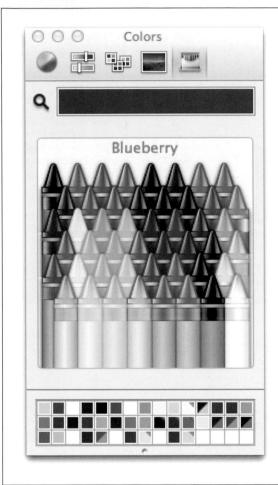

FIGURE 10-12

Some styling options can get ridiculous. When you request a different color for an underline or strikethrough, iMovie launches the OS X Color Picker, which gives you a million ways to dial up a precise shade. (If your computer doesn't offer the toolbar controls shown in this image, make the window wider by dragging the bottom-right corner.)

TIP iMovie doesn't limit you to TV-safe colors. But be careful. If colors are too bright (saturated), the edges of the letters can smear and tear when played back on a TV.

- **Document color.** The next pop-up rectangle is supposed to let you choose a background color for your text, but it doesn't work in iMovie.

- **Drop shadow.** The rightmost pop-up button is responsible for the shadow that iMovie adds to your titles to help them stand out from the background (Figure 10-13).

FIGURE 10-13

In the OS X Fonts window, the four tiny controls to the right of the Shadow button style the shadow itself: its opacity, degree of "spread," distance from the main characters (controls how far away the "page" looks from the text), and the angle of the light that's casting the shadow. (If you don't see these controls, drag the window's bottom-right corner until they appear.)

General Guidelines

As you choose fonts and type effects for the various credits in your movie, consider these guidelines:

- **Be consistent.** Using the same typeface for all the titles in your movie lends consistency and professionalism to the project.

- **Remember the QuickTime effect.** If you plan to distribute your finished movie as a QuickTime file—an electronic movie file that you can share with others—use the biggest, boldest, cleanest fonts you have. Avoid spindly, delicate fonts or script fonts. When QuickTime compresses your movie down, what looks terrific in your Viewer will be so small it may become illegible.

  Come to think of it, you might want to choose big, bold, clean fonts even if you're going to play the finished movie on a TV with a resolution far lower than that of your computer screen. Be especially careful if you use one of the text effects that includes a subtitle, as iMovie subtitles often use an even smaller typeface than the one for the primary title, and you may lose legibility if the font has too much filigree.

  Finally, favor *sans serif* fonts—typefaces that don't have the tiny *serifs*, or "hats and feet," at the ends of the character strokes. The typeface you're reading now is a sans serif font, one that's more likely to remain legible in a QuickTime movie.

The Color Picker

Here and there—not just in iMovie, but also in System Prefer-ences, TextEdit, Microsoft Office, and many other programs—OS X offers you the opportunity to choose a *color* for some ele-ment, like your desktop background, a window, and so on.

The Colors dialog box (Figure 10-12) offers a miniature color lab that lets you dial in any color in the Mac's rainbow. *Several* color labs, actually, arrayed across the top, are designed to make color-choosing easier in certain circumstances:

- **Color Wheel.** Drag the scroll bar vertically to adjust the brightness, and then drag your cursor around the ball to pick the shade.

- **Color Sliders.** From the pop-up menu, choose the color-mixing method you prefer. *CMYK* stands for cyan, magenta, yellow, and black. People in the printing industry will feel immediately at home, because these four colors are the component inks for color printing. (These people may also be able to explain why K stands for black.) *RGB* is how a TV or computer monitor thinks of colors: as proportions of red, green, and blue. *HSV* is hue, saturation, and value—a favorite color-specifying scheme in scientific circles. In each case, just drag the sliders to mix up the color you want, or type in the percentages of each component.

- **Color Palettes.** These palettes present canned sets of color swatches. They're primarily for programmers who want quick access to the standard colors in OS X.

- **Image Palettes.** Image palettes offer the visible rainbow arrayed yet another way—as cloudy, color-arranged streaks.

- **Crayons.** Now *this* is a handy tool. You can click each crayon to see its color name: Mocha, Cayenne, Fern, and so on. (Some interior decorator in Cupertino had a field day naming these crayons.)

In any of these color pickers, you can also "sample" a color that's *outside* the dialog box—a color in your clip, for example, or one that you found on a web page. Just click the magnifying glass and then move your cursor around the screen. You'll see the sliders and numbers automatically change inside the dialog box when you click.

Finally, note that you can store frequently used (or frequently admired) colors in the mini-palette squares at the bottom. To do that, drag the big rectangular color swatch (next to the magnifying glass) directly down into one of the little squares, where it will stay fresh for weeks.

The beauty of iMovie's titling feature is that the fonts you choose become embed-ded in the actual digital picture. In other words, when you distribute your movie as a QuickTime file, you don't have to worry that your recipients may not have the same fonts you used to create the file. They'll see on their screens exactly what you see on yours.

> **TIP** Don't forget that you can superimpose text on a *still* image, too (Chapter 12)—such as a photo or some gradient fill you created in, say, Photoshop Elements.

Add a Custom Title

The Titles feature isn't the only way to create text effects. Using a graphics program like Photoshop or Photoshop Elements, you can create text "slides" with far more flexibility than you can find in the Titles feature. You're free to use any text color and any font size you want, and you can import the resulting file into iMovie as a title card (read on). You can even dress up such titles with clip art, 3D effects, and whatever other features your graphics software offers. Figure 10-14 (bottom) shows the idea.

Creating a title like this involves creating an *alpha-channel PNG* file. A little Photoshop experience is helpful, but here's the gist:

Use the text tool to type and format the text in Photoshop. In the Layers palette, ⌘-click the text layer's thumbnail to select it. Then, at the bottom of the Channels palette, click the "Save Selection as Channel" button. Finally, choose File→Save As.

Choose PNG as the format, and Photoshop makes you save the file as a copy. (Don't worry, the transparency should be preserved.) Name the title and save it to your desktop.

Now just drag the title graphic off your desktop and just above the clip you want titled, as shown in Figure 10-14, top. iMovie adds the graphic as a Cutaway (page 113); your PNG graphic will now look like a title to anyone who watches your movie.

FIGURE 10-14

Top: Drag your alpha-channel PNG title graphic right off the desktop and onto a filmstrip.

Bottom: iMovie treats the graphic like a cutaway to a photo and superimposes it on your video. To the rest of the world, though, it looks like a snazzy title.

Check the Results

As you edit a title, you can see how it looks in context by clicking the ▶ button in the Viewer. Or, once you finish your title, point to a spot in the storyboard just before the title and then press the space bar to view the title in the context of the movie. You can also simply move your cursor back and forth across the title in the storyboard without clicking to see how it looks.

If the title isn't quite what you wanted—if it's the wrong length, style, or font, or if there's a typo, for example—you can change its settings as described in the next section. If the title wasn't *at all* what you wanted—if it's the wrong title style, for example—you can undo the entire process by highlighting the purple title stripe and pressing the Delete key (or choosing Edit→Undo, if you added the title recently).

Edit or Delete a Title

If you don't like the title style you chose, just drag another one from the Titles pane and drop it right on top of the one you want to replace. iMovie updates the title instantly to reflect the change.

> **TIP** You can also change a title's style quickly by selecting it and then double-clicking a new title style in the Titles pane.

Making other changes to a title is easy:

- **Change the start or end points** by dragging the endpoints of the purple stripe in the storyboard.

- **Move the entire title earlier or later** by dragging its stripe left or right in the storyboard.

- **Edit the text or its typography** by clicking the title's purple stripe in the storyboard. The text boxes appear immediately in the Viewer. Follow the steps starting on page 160 if you need to change the color, font, or other typographical niceties.

- **Delete a title** by clicking its purple stripe and then pressing the Delete key.

Music, Sound Effects, and Narration

If you're lucky, you may someday get the chance to watch a movie whose soundtrack isn't yet finished. Maybe you'll be scanning TV channels and stumble across a special about how movies are made, or you'll see a tribute to a film composer, or you'll rent a movie that includes a "making of" documentary. These shows sometimes include a couple of minutes of the finished movie as it looked *before* the music and sound effects were added.

At that moment, your understanding of the film medium will take an enormous leap forward. "Jeez," you'll say, "without music and sound effects, this $100 million Hollywood film has no more emotional impact than...my home movies!"

And you'd be right. It's true that the *visual* component of a film is the most, well, visible. Movie stars and directors become household names, but not the sound editors, composers, *foley* (sound effects) artists, and others who devote their careers to the audio experience of film.

But without music, sound effects (called SFX for short), and sound editing, even the best Hollywood movie will leave you cold and unimpressed.

iMovie's more powerful than it's ever been at editing your movie's audio. You can use traditional methods to make simple volume changes, like the classic rubber-band tool (page 171), or advanced techniques that reduce background noise (page 198). This chapter explains everything iMovie has to offer in audio editing.

■ Three Kinds of Audio

You'll work with three kinds of audio in iMovie: clip audio, background music, and connected audio.

Clip Audio

Clip audio gets recorded with your video footage. It stays fixed to the clip unless you ask iMovie to "detach" it—see page 191 for how and why you'd want to do that.

Background Music

A lot of iMovie owners like to add music to their movies. It's a fun way to augment otherwise mundane shots, and can evoke the feeling of the moment. (Think of an end-of-year slideshow set to "Gangnam Style," or whatever song was big that year.)

To make editing music easier, iMovie can set it as *background music*, a solid block of audio that sits "under" the clips in your project, playing through everything, no matter how you shuffle the clips around. You can even line up a playlist of several songs; iMovie plays them consecutively, with a nice crossfade in between.

> **NOTE** There's much more on editing to music in this chapter, starting on page 182.

Connected Audio

Background music remains steadily in place no matter how you rearrange your footage, but some audio *should* move with your video. When you add a *connected* audio clip, you attach an audio file to a specific spot in your video. You'd use connected audio for things like sound effects, to trigger a laugh track, for example, or the roar of applause. As you rearrange your clips during the editing process, the connected audio goes along for the ride.

> **NOTE** There's no difference between the *kinds* of audio you can use as background music and connected audio. *Any* audio, including sound effects, can serve as background music, and *any* audio, including music, can work as a connected clip. You'll learn the details later in this chapter.

Audio Sources

In addition to the audio built into every video clip, you can *add* sound to a project from any of these sources:

- **Video camera audio.** You can extract the audio from a camera video clip to use as an independent sound clip, for use somewhere else in your movie.

- **iTunes tracks.** Adding background music to your movie is easy. As described later in this chapter, iMovie displays your iTunes music collection, playlists and all. (iMovie's integration with iTunes is an example of what makes Apple's iLife software a *suite*, and not just a handful of separate programs.)

- **Sound effects.** Choose these effects (gunshots, glass breaking, applause, and so on) from iMovie's Audio palette.

- **Narration.** This can be anything you record with a microphone.

- **MP3, WAV, AIFF, and AAC files.** iMovie can directly import files in these popular music formats. You can drag them in from the Finder or bring them in from iTunes.

This chapter covers all these sound varieties.

NOSTALGIA CORNER

Importing Music from a CD

For several versions of iMovie, you could import songs from a CD directly into iMovie. You'd insert your favorite music CD (The Rolling Stones, the Cleveland Orchestra, or whatever), choose the track you wanted, and the deed was done.

That feature mysteriously disappeared from iMovie starting in version 6. Now you're supposed to switch to iTunes, import the CD into your music collection there, and then return to iMovie to import the songs.

■ Volume Adjustments

This section covers all the ways you can adjust the volume in your movie.

The Rubber Band

If "rubber-banding" makes you think of office supplies instead of volume levels, then meet an iMovie tool that's super useful. (Audio editors call volume adjustments "rubber-banding" because the line you grab to adjust the fade-in and fade-out points in an audio track seems to stretch as you fine-tune those points.)

■ FINDING THE RUBBER BAND

To see the rubber-band tool, turn on the Show Waveforms checkbox, hidden in the Clip Size slider you read about on page 50 (see Figure 11-1).

NOTE A "waveform" shows volume changes in your audio. It looks like a bunch of peaks and valleys (see Figure 11-1). Waveforms let you visualize sound changes without having to listen to them.

When you do, iMovie displays an audio track just below your filmstrip. It represents the audio levels for everything in your project that produces sound.

A single, thin line runs horizontally across your waveform, looking as though it wants to chop off their tips (Figure 11-1). That's the rubber-band tool.

FIGURE 11-1

Behold the once-missed rubber band! To see a clip's waveforms and this handy little audio tool, turn on the Show Waveforms checkbox.

Rubber Band tool Waveform

■ USE THE RUBBER BAND

The height of the rubber band determines the volume of your clip. The higher the line, the louder the clip. The band's starting position, about a third of the way down from the top, is the standard 100% volume. If you drag the line higher or lower, iMovie displays a floating bubble that shows you the new volume level (Figure 11-2).

If all you could do was change the height of the line for the entire clip, there wouldn't be much point to the tool. (After all, you can change the volume of a clip in the Adjustments pane.) The beauty of it comes when you stretch it up or down on just *part* of your clip. You can, for example, soften the background music when Grandma

Alice tells her story. Alternatively, you can increase the volume when a soft-spoken interviewee appears onscreen.

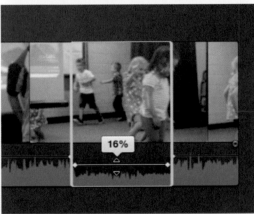

FIGURE 11-2

Top: If you drag the entire rubber band up or down, iMovie shows you the new volume level in a floating window.

Middle: To adjust the volume for just part of a clip, click and hold the mouse button down until you see a yellow line. Drag the line to select the part of the clip you want; as you do, the line changes to a highlight box. Now you can drag the rubber band inside the box to change the volume for that part of the clip only.

Bottom: To adjust the fade for volume changes, making them gradual or abrupt, grab the small yellow diamond on either side of the volume change. Drag them outward to fade gradually, inward to fade abruptly.

To make these adjustments, first select the part of a clip you want to affect. To do that, click the clip and hold down the mouse button until a vertical yellow line appears. Then drag your mouse—as you drag, the yellow line expands into a box that selects the underlying clip fragment (Figure 11-2, middle). Drag the rubber band within that selected area to adjust the volume. You can see the rubber band move up and down as you drag.

NOTE Any whole or partial volume adjustments you make in your project are project-specific. That is, other projects that use the same clip don't see (or hear) the changes. That's not true, however, for volume changes you make to clips in the Event library. Any volume changes to Event footage affect every project that uses that footage.

Once you deselect the clip fragment by clicking anywhere else in the storyboard, you can see the "stretched" parts of the rubber band, where iMovie fades the volume in or out to reach the fragment's setting.

To change the length of the fade—that is, to make it gradual or abrupt—grab the little yellow diamonds on either end of the adjustment and drag them horizontally (Figure 11-2, bottom). Dragging them outward makes the volume change more gradually. Dragging them inward makes the volume change more suddenly, which you might do, for example, to make a song pop back in really loudly.

NOTE You might have noticed that some of the waveform waves go above the rubber-band line, while most stay below it. That's because the rubber band just sets the base volume for your clip. Every movie still has loud parts and quiet parts, no matter where you set the volume. The high peaks in your waveforms are the loud parts.

Finally, you can add your own yellow diamonds—iMovie calls them *keyframes*—by Option-clicking the volume-level line. You can drag these added keyframes the same way you do the iMovie-generated diamonds, and to the same effect—fading the volume in or out.

To delete a keyframe, right-click it and then select Delete Keyframe, or select the keyframe and then choose Edit→Delete Keyframes, or press Shift-Option-Delete.

Ducking

Anytime you hear competing audio tracks in a movie, the editor has probably dropped the volume in one track so you could hear the sound in the other. (You've seen this when actors in a music montage stop for a moment to have a brief discussion. The music dips down so you can understand the dialogue.) This is called *ducking*, where you "duck," or drop the volume in, one audio track to make room for the audio in another.

Ducking is a convenient way to make sure your audience hears your audio, regardless of where the rubber band is—that's because ducking makes the volume adjustments for you. It really all comes down to a checkbox and a slider.

NOTE Ducking works only for entire clips. You can't choose part of a clip and duck the other audio competing with that part. The ducking slider will reduce the volume for anything competing with the entire clip.

If you want to reduce the volume of competing clips for just part of your main clip, you'll have to select the parts of the competing clips and reduce their volume directly with the rubber band, as explained on page 171.

To make sure that one of your audio tracks is always heard, do the following:

1. **Select the clip whose audio you want to change.**

   You might want to adjust the clip's native audio, or the volume of an audio track you added to the clip, such as a background track or a connected audio clip (all explained on page 170).

2. **In the Viewer toolbar, click the Adjust button, followed by the Volume button (the speaker icon).**

   iMovie displays the volume adjustment tools, where you can change the clip's audio in multiple ways (Figure 11-3).

FIGURE 11-3

Check the "Lower volume of other clips" checkbox to make the sound in the selected clip supersede that of other clips.

3. **Turn on the "Lower volume of other clips" checkbox and then adjust the slider to your liking.**

   The lower you move the slider, the quieter other audio clips become. You can skim and play your project to make sure you've got the right setting.

TIP If you're making volume adjustments and for some reason you can't get one loud enough, it may be because another clip competing with it has the ducking feature turned on.

To undo the ducking on a track, turn off the "Lower volume of other clips" checkbox.

Music

If you drag a piece of music to the *very bottom* of your storyboard—where you see a clip silhouette with a musical note in it—the clip turns into long green waveform (Figure 11-4). That's your clue that you just added a piece of what Apple calls background music. (Make sure you drag the song all the way to the bottom of the storyboard and not immediately under the video clip—that would make it a connected audio clip, as explained on page 170.)

FIGURE 11-4

A background music track. When you add music to the very bottom of your storyboard, iMovie keeps it separate from your other clips, which preserves its timing and placement in your project.

3.8m – Here Comes the Sun

Understanding what, exactly, Apple means by this term—and figuring out how it differs from *connected audio*—isn't especially easy. This much, though, is clear:

- **Background music generally plays from the beginning of your movie.** You can drag it to a different spot, however, as described in a moment.

- **If you add two pieces of background music, one after the other, iMovie plays them consecutively, with a crossfade in between.** You add the second piece the same way you added the first one, by dragging it. (Two pieces of background music can never overlap, though.)

Putting your background music in its own track makes sense because the music is usually ancillary to the story you're telling (unless you're editing a video to music, as described on page 182). Adding the song as a background track puts it conveniently out of your way, impervious to whatever video edits you make.

Music Sources

Before getting into the details of how background music works, you need to add a song to your project. iMovie gives you three ways to do that: via iTunes, Garage-Band, and the Finder.

■ ITUNES

When you have a project open, iMovie displays a list of media sources in the Content Library in the bottom-left corner of the window. One of the options is your iTunes library, where you can tap into your entire iTunes song list, without actually having to open iTunes itself, a real convenience.

When you click iTunes in the Content Library. iMovie replaces the Event browser with a music browser (Figure 11-5) that displays your song list and a waveform representing the currently selected tune. A dropdown menu lets you sort your music by stock iTunes listings (My Top Rated, Recently Played, and so on) or by playlist.

TIP Playlists are a great way to store music you want to use in your movie. Just create the playlist in iTunes and then choose it from the drop-down menu in iMovie. Voilà! All your movie music in one place.

If you can't find the song you want, use the search field in the top-right corner of the music browser. As you type, iMovie narrows your choices. You can search song titles, album titles, and artist names all at once. (Typing "fun" would show the results for the band Fun., the album "Funeral" by Arcade Fire, and the song "Girls Just Want to Have Fun.")

NOTE iTunes holds videos in addition to music, and you can bring those into iMovie through the music browser, too, so long as the movies aren't copy-protected iTunes purchases or rentals.

FIGURE 11-5

The music browser. This image shows your iTunes library, which you can see without having to open iTunes itself. You can winnow the song list using the search field, and preview songs here as well.

Fun with Copyright Law

Don't I break some kind of law when I use iTunes music in one of my movies?

Exactly what constitutes stealing music is a hot-button issue that has tied millions of people (and recording executives) in knots. That's why some iMovie fans hesitate to distribute their films in places where lawyers might see them—like the Internet.

Frankly, though, record company lawyers have bigger fish to fry than small-time amateur operators like you. You're perfectly safe showing your movies to family and friends, your user group, and other limited circles of viewers. In fact, Apple *encourages* you to use iTunes Music Store purchases in your movies. After all, Apple is the one who made them available right in iMovie.

You'll risk trouble only if you go commercial, making money from movies that incorporate copyrighted music.

Still, if your conscience nags you, you can always use a GarageBand composition (see page 179). And even if you're not especially musical, the world is filled with royalty-free music—music that artists compose and record expressly for the purpose of letting filmmakers add it to their work without having to pay a licensing fee every time they do (they pay a one-time fee). Some of it's even truly free. You'll find 200 free music pieces in the Jingles folder of your Sound Effects browser, for example, ready to use.

Or check out *www.freeplaymusic.com*, a website filled with prerecorded music in every conceivable style. You're welcome to use it in your movies at no charge for noncommercial use.

If that's not enough for you, visit a search engine like Google (*www.google.com*), look for *music library* or *royalty-free music*, and start clicking your way to the hundreds of sites that offer information about (and audio samples of) music that you can buy and use without fear.

■ GARAGEBAND

If you're a GarageBand composer, you can access your compositions from within iMovie. With a project open, choose GarageBand from the Content Library in the bottom-left corner. The music browser for GarageBand looks and acts just like the one for iTunes, described previously. For more on using GarageBand, see page 200.

■ THE FINDER

If you have a music file that's on your hard drive but not in iTunes or GarageBand, you can always just drag it into the iMovie storyboard from the Finder. You don't get the benefit of a handy music browser, but once you add the file to your project, it behaves just like any iTunes or GarageBand song.

Preview a Song

As you go over your list of songs in the music browser, position your mouse over any one of them and a small Play button appears on the left. Click it to play back the song and see its waveform. (Double-clicking the song does the same thing.) A playhead line drifts over the waveform.

You can skim the playhead to any point in the song and hit the space bar to start playback from that spot.

Add All of a Song

You can add an entire song to your project in two ways. One is to drag the tune from the song list to the very bottom of your storyboard, where you see the clip silhouette that has the musical note in it.

The other is to click the + button in the song's waveform in the music browser (Figure 11-6). That has the added advantage of automatically trimming the end of your song should it go longer than your project.

You can add multiple songs to your project's background track. If you do that through the + button in the waveform, iMovie lines them up sequentially. If you already have a background song in your project and drag another one in, iMovie starts playing it at whatever point you drop it, even if it has to trim the song added beforehand.

> **NOTE** iMovie can play only one background song at a time, so multiple songs in the background track play sequentially.

Add Part of a Song

You can use the green waveform to select just *part* of a song, too.

Drag the mouse across the waveform to highlight the song section with a yellow border (Figure 11-6). You can refine the selection by dragging either end of the border. Once you finish, click the + button or drag the selection into your project.

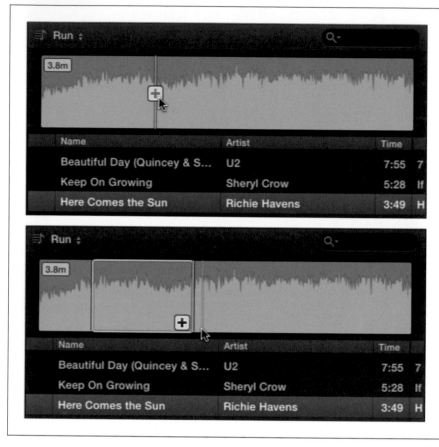

FIGURE 11-6

Top: To add a song to your project, drag it from the list into your storyboard, or click the + button (pictured).

Bottom: To add just part of a song, drag in the waveform to select the section you want, and then click the + button; iMovie adds just that part to your project.

Trim a Song

Once you have a song in the storyboard, you're not stuck with it. In fact, the awesome editing-by-reference trick that iMovie does with video (page 35) works on music, too.

To trim a song, move your mouse over the beginning or end of the clip. When you do, iMovie changes your cursor from an arrow to two arrows with a line between them. Drag to trim or extend that part of the song.

That approach isn't nearly as versatile as the Clip Trimmer, which you can use to fine-tune your track edit, as explained in the sidebar here.

Move a Song

By default, iMovie starts your song at the beginning of your project, but you can drag it to whatever starting point you want.

Change the Volume of a Song

You change the volume of background music the same way you change the volume of any other clip. Use one of the methods described on page 171.

The Clip Trimmer

Most people treat background music in iMovie as a set-it-and-forget-it affair. You drop the track into the storyboard, it plays as long as necessary to cover your video, and end of story.

Truth is, though, you have a little more control than that. Exhibit A: You can start playing any piece of music from someplace *other* than the song's beginning (and stop it before the song ends). If you have an iTunes track that begins with an annoying 35-second drum solo, for example, you can lop it off, so that the music (and your movie) begin with the actual hook of the song—the main part.

To edit background audio, double-click the green clip anywhere. That launches the Clip Trimmer, which you read about back on page 67 (Figure 11-7). The waves you'll hear as your movie plays back appear light green. If the music lasts longer than your project, iMovie shades the parts you won't hear dark green.

The bright, white, vertical lines tell you where the music starts and stops in your project. To trim the music, adjust the position of the white vertical lines. Drag the first one to the right if you want the music to begin at a point that's later in the song; drag the final one to the left if you want the music to end before the end of the song. You can skim or play to hear where you are in the piece.

Click Close Clip Trimmer when you finish, or click anywhere in your storyboard.

Incidentally, this trick also works on cutaway audio (page 113), narration, and so on.

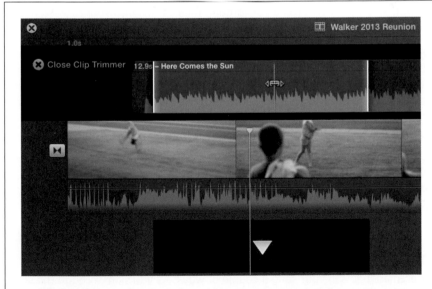

FIGURE 11-7

You can use the Clip Trimmer to trim audio clips just as you do video clips.

Delete a Song

To delete background music, select the clip in your storyboard and then press Delete.

▇ Edit to the Beat

If you've ever made a music video, you know how easy it is to pull your hair out trying to match a transition with a beat in the background. To make sure you don't go bald, iMovie offers a subtle but very powerful tool called a *marker*.

Markers are specially designed indicators you add to your movie that correspond to particular moments. You can use markers for all sorts of editing strategies, like noting when you want a title to appear or a clip to end. You can also use markers to tap out beats in a song. Then, as you add video clips to your project, you can easily match the clips' length and cuts to the beat of the music. The markers even work with adjustments you make using the Precision Editor (page 68)—those edits will also snap to line up with the beats you mark.

The truth is, markers are one of the coolest iMovie features that no one talks about. But what markers lack in recognition, they make up for in power. They'll save you huge swaths of time editing a movie to the beat of a song.

> **TIP** You can mark beats in *any* kind of audio track: pinned, unpinned, sound effect, or even a voiceover.

Editing to the beat is a three-phase process. Before you dive in, make sure you have snapping enabled by heading to View→Snapping (you'll see a checkmark if you have Snapping turned on).

Phase 1: Add Your Background Music

Start with a new project. Drop a background music track into your project, as described on page 176.

"Wait a minute!" you may protest. "I don't even have any video clips in place!" Your concern is justified—your song appears like a lonely green blob in your timeline. But there's a good reason to put the song in first: You can resize the video clips and photos you place later to match the beat markers you're about to add to the song. In addition, you can edit the song itself to make audio adjustments (page 171) or change its start and end points using the Clip Trimmer (page 67).

> **TIP** You can add markers to projects you've *already* created, and then resize your clips to fit the beats. But as you do, the changes you make cascade throughout your movie, potentially wreaking havoc on the timing of the visuals you so carefully assembled. If you plan to cut a movie to a song's rhythm, it's best to mark all the beats from the start.

Phase 2: Insert Markers to the Beat

You can mark beats in your song a couple of ways. As you skim through the song, you can hear and spot (using the song's waveform) places where the beat would make a well-timed cut. As you line up your playhead on that spot, choose Mark→Add Marker (or press the letter M key on your keyboard).

In addition to tagging beats, mark any spot you want to get special attention as you edit, like a big musical swell or key bit in the lyrics.

The markers show up as tiny blue tags resting on top of your song (Figure 11-8).

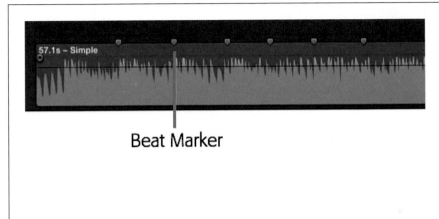

Beat Marker

FIGURE 11-8

iMovie's markers let you identify beats in a song. The markers appear as small, blue tags in your storyboard. You can move them by dragging them around. To delete one, drag it above the clip and then release the mouse button, or right-click it and then choose Delete, or select it and then choose Shift-Control-M.

Alternatively, you might find it a lot simpler to just hit the letter M key as your song plays. That way, you can have all your markers in place by just going through the song.

Play the audio track from the beginning. As it plays, tap the M key on every beat where you want the video to cut to a new shot. (It's OK to boogie in your chair; no one is watching.)

Once you tap out the whole song, take a moment to review your markers and fix mistakes. Beat markers are draggable, even after you place them. You can remove a marker by dragging it off the top of the clip, or by right-clicking it and selecting Delete from the shortcut menu. There's no way to get rid of all the markers at once, however. If you want to start over, delete the entire song from your project. Then add the song back into your project and begin again.

TIP Usually, if you cut right on the beat, the cut will appear to be late. If you practice tapping the M key just barely *before* the beats, your cuts will look just right.

Don't group your markers too closely together unless you're trying to get a very fast-paced effect. If the video cuts happen *too* quickly, your viewers won't be able to absorb them.

Once you're happy with the beat placements, it's time to start adding video clips.

Phase 3: Add and Resize Clips

You should be back in your Event browser now, having a basically blank project awaiting some footage. Grab a video chunk from the browser and add it to your project.

Now you need to resize it to match the beat. Grab the end of the clip and drag it toward the closest marker. As you get close, the yellow line you're dragging snaps to the closest marker as though it were magnetized.

Because of a quirk in the way iMovie works, it might look like trimming the video displaces your marker (the marker appears to jump to the right of the yellow border). But when you play back your project, you'll find that the clip ends right on the beat. Try it with a photo now (page 210). Isn't that cool? (If you don't see any snapping, make sure you have View→Snapping turned on.)

You can use the Precision Editor (page 68) to make sure the right moments in your video line up with the right beats. Snapping works here, too.

After very little work, your project will look something like the one in Figure 11-9.

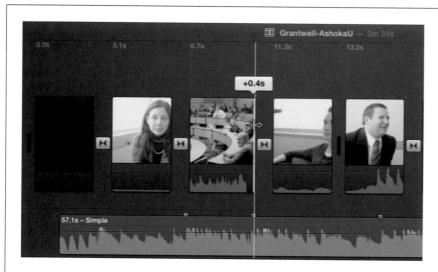

FIGURE 11-9

To edit to the beat of music, you often need to resize clips to create a cut on the beat.

Notice how the markers show up in your project? That reminds you that you cut to the beat there, in case you want to make an edit that would displace the cut.

Snap to Beats in Your Project

With snapping turned on, your markers in place, and your footage added, you can start adding things like titles and sound effects. As you drag these elements around, they, too, snap into position against markers, as though magnetically attracted. (Turn off View→Snapping if this is getting in the way.) You can adjust their timing too, so they match the beats in your project.

> **TIP** You can add all kinds of other project elements, but *transitions* will disrupt your timed cuts, as described next.

Beat Markers in the Precision Editor

What if you added beat markers *after* you added your footage? Or what if your video doesn't display the exact image you want on the beat? That's where the Precision Editor can help.

With your song at the bottom of the project window and all its beat markers in place, double-click any empty space between two video clips to launch the Precision Editor. Page 68 covers the basic operation of the editor, but you should know that it offers some handy extras when you work with beat markers (Figure 11-10).

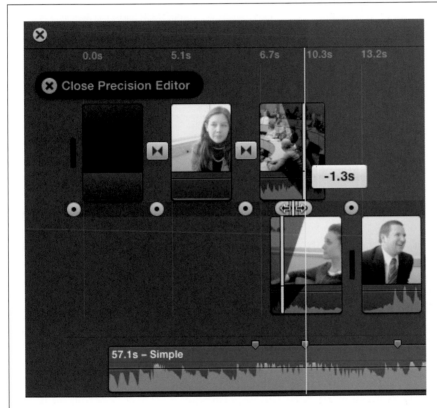

FIGURE 11-10

With markers in your song and snapping turned on, the Precision Editor takes on a new twist. As you move the transition bubble toward a marker, it snaps to the marker.

To line up a transition with a beat, drag the gray transition bubble around. Each time it approaches a beat marker in the song, the bubble snaps to the marker.

Here's a rundown of how you could use beat markers in the Precision Editor:

- If you added beat markers after you added your clips, you can go back through the movie to make sure the cuts work in sync with the background music.

- You can line up video elements, like a poignant image or a title, to match a beat.

- You can override the snapping effect to line up a video moment with the music (and that moment, like the crack of a bat at a ball game, may take place in the *middle* of a clip).

Beats and Transitions

If you use transitions in your movie, as described on page 83, here's some timely advice.

A simple cut to a beat almost always looks good, because the cut is just as quick as the beat itself. But transitions, like cross dissolves (page 92), generally last longer than a beat, so they won't line up with the beat as precisely.

You'll encounter this problem no matter what kind of transition you use. When you add a transition between two beat-aligned clips (by placing it yourself or by having automatic transitions turned on [page 91]), iMovie puts the beat in the middle of the transition. To correct for this, you can adjust your clips in the storyboard or with the Precision Editor.

◼ Connected Audio

Background music works when you want a song to play behind whatever is onscreen, but sometimes you want to marry an audio file to a particular moment in your video. You might, for example, want a laugh track to start right after your actor tells a joke.

That's where connected audio comes in. It lets you pin audio to video. (It's analogous to connected video clips, explained on page 112.) If you move the video clip, the audio track goes with it. This gets super handy when you shuffle clips around or change your project timing with added transitions (see page 88 for transitions and project timing).

Sound Effects

This is a great time to introduce iMovie sound effects, since you'll almost always use them as connected audio. With a project open, you'll see the Content Library in the bottom-right corner of the iMovie window. One of the sources listed is Sound Effects.

When you click it, iMovie opens the music browser you saw for iTunes, now full of premade sound effects (Figure 11-11). There are hundreds to choose from, so use the search box and/or the drop-down menu to narrow things down.

NOTE   The best part of iMovie's sound effects is that they're not only free (they come with iMovie), but they're *royalty-free*, too, which means you can use them in any movies you create, for commercial purposes or not, without ever paying Apple.

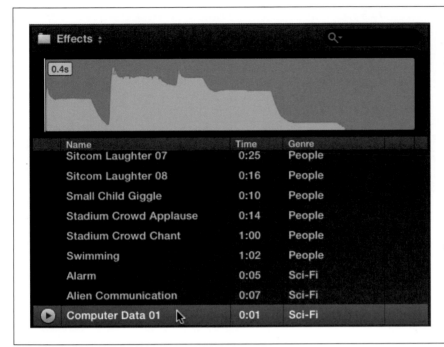

FIGURE 11-11

Apple offers hundreds of royalty-free sound effects, with everything from laugh tracks and canned applause to explosions, telephone rings, and cute little jingles.

Name	Time	Genre
Sitcom Laughter 07	0:25	People
Sitcom Laughter 08	0:16	People
Small Child Giggle	0:10	People
Stadium Crowd Applause	0:14	People
Stadium Crowd Chant	1:00	People
Swimming	1:02	People
Alarm	0:05	Sci-Fi
Alien Communication	0:07	Sci-Fi
Computer Data 01	0:01	Sci-Fi

Add and Edit Connected Audio

To add all or part of an audio track as a connected clip, you have to drag it into your project. (Don't use the white + button that appears in the waveform preview—that adds the track as background music.) Drop the audio onto your video clip where you want to connect it.

A few things about connected audio clips:

- While background songs can't overlap, connected audio clips can. You can stack multiple ones on top of one another.

- Connected audio attaches to your video clips with a little green flag staking their ground (Figure 11-12). The position of the flag tells you when the clip will play.

- You can edit connected audio clips just as you do background music. Drag either end to lengthen or shorten the clip. Double-click it to use the Clip Trimmer. Move it by dragging it with your mouse.

- All the volume-adjustment tools (described on page 171) work on connected audio clips.

- Delete a connected audio clip by right-clicking it and choosing Delete, or by selecting it and pressing the Delete key.

FIGURE 11-12

A connected audio clip looks a lot like a background music clip, but it has a green flag that shows you when the audio kicks in. If you drag the video clip to another part of your project, the connected audio clip comes with it.

Narration

If anyone ever belittles iMovie for being underpowered, point out an iMovie feature that isn't even available in many more expensive video-editing programs: the ability to record narration while you watch your movie play back. If your Mac has a microphone, you can easily create any of these effects:

- **A reminiscence.** As your footage shows children playing, we hear you saying, "It was the year 2009. It was a time of innocence. Of sunlight. Of children at play. In the years before the Great Asteroid, nobody imagined that one 6-year-old child would become a goddess to her people. This, then, is her story."

- **Voiceover.** The technique of superimposing an unseen narrator's voice over video is called a *voiceover*. It's incredibly popular in TV, commercials, and movies (such as *Saving Private Ryan*, *Sin City*, and, of course, the *Look Who's Talking* movies).

- **Identify the scene.** Even if your movie isn't one with a story line, iMovie's narration feature offers an extremely convenient way to identify your home movies. Think about it: When you used to get photos developed at the drugstore, the date was stamped across the back. Even years later, you knew when you took the photo.

Some video cameras offer an optional date-stamp feature, but it's a crude, ugly, digital readout that permanently mars your footage. And few people are compulsive enough to film, before each new shot, somebody saying, "It's Halloween 2014, and little Chrissie is going out for her very first trick-or-treating. Mommy made the costume out of some fishnet stockings and a melon."

Using iMovie, it's easy to add a few words of shot-identification narration over your establishing shot. (To find out the time and date when you shot the footage, double-click the clip.)

- **Provide new information.** For professional work, narration is an excellent way to add another layer of information to whatever is playing onscreen. Doctors use iMovie to create narrated slideshows, having created a storyboard filled with still images of scanned slides (see Chapter 12). Real-estate agents feature footage of houses for sale, narrating key features that can't be seen ("Built in 1869, this house was extensively renovated in 1880…"). And it doesn't take much imagination to think of how *lawyers* can exploit iMovie.

To create a *voiceover* (a narration), follow these steps:

1. **Choose Window→Record Voiceover, or press the letter-V key.**

   The Viewer displays iMovie's voiceover tools (Figure 11-13).

2. **Click the Voiceover Options button to choose a sound source.**

   Your Mac's microphone takes one of two forms: built-in or external. The built-in mic, a tiny hole in the facade of the iMac, eMac, or MacBook, couldn't be more convenient. It's always with you, and always turned on.

   If your Mac doesn't have a built-in microphone, you can plug in an external USB microphone or a standard microphone with an adapter (like the iMic from Griffin Technology [*www.griffintechnology.com*]).

   The Input Source menu lists all the audio sources the Mac knows about—Built-in Microphone, Built-in Input (meaning the audio-input jack on the back or side), USB Microphone, or whatever you've connected.

> **NOTE** The selection you make here is independent of the input currently selected in System Preferences.

3. **Set the input level.**

   That is, move close to the microphone and practice your spiel. If the green sound meter inside the little microphone (Figure 11-13) is too low (say, just a couple of bars), your narration isn't loud enough. On playback, it'll probably get drowned out by the other audio track.

   If the meter turns bright red, you're too loud, and the recording will have an unpleasant, "overdriven" distortion.

   To change the recording volume, drag the Volume slider left or right. (You can learn tricks for boosting the volume of audio tracks later in this chapter, but it's much better to get the level right the first time.)

FIGURE 11-13
Choose Window→Record Voiceover (or press V on the keyboard) to narrate a clip. The voiceover tool (pictured) appears in the Viewer. When you press the microphone button to start recording, you get a brief countdown followed by a growing, burning-red audio clip that cools to green as you continue talking. Speak clearly into the mic, and then click the microphone button again to stop recording.

Close Voiceover button | Voiceover Options button

Start/Stop Recording button

4. **Turn the Mute Project checkbox on or off.**

   The question you're answering here is this: Do you want to hear the audio from your movie playing back while you record? Usually, the answer is "Yes" (so you want to turn off this checkbox), because you don't want to talk over the on-camera conversation, and you can time your own utterances to perfection. The problem is, your microphone *hears* the movie playback coming out of your Mac's speakers and records it anyway, or even triggers squealing feedback.

Therefore, turn off the Mute Project checkbox only if you're wearing headphones to monitor playback.

5. **Find the spot in your video where you want to start narrating.**

You can use all the usual techniques to navigate your clips: skim (point without clicking), press the space bar to play the movie, and so on.

6. **When you find the right spot, click the microphone button (Figure 11-13).**

A big, orange 3-2-1 countdown timer appears in the Viewer, accompanied by attention-getting countdown beeps. You even see preroll—the Viewer shows the 3 seconds of video that *lead up* to the point you clicked. All of this is intended to help you get ready to speak at the spot you selected.

7. **Once the numbers in the Viewer disappear, start talking. Press the space bar (or click the glowing red microphone button) to stop.**

A new connected audio clip appears below your filmstrip, bearing the label "VO-1:" and your project name, as shown in Figure 11-13. (VO stands for "voiceover.") As you speak, the audio stripe starts off a burning red and then cools into the standard audio green as you continue narrating. After you finish recording, point to a spot just before the beginning of the new recording, and then press the space bar to listen to your voiceover.

8. **Close the Narration window (press the letter V key).**

If the narration wasn't everything you hoped for, it's easy enough to record another take. Just hit ⌘-Z (Undo) or highlight the green voiceover stripe, and then press Delete. Then repeat this process.

You can record as many overlapping narration takes as you like. The green stripes just pile up, and they behave exactly like the sound-effects stripes described on page 186. That is, you can do the following:

- Delete a stripe by clicking it and then pressing the Delete key.

- Shorten a stripe by dragging its endpoints (or by double-clicking the stripe, and then using the Clip Trimmer, as described on page 67).

- Move a stripe by dragging it to a new spot, using the middle of it as the handle.

- Change the volume using the tricks explained on page 171.

Detach Clip Audio

iMovie is perfectly capable of letting you add just the audio portion of a piece of video footage to your storyboard. The recorded audio shows up as an independent, connected audio clip. Its green flag indicates that it's locked to wherever in the storyboard you dropped it. Figure 11-14 shows the process.

FIGURE 11-14

Top: Highlight part of a filmstrip in your Event browser, and then drag the selection below *a video clip in your storyboard. Before you let go, iMovie illustrates that you're adding just the audio portion of the clip by displaying its green waveform.*

Bottom: The video's audio appears as a connected clip, which you can manipulate just like any other audio clip: delete it, shorten it, trim it, move it, and so on.

Adding just a clip's audio to your project unleashes all kinds of useful new tricks that are impossible to achieve any other way:

- **Create an echo.** This is a cool one. Park the extracted audio clip a few frames to the right of the original. Use the volume controls (page 171) to make it slightly quieter than the original. Repeat a few more times, until you get a realistic echo or reverb sound.

TIP If you're not picky about fine-tuning the echo effect, consider using the Echo or Cathedral audio effects, covered on page 194.

- **Reuse the sound.** You can put the extracted audio elsewhere in your movie. You've probably seen this technique used in dozens of Hollywood films: About 15 minutes before the end of the movie, the main character, lying beaten and defeated in an alley, suddenly pieces together the solution to the central plot, as snippets of dialog we've already heard float through his brain, finally adding up.

TIP You may be tempted to extract audio to create a *cutaway*, something like you see in documentaries. An interviewee starts on-camera, but historic pictures soon replace the video while the interviewee's voice forges on excitedly about the history of dirt.

Don't. Cutaways like these are much easier to make using the dedicated Cutaway feature, covered on page 113.

- **Grab some ambient sound.** In real movie-editing studios, it happens all the time: A perfect take is ruined by the sound of a passing bus during a tender kiss and you don't discover it until you're in the editing room, long after the actors and crew have moved on to other projects.

  You can eliminate the final seconds of sound from a scene by cropping or splitting the clip, of course, but that won't result in a satisfying solution—you'll have three seconds of *silence* during the kiss. The real world isn't truly silent, even when there's no talking. The air is always filled with *ambient sound*, such as breezes, distant traffic, or the hum of fluorescent lights.

  Even inside, in a perfectly still room, there's *room tone*. When you want to replace a portion of an audio track with silence, what you usually want, in fact, is ambient sound.

  Professionals always record about 30 seconds of room tone or ambient sound just so they'll have material to use in case of an emergency. You may not need to go to that extreme; you may well be able to grab some sound from a different part of the same shot (when nobody is talking). The point is that by extracting the audio from another part of the scene, you've got yourself a useful piece of ambient sound footage you can use to patch over unwanted portions of the originally recorded audio.

- **Add narration.** The technique described on page 188 is ideal for narration that you record at one sitting, in a quiet room. But you can add narration via video camera, too. Just record yourself speaking, import the footage into iMovie, extract the audio, and then throw away the video. You may want to do this if you're editing on a mic-less Mac, or if you want the new narration to better match the video camera's original sound.

It's important to note that iMovie never *removes* the audio from the original video clip. You'll never be placed into the frantic situation of wishing that you'd never done the extraction at all, unable to sync the audio and video together again (which sometimes happens in "more powerful" video-editing programs).

Instead, iMovie places a *copy* of the audio in the storyboard. The original video clip retains its original audio. As a result, you can extract audio from the same clip over and over again, if you like. iMovie simply spins out another copy of the audio each time.

TIP If you want to detach the audio of a clip already in your project, select the clip and choose Modify→Detach Audio (Option-⌘-B). The detached audio shows up like any other connected audio clip.

■ A Word on Audio and Transitions

When you transition between video clips, the audio needs to transition, too. With video transitions, you get to choose how they look because you choose from any of iMovie's many transitions (page 92).

In the case of audio, iMovie always crossfades between clips for the duration of the transition. That means a 2-second transition will cause a 2-second audio crossfade between clips.

If you don't want this, you can always use the Precision Editor to change when the audio changes between clips, as explained on page 68.

■ Audio Effects and Enhancements

If all iMovie could do in the audio department is make volume changes and add some music, it would be good enough. But who wants good enough? Apple makes iMovie even more formidable, audio-wise, by adding a slew of effects and enhancements.

Audio Effects

iMovie's audio effects are really cool and a ton of fun to play with. Want your dad to sound like a mouse? Piece of cake. Want your baby to sound like a robot? Easy-peasy. Want to be able to sing like T-Pain, the rapper who made autotuning famous? You get the idea.

■ APPLYING AN AUDIO EFFECT

Here's how you apply an audio effect to a clip, song, sound effect, or voiceover.

1. **Select the clip, song, sound effect, or voiceover track; click Adjust in the Viewer toolbar; and then choose the Video and Audio Effects tool (the overlaid film strip).**

   The Viewer displays buttons for both video effects and audio effects. You read about video effects on page 107; audio effects work almost the same way.

   TIP   You can't apply an audio effect to part of a clip or song. You have to split the clip or song in question first. To do so, put the playhead right where you want the effect to start or end, and then right-click (or Control-click) that spot and choose Split Clip (⌘-B) from the shortcut menu. (You might need to repeat this step if you cut out a piece from the middle of something.) Once you have the bit you need separated from the rest, proceed with the steps that follow.

   ---

2. **In the Viewer, click Audio Effect.**

   iMovie displays a grid of skimmable effects (Figure 11-15), not unlike the one for video effects (page 110). As you skim, iMovie previews the audio effect. Pause for a moment to enjoy the fact that this takes zero rendering time.

3. **Skim through the effects, and then click the one you want.**

   Once you choose an audio effect, iMovie applies it to your entire clip or song.

If you change your mind and want the clip's audio back to normal, choose None from the Audio Effect grid.

■ THE AUDIO EFFECTS CATALOG

Although you've got the adorable little stick figures doing interpretive performances of each effect (Figure 11-15), you might still like a rundown of each effect and what it accomplishes:

- **Muffled.** This makes people sound like they're talking through a pillow.

- **Robot.** If you're making a throwback B-movie about robots attacking earth, this will overlay your actors' voices with a monotone, buzzing noise that sounds, well, robotic.

- **Cosmic.** Imagine taking an FM radio dial and turning it from bottom to top to bottom. The Cosmic effect makes your voice sound as though it were coming from a radio. (It also adds a monotone effect to enhance the cosmicness.)

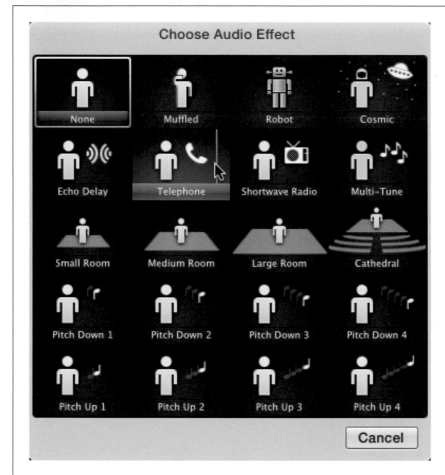

FIGURE 11-15

iMovie offers a range of audio effects, from muffled to cosmic and from mannish to mousy. Note the stick figures illustrating what each effect does.

- **Echo.** Although iMovie calls this effect Echo, it sounds a lot more like reverb, because the "echo" is fast and doesn't fade the way an echo would in a large space.

- **Telephone.** This option slightly muffles the sound to match what you'd hear over the phone. A great way to simulate a phone conversation if your actor is on the phone and you can hear the audio track of the other person on the line.

- **Shortwave Radio.** A lot like the Cosmic effect, just tamed down.

- **Multi-Tune.** You've heard this effect before, even if you don't know it. The rest of the world calls it autotune; it was popularized by rapper T-Pain, Auto-Tune the News, and others. It tunes your voice (or any sound) to the nearest musical tone, rounding off the pitch to the nearest piano-key note. Autotune is applied gently to just about every pop singer's recording to fix the pitch, but turned up all the way, it creates a distinctive mechanical, clicky edginess to the singing. Normal speaking doesn't really show off this effect, but singing, or drawn-out vocal sounds, make it sound really cool. Play around with this effect just for the fun of it.

- **Small/Medium/Large Room.** These three options create the same level of echo you'd encounter in a correspondingly sized room.

- **Cathedral.** Like the Small/Medium/Large room effects, but in a *really* big room. This is a nice alternative to the Echo effect.

- **Pitch Down/Up.** These effects lower or raise a person's voice by an amount that you can control by choosing one of the four pitch up/down options. Here you can make your 5-year-old daughter sound like a man—or your bowling buddy sound like your 5-year-old daughter.

Auto Enhance

You enhance the audio in your movie one of two ways. If you click the Enhance button in the Viewer toolbar, iMovie makes all the video enhancements it can, along with all the audio enhancements it can make, too.

To work on the audio portion of your movie only, click the Adjust button in the Viewer toolbar and then select the Volume tool (the speaker icon). Click the Auto button there, and iMovie adjusts just your audio track to produce what it thinks is the best sound possible.

> **NOTE**   If you don't like the way iMovie enhances your audio, turn off the Auto button (select it a second time) and then try one of the tools described here.

The Equalizer

Traditionally, an equalizer is a set of sliders that lets you increase or reduce the low, medium, and high tones in an audio track. They've been around for years, but most people don't ever use them.

That's because most people don't need them. Usually they show up only in music-playback software like iTunes. If you have decent speakers and the song was recorded professionally, there's little point in messing around with audio levels. The balancing work has been done for you.

Your camera's audio, on the other hand, hasn't been professionally adjusted. As a result, you might find that the bass guitar at the concert you're (legally) recording sticks out like a sore thumb. That's where the equalizer comes in handy. You can reduce the low-end sounds to make everything balance out.

iMovie doesn't want to bother you with sliders, but it still helps you improve a clip's sound the way an equalizer can. Figure 11-16 shows you the iMovie equalizer menu.

You get to it by clicking Adjust, and then the bar graph icon, a.k.a. the "Noise reduction and equalizer" button.

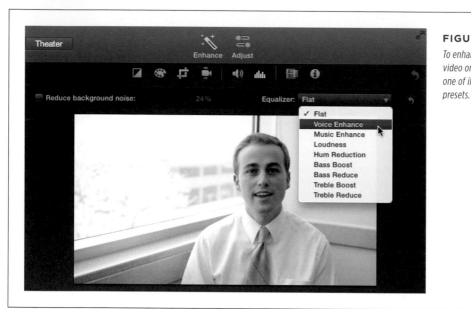

FIGURE 11-16

To enhance the sound of a video or audio clip, choose one of iMovie's equalizer presets.

If you're not sure which Equalizer menu option to choose, try one. If you choose Bass Reduce, for example, the lower-tone sounds in your clip drop away. You can preview the result by clicking a spot in your audio and then pressing the space bar. Change your equalizer setting at any time; iMovie makes the change instantly, with no rendering.

Reduce Background Noise

File this feature under "Amazing power turned on with a mere checkbox." Among iMovie's many cool tricks, this is one of the coolest. All of us suffer from the problem this feature fixes.

Other than shaky video (page 130), the surest sign of amateur video is bad audio. Most people pay so much attention to what they're filming that they tune out the sound they're recording. So without your even noticing it, your camera's microphone can pick up the hum of fluorescent lights, the drone of a clothes dryer, or even the whir of its own zoom lens. Professionals know all this, and that's why they're famous for shouting, "Quiet on the set!" They know that you can point a camera lens right where you want it, but microphones aren't so discriminating.

As you're out and about filming, unless you've brought professional audio equipment like a boom mike and a mixing board, you're using the microphone in your camera. Unfortunately, built-in mics have a reputation for being undiscerning. That is, they generously record any and every sound that hits them. That's no big deal if you're recording an interview in a quiet room, but it really stinks if the air conditioner in the room kicks in. The drone in the background makes the whole clip sound like amateur hour.

So if you're at the beach and just got a great little shot of your 4-year-old singing "Bob the Builder" over his sand castle, you want to hear the singing and not the wind or waves. Here's where iMovie steps in to save the day. It magically scrubs your audio, removing sounds like waves, fan noise, traffic, and other messiness.

NOTE While this tool can reduce even a roaring waterfall to a low hum, it can't entirely eliminate many background noises. In fact, if you ratchet the effect too high, it makes your clip sound like it's playing from a set of broken speakers.

To use this feature, select the audio clip and then click the Adjust button. Choose the "Noise reduction and equalizer" tool (the bar graph) shown in Figure 11-17, and then turn on the checkbox labeled "Reduce background noise."

FIGURE 11-17

You can minimize the interference of background noise by checking the "Reduce background noise" box and adjusting the effect with the slider. But don't overdo it, or your actor will sound like a robot.

Your clip immediately sounds cleaner. If it's not clean enough (or if it's too clean to sound real for the surroundings), then move the slider left or right to change the amount of noise reduction.

Multiple Audio Adjustments

Let's say you make a few audio adjustments to a clip: upped the volume, ducked other tracks, and added an effect. Now you want to do the same to a lot of other clips. Luckily for you, iMovie saves you the many clicks it would take to repeat the process. You can copy and paste the audio adjustments in one clip to a bunch of others.

Select the clip you've adjusted and choose Edit→Copy (⌘-C). Then select the clip(s) you want to adjust and choose Edit→Paste Adjustments. In the menu that appears, you can choose Volume (Option-⌘-A) or Audio Effect (Option-⌘-O). The first pastes all the volume adjustments, including rubber-band changes, auto enhance, and ducking, and the second pastes whatever audio effect you applied to the copied clip.

> **NOTE**   Unfortunately, you can't copy and paste changes in the equalizer or background noise settings. You have to do those by hand.

Because you can select multiple clips at once (page 54), you can make all these audio changes in one fell swoop.

Editing Audio in GarageBand

What if you *really* want to dig into your movie's audio? iMovie's audio tools are great and all, but they could leave you wanting. What you need is an audio-editing program. Perhaps one like the application that *Apple offers for free in the App Store!*

That would be GarageBand, the music composition program that's part of iLife. It offers all kinds of audio-specific tools not found in iMovie, the most prominent being the composition tools you can use to create your own movie scores.

Fortunately, you can export your movie to GarageBand to edit the soundtrack with its much more powerful tools. Don't read any further, however, until you absorb these two warnings:

* Your movie arrives in GarageBand with only a single, boiled-down audio track. You can't adjust the video camera's audio and the iMovie music independently. (That's a good argument for avoiding adding *any* music in iMovie—wait until you're in GarageBand to add all music and sound effects.)

* The iMovie→GarageBand train goes only one way. Once you work with a movie in GarageBand, you can no longer return to iMovie for further edits, either video or audio. You *can* return to iMovie, edit the video, and re-export the whole thing, but you lose all the audio work you did in GarageBand the first time.

GarageBand Basics

GarageBand is a music composition program containing dozens of powerful tools. It lets you combine multiple audio tracks, giving you fine control over each track's sound effects, volume, and even stereo panning.

But if you're like most people, you've never even set foot in GarageBand. (Apple says GarageBand is the second least-used iLife program.) Here's a crash course:

1. **Export your movie from iMovie.**

   Use one of the file export options explained in Chapter 15.

2. **Open GarageBand.**

GarageBand's icon looks like an electric guitar; it's in your Applications folder. If this is your first time in GarageBand, a welcome screen greets you with a list of choices. If you *have* worked in GarageBand, it opens the last project you worked on.

3. **Create a new project.**

Choose File→New and then select Empty Project from the window that appears (Figure 11-18).

iMovie asks you what kind of audio track you want to start with. Choose Software Instrument and then click Create.

FIGURE 11-18

GarageBand appears to be designed for either the short-sighted or for those with really bad mouse aim. Either way, double-click the icon labeled "Empty Project" to create a new movie project.

4. **Add your movie from the Finder.**

Find your movie in the Finder, and then drag it into the big, empty part of the GarageBand window. (At this point, GarageBand opens a preview window showing your movie. You can close this by clicking the X in the top-left corner.)

GarageBand creates its own thumbnails to represent your movie.

5. **Edit your movie's audio track.**

Once GarageBand imports your movie, you'll see an audio track directly under the video track. This is the audio from your exported movie. It contains *all* your movie's audio, merged into one track. Now that it's in GarageBand, you can manipulate the audio in a multitude of ways. At the left edge of the window, under your movie, tiny icons let you mute, isolate, lock, and pan the audio (shift the stereo sound right or left). You can also make the volume rise and fall at particular points, as shown in Figure 11-19.

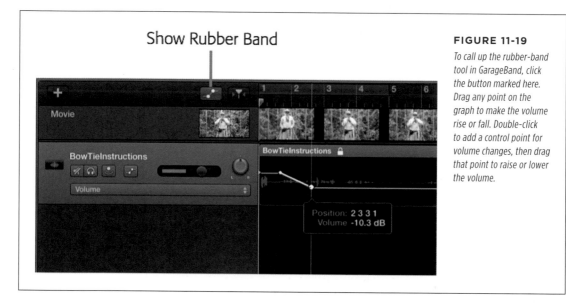

Show Rubber Band

FIGURE 11-19

To call up the rubber-band tool in GarageBand, click the button marked here. Drag any point on the graph to make the volume rise or fall. Double-click to add a control point for volume changes, then drag that point to raise or lower the volume.

6. **Add audio tracks.**

   Add additional tracks, if you like, by choosing Track→New Track (Option-⌘-N), or by clicking the + button in the toolbar. You might use these new tracks to create a custom score (read on). In GarageBand, you can create as many parallel audio tracks as you like, although a huge number slows your Mac to a crawl.

   You can also drag songs from the Media Browser (View→Show Media Browser) right into a blank area of the GarageBand window. GarageBand automatically creates a new track and places the song in it.

   NOTE Copy-protected songs you bought from the iTunes store (back when Apple sold protected music) won't work. GarageBand isn't on the guest list for protected songs. In fact, protected songs won't even show up in the iTunes list in GarageBand.

7. **Export your movie.**

   Once you finish editing the audio, send the movie out into the world by choosing File→Movie→"Export Audio to Movie." Save the file to your computer, and now it's ready to use for whatever you had in mind.

Scoring in GarageBand

Because GarageBand is a music program, its greatest strength is its ability to help you create a custom score for your movie. You can actually record or compose music crafted to run in perfect harmony with your video, turning you into a regular John Williams. (Actual musical ability may vary.) GarageBand shows the movie in the timeline, frame by frame, so you know exactly where to add a cymbal crash or a guitar riff.

Here's a super-condensed review of the different tools for scoring:

- **Use prerecorded loops.** Choose View→Show Apple Loops to see all the different categories of prerecorded *loops* (music building blocks) you can drag directly into new tracks beneath your video. Once you add it, you can drag the upper-right corner of a loop to make it repeat over and over, for as long as you drag to the right. (This works well with drum parts.)

- **Record a MIDI instrument.** If you have a MIDI instrument connected to your Mac (usually a keyboard or a synthesizer), choose Track→New Track, click Software Instrument, and then click Create. Now you can choose an instrument sound from the list that appears at the lower right, and then click the red, round Record button to begin recording as you play. You can even use the Tempo control (hold your mouse down on the digits) to make the movie play back more slowly, so that you have a better chance at a perfect performance. After you finish playing, you can crank the tempo back up to its original speed.

- **Record a live instrument or voice.** GarageBand can record live sounds, like your own singing or saxophone playing. Choose Track→New Track, click either choice under Audio, and then click Create. Next, choose a reverb preset from the list at the left (like Female Basic or Male Rock Vocals). Click the Record button to begin recording.

When you finish the soundtrack, export the results using the instructions given previously. With enough practice, you might eventually wind up on Steven Spielberg's speed dial.

Photos

You may think that iMovie's primary purpose in life is working with video, but the truth is, it's quite handy with photos and graphics, too. For example, you can add images to your movie from iPhoto, Aperture, or your hard drive to use as still shots, which you can then pan and zoom for an authentic, documentary-style effect. You can also use images and graphics to create slideshows. And you can turn individual frames of your movie *into* still images for use as freeze-frames. This chapter tells all.

■ Using Photos and Graphics

You may want to import a photos or graphics into iMovie for any number of reasons. For example:

- You can use a graphic, digital photo, or other still image as a backdrop for movie credit rolls (Chapter 10). A still image behind your text is less distracting than moving footage.

- You can use a graphics file for your credits themselves *instead* of using iMovie's titling feature. As noted in Chapter 10, iMovie's titling effect offers a number of powerful features, but it also has a number of limitations. For example, you have only rudimentary control over the title's placement in the frame (see Figure 12-1).

  Preparing your own title graphic in, say, Photoshop or Photoshop Elements gives you a lot of flexibility that iMovie titling doesn't. You get complete control over the size, color, and placement of text, and you can add graphic touches or a unique background.

FIGURE 12-1

Preparing your title cards in a graphics program gives you far more typographical and design flexibility than iMovie's own titling feature. Using graphics software, for example, you can enhance your titles with drop shadows, a 3D look, or clip art.

- One of the most compelling uses of video is the *video photo album*: a smoothly integrated succession of photos, joined by crossfades, enhanced by titles, and accompanied by music. Thanks to iMovie's ability to import photos directly—either from the iPhoto or Aperture photo-management programs, or your hard drive—creating this kind of slideshow is a piece of cake.

NOTE   Of course, you can create video photo albums in iPhoto, too. And iPhoto lets you loop a slideshow, while iMovie doesn't. Rearranging and regrouping photos is much easier in iPhoto, too.

So why consider iMovie? Building a slideshow in a movie has several advantages. First, you have many more audio options; you can record narration as you play the slideshow, for example. And you have a full arsenal of tools for creating titles, credits, and special effects.

As your life with iMovie proceeds, you may encounter other uses for its picture-importing feature. Maybe, when you edit a home movie of your kids tussling in the living room, you decide it would be hilarious to insert some *Batman*-style fight-sound title cards ("BAM!") into the footage. Maybe you need an establishing shot of, say, a storefront or apartment building, and realize that you could save production money by inserting a still photo that passes for live video in which there's nothing moving. Or maybe you want to end your movie with a fade-out—not to black, but to maroon (an effect described later in this chapter).

Photo Sources

You can bring still photos into a project two ways. If you use either of Apple's photo-management programs, iPhoto for consumers or Aperture for pros, the first and most convenient way is to choose from their libraries, which you can tap into directly from iMovie (see the next section). If you don't use either program, you can import pictures directly from your hard drive.

The iPhoto Library

The more you work with iMovie, the more you appreciate the way Apple integrates related programs like iTunes. If you use iPhoto or Aperture, you'll experience another case of synergy.

In iMovie's Libraries list, the first offering is your iPhoto library. Select it and you see what amounts to iPhoto Lite: a panel of thumbnail images of shots from your iPhoto library. Using the drop-down menu just above the thumbnails, you can browse your photos by event, album, folder, or according to other iPhoto presets (like flagged photos or photos added during your last import). You can filter your photos based on Faces or Places you identified in iPhoto. too. And you can view any Facebook albums you synced with iPhoto.

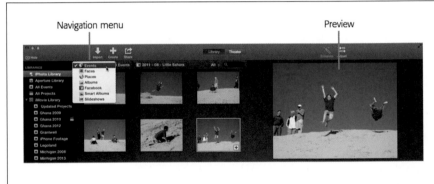

Navigation menu   Preview

FIGURE 12-2

The photo browser displays all the pictures you have in iPhoto or Aperture. Use the drop-down menu to find photos from certain albums or folders only. Use the filter menu to view just photos, videos, or flagged items. Note the search box on the right. As you type into it, iMovie narrows your choices to photos that have matching titles or keywords. It's an amazingly quick way to pinpoint one photo out of several thousand.

TIP Events in iPhoto are a lot like events in iMovie. That is, iPhoto groups all the photos the way you tell it to. Each photo can be in only one event.

NOTE Albums are different; they're more like iMovie's "projects." A photo can be in as many albums as you like. You create one by choosing File→New Album (or by clicking the + button in the lower-left corner). Complete details are in *iPhoto: The Missing Manual* (O'Reilly).

Here are more handy photo browser tips:

- iMovie shows your photos as a row of thumbnails. Unfortunately, there's no way to resize these thumbnails like you can filmstrips.

- When you click a photo to select it, iMovie displays it in the Viewer, giving you a chance to review it.

- iMovie supports iPhoto's cool Places feature. If you choose Places from iMovie's drop-down navigation menu, you get a map with pushpins identifying where photos were shot, just like you see in iPhoto.

- If you flag photos in iPhoto, you can limit what iMovie shows you by choosing Flagged from iMovie's drop-down menu (Figure 12-3).

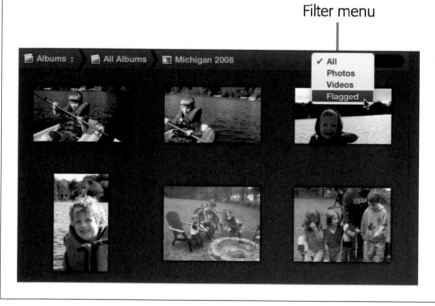

FIGURE 12-3

You can have iMovie display all your iPhoto or Aperture visuals, or restrict them to just photos, videos, or flagged items.

The Aperture Library

Your Aperture library works in iMovie just like the iPhoto library does. The navigation menu in Figure 12-2 works the same way. The only difference is that it shows Projects instead of the iPhoto-equivalent events. Other than that, everything works identically.

Import from the Finder

If you don't have iPhoto or Aperture, you add images to your movie by locating them in the Finder and dragging them into your project window.

> **TIP** iMovie can import graphics in any format that QuickTime can understand, which includes PICT, JPEG, GIF, PNG, Photoshop files, and even PDF files (for when you want to display an IRS form in your movie). Avoid the GIF format for photos, which limits the number of colors available to the image; otherwise, just about any format is good still-image material.

Once you add a photo to iMovie, you don't have to keep track of the original. Behind the scenes, iMovie copies the image to your project (hidden in the huge library file explained on page 41). So even if you delete a photo from iPhoto or your hard drive, it still exists in your project files.

iMovie Backgrounds and Maps

Generations of iMovie fans have dressed up their opening credits and chapter titles by creating custom backgrounds, so that text appears in front of red curtains or a Hollywood opening-night spotlight instead of plain black. To save you that hassle, iMovie comes with a handsome set of premade background images (Figure 12-4). Some are even animated; for example, the Underwater background shows shimmering rays of sunlight filtering through the water.

> **TIP** You can use background images and animations for your green-screen work, too (page 115). So, instead of revealing that you shot your newscaster skit in your pathetic basement, you can insert one of these much more handsome backgrounds.

FIGURE 12-4

Behold the Maps & Background browser. It gives you 24 high-quality backgrounds to jazz up your project.

To use a background image, drag it out of the Content Library's Maps & Backgrounds browser and into any empty area of your project—between two clips, after a clip, or on top of a clip (which will make it a cutaway; see page 113). It appears as a 4-second clip, though you can adjust the timing (see page 214).

Connected Photos

Alternatively, you can drag a photo *above* a video clip to make it a connected photo. It works just like a connected video clip, as explained on page 112.

The most common use of connected photos is as a cutaway (Figure 12-6), a documentary-style effect discussed on page 113. When you use a photo as a cutaway, iMovie sticks it right on top of the underlying clip in the timeline.

NOTE Connected photos get close to full iMovie citizenship. You can crop, rotate, and apply effects to them to adjust the color of the cutaways. What you *can't* do is adjust audio, since photos don't have it.

Of course, it also covers up the video in the movie itself. So if the photo blocks the video, what good is it? Why not just create a photo filmstrip?

A connected photo has four advantages over a photo clip:

- **Connected photos are much easier to adjust.** You can slide a connected photo left or right, earlier or later in the movie, with the touch of the mouse. And you can shorten or lengthen it by dragging its ends. (Oddly, this last trick works only when the clip is *not* selected.)

- **You can make photo cutaways transparent.** Because iMovie lets you adjust the transparency of a photo cutaway (see page 114 for instructions), you can dial it back, turning the photo into a translucent layer. You might take a photo of clouds, dial back the opacity, and—bam!—you have fog covering the clip underneath.

- **Photo cutaways are incredibly useful.** You've seen it a million times on TV. Someone starts talking; as the narration continues, the camera *cuts away* to a still shot, and then we return to the original person speaking.

  It's actually pretty remarkable how easy iMovie makes this. Instead of having to extract audio from your video clip and then create a still image to plug in the middle, you just drop a photo above the top of the video clip. The result is a cutaway (with a cross dissolve, if you like) that looks like it took a lot more work than it actually did.

- **You can poke holes in it.** This tip is for Photoshop (or Photoshop Elements) mavens, but it's wicked cool. It lets you create see-through *pieces* of a photo— while the video behind it plays through the holes. (It's not the same as the whole-photo transparency setting already described.) The steps for creating this fantastic effect appear in Figure 12-7.

  This trick opens up a host of effects that iMovie can't do with its built-in tools. You could, for example, create a black image with two holes in it that make it look like you're peering through a pair of binoculars. (A great way to pump up your 10-year-old's spy movie!)

FIGURE 12-6

By dialing back the opacity of a photo cutaway, you can add cool effects, like the "fog" covering the bottom clip. You create this effect with a cutaway picture of clouds set at half transparency. You can use it for a "Scooby-Doo and the Haunted Forest" remake.

FIGURE 12-7

This effect pops up often in opening credits for TV shows (at least those from the 1970s) and the occasional cheesy movie. Make a graphic in Photoshop that contains cutouts. Select the pieces that you don't want to be transparent; ⌘-click the "Save selection as channel" button on the Channels palette, and save the result as a PNG graphic with an alpha channel. Drag the resulting file right off the desktop above any filmstrip in iMovie. Once it becomes a photo cutaway in iMovie, the underlying video plays through the holes!

Use this trick to put a pair of nose glasses or a funny hat on someone. Or create text titles, like *Batman*-style "BAM!"s and "KAPOW!"s superimposed on your footage. As long as you use the PNG image format (which recognizes transparency), a little creativity can lead to all kinds of cool effects. (iMovie also supports transparency in TIFF files.)

■ Timing Changes

When you add a photo to a movie, it gets something regular photos don't have: a *duration*. You want your picture to remain onscreen for just the right amount of time, so follow these steps to change a photo's duration.

Standard Photo Timing

Long ago, iMovie's designers made the decision that the optimal length for just about any clip or photo is 4 seconds. That's why, when you add a photo to your project, the proposed length is 4 seconds. (iMovie even used to scold you with a warning if you added a whole video clip from the Event browser instead of selecting part of it.)

This default timing quickly becomes a pain if you're making a photo slideshow and want each photo to last, say, 5 seconds. Save yourself the hassle of adjusting each photo by changing the standard timing before you add photos to your project. Go to Window→Movie Properties (⌘-J)→Settings and move the Clips slider to anything from 1 to 10 seconds. Now all the photos you add will show up at the length you set.

TIP If you later change the Clips slider, only *new* photos will carry the new setting. Photos already in the storyboard keep their old duration.

Adjust Timing

To retime a photo already in your storyboard, drag the end to add or subtract time from it (Figure 12-8). This works just like adding or subtracting video footage (page 65). iMovie displays a window that tells you how much time you're adding or subtracting. You resize photo clips and connected photos the same way. Unlike video, however, it doesn't matter which end you drag, because whatever iMovie adds or trims will look the same.

■ RETIME MULTIPLE PHOTOS

If you added multiple photos that need to go from, say, 10 seconds to 5, you can retime them all at once:

1. **Choose all the photos to be retimed.**

   You can select multiple photos in your storyboard by ⌘-clicking them.

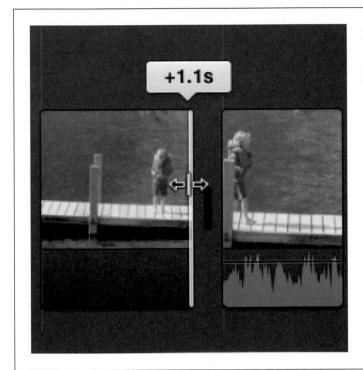

FIGURE 12-8

To retime a photo, drag either end of it. iMovie shows you how much time you're adding or removing.

2. **Click the Adjust button, followed by the ❶ button.**

    In the Viewer, iMovie tells you how many photos you selected and displays a Duration box.

3. **Type in the new duration (in seconds) and then hit Return.**

    iMovie retimes all the photos you selected.

TIP   This is a nice fix if your default timing (page 58) wasn't what you wanted when you started adding photos to your project.

The Dimensions of an iMovie Photo

If you're designing a custom image for your movie, you generally want it to have the same dimensions as your video. Otherwise, iMovie crops the photo or inserts black bars to make it fit.

iMovie makes movies only in widescreen format (16:9). (See page 72 for a complete discussion.) That's not a normal dimension for most photos, which are usually around a standard 4:3 format. For now, here's how big to make your photos so that they fit a widescreen movie frame.

Your imported photo should be at least 1,920 pixels wide and 1,080 pixels tall. Your footage may actually be the smaller 1,280 by 720 kind, but iMovie will shrink your photo down, if needed.

If you have an image that wasn't born with the right dimensions, don't worry. The powerful Crop tool (page 143) and the Ken Burns effect (page 217) can help you compensate.

UP TO SPEED

Avoiding Pixelated Images

You may have tried adding an image to iMovie and found that it looked pretty rotten. Blurry, pixelated, or jagged images are ugly and jarring in a movie surrounded by pristine video footage.

Sloppy-looking images like these usually result from using a photo whose resolution is too low to begin with. For example, you might have taken a hilarious little shot with an old camera-phone—emphasis on *little*. Images downloaded from the Web are often low resolution, too.

iMovie, thinking it's doing you a favor, stretches that photo from its original size to make it fit the movie frame, and ugly-looking coarseness results.

If you absolutely must use a small image, consider framing your picture inside a larger image, like a background graphic, of the proper dimensions. iMovie shows the small picture with the frame surrounding it, preventing the jagged, blurry resizing you'd otherwise see.

◼ Fit, Crop, and Rotate Photos

One of iMovie's greatest virtues is its resolution agnosticism. You can combine widescreen footage from your new HD video camera with standard-def footage from your old DV camera in the same movie; iMovie gracefully handles their different dimensions.

This adaptability extends to photos. Chapter 9 includes a detailed discussion of cropping *video* to fit the frame (or to draw emphasis to a certain part of the picture) by adding letterbox bars and even rotating it.

Well, surprise, surprise: iMovie makes *exactly* the same features available for photo clips. See page 143 for the full discussion.

TIP You can crop, fit, and rotate both photo clips and connected photos, like cutaways. The process is exactly the same.

The Ken Burns Effect

The only problem with using still photos in a movie is that they're *still*. They just sit there without motion or sound, wasting much of the dynamic potential of video.

For years, professionals addressed the problem using special sliding camera rigs that produce gradual zooming, panning, or both, to bring photographs to life.

But this smooth motion isn't just about adding animation to photos for its own sake. It also lets you draw the viewer's attention where you want it, *when* you want it. For example: "Little Harry graduated from junior high school in 1963"—slow pan to someone else in the school photo, a little girl with a ribbon in her hair—"little suspecting that the woman who would one day become his tormentor was standing only a few feet away."

Among the most famous practitioners of this art is Ken Burns, the creator of PBS documentaries like *The Civil War* and *Baseball*, which is why Apple named the feature after him.

> **TIP** In iMovie, you can also apply the Ken Burns effect to video. You can create very smooth pans and zooms in footage where the camera didn't actually move an inch. Powerful feature! (Familiarize yourself with the Ken Burns tools here, then see page 146 for more info.)

Apply the Ken Burns Effect

iMovie's Ken Burns controls are pretty easy to get the hang of. Here's how you use them:

> **TIP** By default, iMovie applies the Ken Burns effect to all the photos you add to a project, varying the panning and zooming in each one. If you don't like what iMovie does with a particular photo, these steps let you adjust the effect.

1. **Click a photo clip or cutaway.**

   A yellow border appears.

2. **Click Adjust in the Viewer toolbar, followed by the Crop button.**

   This unveils the Style menu with the Fit/Crop/Ken Burns buttons.

3. **Click the Ken Burns button.**

   iMovie superimposes two rectangles over your photo, one marked "Start" and the other labeled "End." They represent the beginning and end frames of your photo. iMovie automatically produces the animation required to smoothly pan and/or zoom between them.

4. **Set the photo's starting point.**

   That is, select the Start box by clicking it. Drag its corners to resize the box and drag in the middle to move it.

Set the Start box so it frames the photo as you want your viewers to first see it. For example, if you want to zoom in on the photo, make the Start box big. (Drag its corners to resize it.) If you want an effect that zooms out from the photo, make the Start box small. See Figure 12-9.

5. **Adjust your end point (the End box).**

   Click the End box to select it. Move and resize it just as you did with the Start box.

   If you want your shot to move but not zoom, make sure the End box is the same size as the Start rectangle. Line them up, match their sizes, and then move the End box to the point in the image where you want it to end. With the start and end points the same size, iMovie simply pans from one perspective to the other.

Drag corners to resize. Swap start and end

FIGURE 12-9

Top: In this somewhat confusing display, you adjust the Start box and then the End box to show iMovie how you want to pan and zoom across a photo. The yellow arrow shows the current direction of the pan to help you visualize the motion of the shot.

Bottom: This three-frame sample shows a representation of the pan and zoom the settings above will produce.

6. **Preview your effect and make adjustments.**

   Click ▶ in the Viewer to preview your Ken Burns effect. If you don't like what you see, adjust the boxes accordingly.

If you decide that you want to *reverse* what you set up—you want to zoom out instead of in, or pan left instead of right—click the Swap button identified in Figure 12-9. That turns your Start box into the End box, and vice versa.

7. **Click the checkmark in the Viewer toolbar when you're done.**

You can always adjust the Ken Burns effect by running through these steps again.

> **NOTE** If you drag a group of photos into your project all at once, iMovie creates automatic, *varied* Ken Burns effects, subtly panning and zooming in different directions for each one. Add a sweet little crossfade to all of them simultaneously (page 83), and you've got a gorgeous slideshow. (If you're a killjoy, you can always turn off the automatic Ken Burns feature. Choose Window→Movie Properties followed by the Settings button in the Viewer, and then use the "Photo placement" pop-up menu to choose either Fit or Crop.)

■ Freeze Frames

iMovie doesn't just *accept* still photos, it also *creates* them, from a frame in the storyboard. And why would you want to create a still from your video? Let us count some ways:

- **To create a freeze-frame.** One of the most obvious uses of a still frame is as a *freeze-frame*, in which the movie holds on the final frame of a shot. It's a terrifically effective way to end a movie, particularly if the final shot depicts the shy, unpopular hero in a moment of triumph, arms in the air, hoisted onto the shoulders of the crowd. (Fade to black; bring up the music; roll credits.)

> **TIP** You can also use the automatically created one-step effect called "Flash and Hold Frame" (page 126), which adds a little more flair than a normal freeze frame.

- **For credit sequences.** If you were a fan of 1970s action shows like *Emergency!*, you may remember how the opening credits looked. You'd be watching one of the starring characters frantically at work in some lifesaving situation. As she looked up from her work, just for a moment, the picture would freeze, catching her by lucky happenstance at her most flattering angle. At that instant, you'd see her credit flash on the screen: "Julie London as Dixie McCall, RN."

  That's an easy one to simulate. Just create a freeze frame as described in the next section, and then superimpose a title on it.

- **To create a layered effect.** In many cases, the most creative use of still-image titles comes from using *several* of them, each building on the last. For example, you can make the main title appear, hold for a moment, and then transition into a second still graphic on which a subtitle appears.

  If you have more time on your hands, you can use this trick to create simple animations. Suppose you were to create 10 different title cards, all superimposed on the same background, but each with the words in a different size or position. If you were to place each card onscreen for only half a second (15 frames), joined by very fast crossfades, you'd create a striking visual effect. Similarly, you might consider making the *color* of the lettering shift over time. To do that, create two or three title cards, each with the text in a different color. Insert them into your movie, join them with slow crossfades, and you've got a striking, color-shifting title sequence.

Create a Still Frame

Here's how you extract a still frame from your video:

1. **Position the playhead on the frame you want frozen.**

   You can choose from any clip in the Event browser.

2. **Right-click (or Control-click) the clip where you want to extract the still. From the shortcut menu, choose Add Freeze Frame (Figure 12-10). With your playhead in the right spot, you can also choose Modify→Add Freeze Frame from the menu bar, or Option-F.**

   This command directs iMovie to place a new photo clip at the playhead in your storyboard.

NOTE This *splits* the clip under your playhead. Don't panic, though. As long as you move the photo to another spot and keep the split clips together, your viewers won't know the difference. (Unfortunately, the Modify→Join Clips command won't stitch the split clips back together.)

---

3. **Drag the still clip into place in your storyboard.**

   You can drag it with the mouse just like you would any other photo or video clip in your project.

4. **Adjust the still's duration, cropping, color, and so on.**

   Your still frame behaves like any other photo. You can use the Ken Burns effect, for example, to zoom in on a meaningful part of the shot. (Ever seen a suspense movie, where the director zooms in on the once-vanquished villain watching the hero from the middle of a crowd? Works every time.)

Although you can move a still frame you created, you can always keep the photo in place as a true freeze frame, to great effect. Just imagine that moment when Baby Tommy *finally* smiles into the camera. You could freeze on that spot for a second or two, and then have your video keep going. The smile has 10 times the impact if you can dwell on it just a little.

TIP If you want to create a still from the first or last frame of a clip, move your mouse *just past* the end of the clip and then click to set the playhead on the last frame of that clip before you freeze the frame.

Figuring out how to handle the *audio* in such situations is up to you, since a still frame should have no sound. That's a good argument for starting your closing-credits music *during* the final clip, and making it build to a crescendo for the final freeze frame.

FIGURE 12-10

Top: Add Freeze Frame is one of the commands available from the shortcut menu when you right-click a video clip.

Bottom: iMovie splits the video clip in two and sticks the freeze frame in the middle. Note that iMovie assumes that you want a still image, so it doesn't apply the Ken Burns effect.

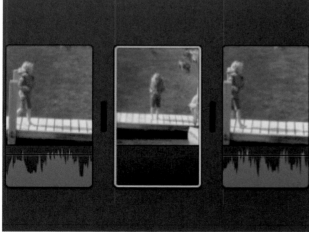

Movie Trailers

From iMovie's beginning, its *raison d'être* has been to take your otherwise boring home movies and make them shine with excitement and professionalism. Features like transitions, themes, video effects, titles, editing to a beat, and the Ken Burns effect give your movies a sleek veneer with very little effort on your part; if you attempted the same tasks manually in high-end editing software, it'd take a lot more time and effort than it does in iMovie.

iMovie's movie-trailers feature is another gigantic leap forward in letting you create awesome movie previews with just a little extra work. In fact, iMovie's trailers represent a merger of all the things that iMovie has done well for a long time: It combines titles, music, transitions, and artwork to give you professional-looking previews made from all your own footage. And iMovie does all the hard work for you!

A trailer is the "Coming Attractions" preview you see before a feature film, or the TV ad that touts "Transformers 7: Hybrids Gone Mad." It tells you enough about a movie so that you want to watch the whole thing. Trailers have become a form of entertainment all their own. For almost a decade, Apple, Yahoo, and other Internet bigwigs have dedicated entire websites to trailers for upcoming movies. Major studios even shoot footage just for a movie's trailer.

iMovie's trailers are 1- or 2-minute videos that look exactly like Hollywood previews, complete with swelling music, animated credits, and fast intercuts of scenes from the actual movie—only this time, the footage is from your life. The results can be hilarious, because your viewers will recognize the format instantly, or actually tantalizing. If anything can make your casual acquaintances want to see your home movies, this is it.

NOTE Apple put a ton of work into making these trailers look and sound great. The background music, for example, was custom-composed for iMovie and recorded by the London Symphony Orchestra. Not bad for a home movie!

■ Trailer Basics

Trailers aren't your typical iMovie project, where you start with a clean slate, and your movie is what you make of it—literally. Trailers are highly structured, and you don't have much control over basic things like shot length, title styles, or other elements.

Once you start playing with iMovie's Trailers feature, you quickly realize that you have rules to follow. For that reason, it's good to know what they are. The next couple of sections tour the trailer-builder, but you can skip ahead to page 231 if you just can't wait to create a preview.

Tour the Trailer-Builder

To see iMovie's trailer project, choose File→New Trailer (Shift-⌘-N) or click the + button in the toolbar and choose Trailer. iMovie opens a window that looks a lot like the one for new movie projects (see Figure 13-1). Here, though, you want to choose a style for your preview. Scroll down to see all your options. (You can read more about each one on page 227.)

FIGURE 13-1

To create a trailer, click File→New Project (Shift-⌘-N), select Trailer from the drop-down menu, and then choose a trailer style. Click the Play button on a trailer to preview it. iMovie even tells you how long each trailer lasts and how many cast members you need.

Once you pick a style, click Create to get started.

You'll immediately notice that you don't see a timeline. Instead, you get a notebook with three tabs: Outline, Storyboard, and Shot List. You use these tabs to build your trailer.

> **TIP** It's easy to spot trailers in iMovie's All Projects list: Their icons look like crossing spotlights instead of the clip icon used for regular projects.

The Outline Tab

You record all the basic information for your preview in the Outline tab—the name of your movie, the starring actor(s), and the production credits (Figure 13-2).

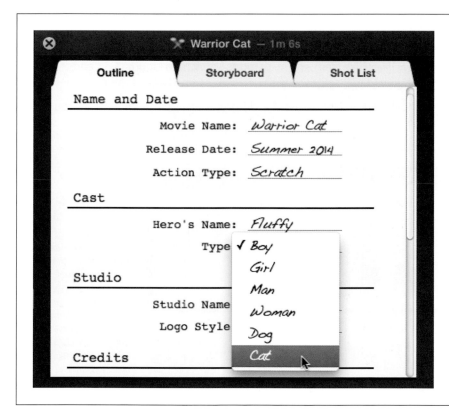

FIGURE 13-2

In the Outline tab, type in your movie's name, the cast name(s), the studio name, and the production credits (not that people actually read those). Each trailer has custom fields; here, the Epic Drama trailer lets you change the hero's identity from "Boy" to "Cat."

You can also name your "studio," and choose from 11 logos for it (like Glowing Pyramid, Sun Rays Through Clouds, and so on). You can change the logo at any point. iMovie models a few of the logos on those from some of the more famous studios (check out Snowy Mountain Peak, for example).

NOTE In iMovie '11, if you selected the Snowy Mountain Peak logo and named your studio "Paramount," or if you typed in "Universal" with the Spinning Earth in Space image, iMovie displayed "---" instead. These styles looked so much like real studios' logos that Apple's lawyers blocked you from duplicating them. Reason has since prevailed, and iMovie no longer blocks those names matched with those logos.

When you move your cursor over the title sections in the Outline tab—Name and Date, Cast, Studio, and Credits—iMovie previews them in the Viewer. It's a nice way to see how they'll look in the final trailer.

The Storyboard Tab

The trailer's Storyboard tab is where you'll do most of the work building your preview. It's the closest thing the trailer-builder has to a timeline. The tab divides your trailer into sections using placeholder headers (like "It's time to go out and play" from the Pets trailer). They show you how your preview will progress from beginning to end. Within each section, you'll find premade slots that describe the type of footage best suited to that part of the preview (Medium and Action, for example). Change the headers if you like (see "And he dared to scratch" in Figure 13-3), and then drop your footage into the slots (you can use as many or as few of them as you like).

As you move your cursor across the clips, you can skim them, just as you would event and project footage.

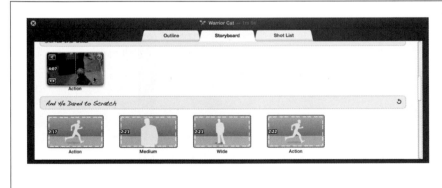

FIGURE 13-3

You do most of your trailer-building in the Storyboard by dropping clips from your Event library into each of the premade slots. You can type in your own text for the headers. Once you drop in a clip, you can unmute it, remove it, or reposition it with the Clip Trimmer (page 67) by using the three little blue buttons shown here.

The Shot List Tab

The Shot List tab displays all the shots that go into your trailer, but in a different way from the Storyboard tab. There, iMovie showed you the trailer's shots according to their sequence in the preview (just as a timeline does). Here, iMovie groups your clips by *kind* of shot (Action, Landscape, and so on; see Figure 13-4). So why the two views of the same information? Organization. The Shot List tells you how many shots of a certain kind you'll need so you can search your Event library for just the right stuff. It also tells you the duration of each clip so you'll know if a shot you're considering is long enough.

iMovie changes the gender in the shot silhouettes based on the gender you enter for the cast member(s) in the Outline tab (when the gender menu appears in the tab, that is—some trailer styles don't let you change the gender). This helps you make sense of which actor you need for which shot.

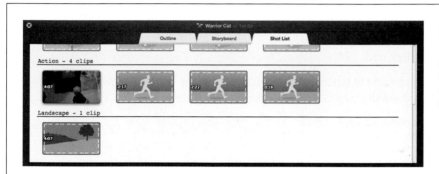

FIGURE 13-4

The Shot List tab groups all your trailer's shots by subject. That way, you know what shots to look for in the Event browser.

■ The Trailers Catalog

Apple was generous with its trailer styles—you get 29 to choose from. Each includes a unique set of titles, transitions, and music. The following catalog gives you a rundown of your choices.

TIP Remember, you can click the Play button on a trailer in the Viewer (Figure 13-1) to preview it—to get a trailer for your trailer, in other words.

- **Action.** *Similar movie: The Fast and the Furious. Cast members*: 2. *Duration*: 0:45 (minutes:seconds).

  Vacation footage never looked so thrilling. Marked by fast-paced techno music and white-on-red titles, the Action trailer is what your vacation would be if you spent it running from international drug cartels.

NOTE Fun fact: The guy featured in this trailer preview is Randy Ubillos, the original designer of the new iMovie. He's an avid traveler, which you can tell from this cool footage of his trip to New Zealand.

- **Adrenaline.** *Similar movie: Inception. Cast members*: Any. *Duration*: 1:04.

  This trailer is all about intensity. The titles and music make you feel like things are going to happen fast, and the heroes will have only one chance to save the day.

- **Adventure.** *Similar movie: Indiana Jones and the Raiders of the Lost Ark. Cast members*: 1. *Duration*: 0:54.

  We all love movie heroes, and this trailer turns you into one. It focuses on a single person and his quest to do something heroic. Feel free to use this trailer ironically if you filmed your husband finally taking out the garbage.

- **Blockbuster.** *Similar movie: Jurassic Park. Cast members*: 2–6. *Duration*: 0:54.

  If you've been to a remote, exotic location facing dangers never before encountered by human beings, or if you just had a blast at the local water park, this is the trailer for you. It features ominous music that swells to a magnificent climax.

- **Bollywood.** *Similar movie: Chennai Express. Cast members*: Any. *Duration*: 1:07.

  Pay tribute to India's booming movie industry. This trailer gives you the chance to make the playful, colorful genre your very own.

- **Coming of Age.** *Similar movie: The Spectacular Now. Cast members*: Any. *Duration*: 1:03.

  Everyone relates to those pivotal growing-up moments. This trailer evokes all those precious memories.

- **Documentary.** *Similar movie: Deep Blue. Cast members*: 2. *Duration*: 1:07.

  Clean lines and Philip Glass-esque music just scream sophistication. If that's what you're going for, choose the Documentary trailer. It makes even the backyard swing set look pivotal for humanity's future.

- **Epic Drama.** *Similar movie: Gladiator. Cast members*: 1. *Duration*: 1:06.

  If you've ever seen the movie *Gladiator*, you've seen this trailer. The triumphant music is absolutely spot-on. Feel free to use it even if you don't conquer insurmountable odds.

- **Expedition.** *Similar movie: National Treasure. Cast members*: 2–6. *Duration*: 1:02.

  Once upon a time, the world was full of unexplored places, some hiding ancient treasures. Of course, along the way your heroes will overcome dangers unknown, and this trailer does their story justice.

- **Fairy Tale.** *Similar movie: Sleeping Beauty. Cast members*: Any. *Duration*: 1:02.

  A trailer fit for princes and princesses. This one evokes all the magic and splendor of the phrase "Once upon a time."

- **Family.** *Similar movie: Cheaper by the Dozen. Cast members*: 2–6. *Duration*: 1:19.

  Ask any parent. Sometimes the mundane life is anything but. If your family is goofy, hectic, and full of surprises, this trailer style will feel right at home.

- **Film Noir.** *Similar movie: The Maltese Falcon. Cast members*: 2. *Duration*: 1:19.

  Real movie trailers looked like this for about three decades. From *The Maltese Falcon* all the way to *North by Northwest*, this classic trailer pays tribute to the dark, brooding films that defined the noir genre.

- **Friendship.** *Similar movie: The Sisterhood of the Traveling Pants. Cast members*: 2–6. *Duration*: 0:54.

  Sometimes feel-good movies are just what the doctor ordered, and the Friendship trailer has feel-good all over it. You don't even have to come of age or form lifelong bonds to use this cheerful preview.

- **Holiday.** *Similar movie: Deck the Halls. Cast members*: 1. *Duration*: 1:17.

  Sleigh bells. Red-and-white titles. It's a great trailer, even if your Christmas miracle was just surviving the family ski trip.

- **Indie.** *Similar movie: 500 Days of Summer. Cast members*: 2. *Duration*: 0:59.

  Indie movies, short for independent films, are popular. Quirky, fun titles in this trailer style tell a classic but off-beat story of boy meets girl.

- **Love Story.** *Similar movie: The Notebook. Cast members*: 2. *Duration*: 1:31.

  In the movie world, true love is hard to find and easy to lose. You can pay tribute to *real* true love with this trailer. Imagine taking old photos and home movies of your parents and putting this trailer together for their anniversary.

- **Narrative.** *Similar movie: The Impossible. Cast members*: Any. *Duration*: 1:34.

  If you've recently filmed a triumph of the human spirit (maybe your son won the school spelling bee, against all odds), this trailer tells the tale of the accomplishment.

- **Pets.** *Similar movie: My Dog Skip. Cast members*: 1. *Duration*: 1:07.

  If a member of your family is furry (and not because he needs to shave), the Pets trailer is a great way to pay tribute to your four-footed friend. The music is cheerful and meaningful. The paw prints in the titles add a great touch.

TIP At the outset, you see a dog's paw prints in this trailer. But on the Outline tab you can change them to a cat's paw or even a dinosaur's footprints.

- **Retro.** *Similar movie: The Pink Panther. Cast members*: 1. *Duration*: 0:59.

  You'll need a madcap caper for this trailer. With throwback titles from the '60s and a jazzy soundtrack to match, it'll leave you using the word "groovy" a lot.

- **Romance.** *Similar movie: The Time Traveler's Wife. Cast members*: 2. *Duration*: 1:23.

  A lot like the Love Story trailer, this one is all about two people who are destined for each other. The titles here are especially heavenly.

- **Romantic Comedy.** *Similar movie*: Any of dozens of romantic comedies. *Cast members*: 2. *Duration*: 0:50.

  Romantic comedies are a clichéd genre, but that doesn't stop people from enjoying them. This trailer nails the motif, especially with the quirky, lighthearted music that suddenly turns meaningful, just like every romance in these movies.

- **Scary.** *Similar movie: The Saw series. Cast members*: Any. *Duration*: 1:01.

  People like horror movies because they leave you on edge. This trailer stays true to the form with jittery titles and creepy music.

- **Sports.** *Similar movie: Miracle. Cast members*: Any. *Duration*: 0:48.

  Put your kid's soccer game into the annals of sports history with this trailer. It showcases dramatic action shots, cheering crowd noises, flashbulb titles, and inspiring fanfare, all essential elements of a great sports movie.

- **Spy.** *Similar movie*: Any James Bond movie. *Cast members*: 1. *Duration*: 1:16.

  Every little (and big) kid dreams about being a spy like James Bond. This is your chance. Imagine how much fun you'll have creating this beat-heavy, fast-moving preview.

- **Superhero.** *Similar movie: The Incredibles. Cast members*: 2–6. *Duration*: 0:59.

  If you're a superhero and it's time for you to reveal your secret identity, this trailer was made for you. It does a nice job of starting with a mild-mannered intro, then ramps up into full action.

- **Supernatural.** *Similar movie: The Da Vinci Code. Cast members*: Any. *Duration*: 1:27.

  If you recently filmed something mysterious or arcane, like how your baby got out of her crib *again*, this trailer fits the mood nicely, with ominous music and ethereal titles.

- **Swashbuckler.** *Similar movie: Pirates of the Caribbean. Cast members*: Any. *Duration*: 1:03.

  Sailing the seven seas in search of buried treasure? iMovie has you covered. The titles in this trailer feature really cool animated maps like you'd see in any pirate movie worth its (sea) salt.

- **Teen.** *Similar movie:* Something between *High School Musical* and *Juno. Cast members*: 2–6. *Duration*: 1:24.

  Ah, high school. A time when cool kids were cool and nerds were nerds. Of course, friendships define that stage of life just as they define this trailer with cute notebook scribblings for titles and a story about stereotype-defying best friends.

- **Travel.** *Similar movie: Mr. Bean's Holiday. Cast members*: 2–6. *Duration*: 1:22.

  iMovie calls this one a "fast-paced screwball comedy." Here's hoping that not all your vacations fit this description, but if they do, here's your trailer of choice. It features big, brassy music and bright titles.

■ Build Your Trailer

Follow these steps to build your trailer:

1. **Choose File→New Trailer (Shift-⌘-N), select a trailer style, and then click Create.**

   Unlike with themes (page 96), you can't change the style of your trailer if you change your mind later.

2. **Fill out the headers in the Outline tab.**

   This is where you name your movie, cast, studio, and production staff. Click each of the items and type in your custom text.

3. **Click the Shot List tab to review the kind and number of shots you need.**

   Rather than follow the order of the tabs, go to the Shot List tab next to see what kind of footage you need. The work you did marking clips as Favorites (page 77) in Chapter 6 pays off here, big time. Use the Favorite setting from the filter menu to pick your shots using just the good stuff.

   At this point, you can plug your footage into each shot by clicking a frame in the Shot List and then clicking a spot on your Event footage. iMovie automatically inserts the right size footage for you. Be aware that your shots may not appear in the right order (remember, the Shot List organizes your shots by subject, not by the order in which they appear in your preview). If the order of events matters a lot, you might want to fill in your shots after you switch over to the Storyboard tab.

4. **Click the Storyboard tab and then add your remaining shots.**

   Just as with the Shot List tab, click a shot and then click the right moment of footage in your Event browser. As you add a shot to each placeholder, iMovie automatically trims the clip to fit the allotted time.

If iMovie doesn't frame a shot right—say it starts and stops at the wrong times—move your mouse over the clip and click the little blue box that pops up in the bottom-left corner. That brings up the Clip Trimmer (page 67), where you can choose a different section of the clip. You can't, however, change the length of the clip; iMovie locks each clip's timing so that the cuts sync up with the trailer's music and titles. If necessary, click the blue button in the top-right of the clip to eject it and start over.

5. **Fill out the trailer titles.**

   Each trailer includes placeholder titles you can edit (or not) in the Storyboard. If your trailer portrays a boy with special powers embarking on the adventure of a lifetime, for example, you can tell his story in the titles.

   To edit title text, click the title in the Storyboard tab and type in your text. Some titles have more than one text box because the trailer uses multiple font styles and sizes (Figure 13-5).

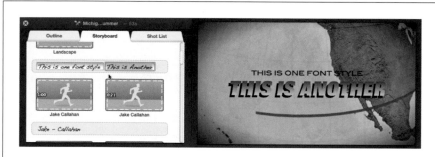

FIGURE 13-5

Some titles use multiple fonts and sizes. iMovie separates those titles into different text boxes (left), and styles each so the titles appear in their proper format in the title itself (right).

6. **Preview your trailer.**

   Click ▶ in the Viewer, and you'll see your trailer in all its glory. At this point, you can customize things using the instructions in the next section.

7. **Share your trailer.**

   You share trailers just like you share movies; see Chapters 15 and 16 for the details.

◼ Customize Your Trailer

Your editing options for trailers are limited. You can't change the length of any of the clips, for example. However, you *can* make some changes in both the Storyboard and Shots List tabs:

- **Change a clip's color settings.**

  As described on page 139, you can adjust a clip's color tone. For example, if the snow in your shot looks a little blue, iMovie's automatic white balance will fix it with just one click.

- **Make audio adjustments to the clip.**

    iMovie automatically mutes the clips you use in trailers so the majesty of the score shines through. To make a clip's audio audible, click Adjust in the Viewer toolbar and then follow the instructions on page 171.

TIP You can quickly unmute a clip by clicking the blue button that appears in the top-left of a clip when you move your cursor over it.

- **Apply a video and/or audio effect.**

    You can apply any of iMovie's cool video effects, like Aged Film or Hard Light (page 107), to trailer clips. The same goes for audio effects, like Cosmic or Telephone (page 194). Click Adjust and then select the effects tool. From there, you can apply whatever effect you want.

NOTE You can apply audio effects until you're blue in the face, but most trailer templates mute your clips, so you won't hear the changes unless you manually unmute your clips, as previously described.

- **Apply stabilization.**

    If, after building your trailer, you realize that your clips are just way too shaky, you can fix them by applying video stabilization, covered on page 130.

Convert a Trailer to a Project

If you feel constrained by the limited editing available in the trailer-builder, you can convert your trailer to a regular iMovie project to get all the control you want. You can then save the result as a movie (page 257), ready for viewing.

TIP If you want to tap into the unique elements of a trailer—animations, music, and titles—for a regular movie, create a "throwaway" trailer project, embed the elements you want in it, and then copy those elements into your movie project.

To make the conversion, open the trailer and choose File→"Convert Trailer to Movie." Your trailer looks and works like a normal video project (Figure 13-6), with a few exceptions. You can't edit the logo titles that begin the trailer. (However, since you're in regular project mode, you can *delete* the logo titles and replace them with titles of your own design.) In addition, you can't change the style of the other titles in the trailer. If you double-click a purple title in the storyboard to edit it (to change the typeface, for example), it looks like the change was made. But when you click the Return key to make the edit permanent, the changes never "take." The only thing iMovie lets you change in a trailer title are the words that appear there.

TIP Although the Title tools are useless for editing trailer titles, you can manipulate them in all kinds of other ways, including dragging them around and lengthening or shortening them.

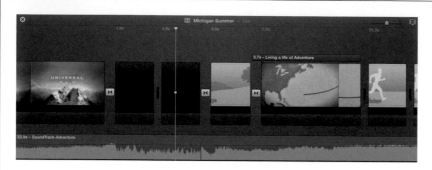

FIGURE 13-6

This looks like a standard movie project now, but it started out as a trailer. To convert a trailer to a project, choose File→"Convert Trailer to Movie." Be careful, though, because once you convert, there's no going back.

And finally, one feature notable for its absence is the ability to add a voiceover (page 188) to your trailer, which is strange because half of all Hollywood previews use a voiceover. But if you convert your trailer to a movie project, you can be your very own Don LaFontaine. (LaFontaine was, perhaps, the most famous voiceover actor ever, narrating the trailers for almost 5,000 movies.)

What you *can* do in a trailer converted to a movie is pretty much everything else—change the music, the length of clips, the transitions, the title backgrounds, and so on.

A word of warning, however: Once you convert a trailer to a project, the move is permanent—you can't turn what is now a movie project back into a trailer. Because this is a one-way street, be sure to add all the elements you want from the trailer-builder before you switch over to the familiar neighborhood of a movie project.

TIP   If you just want to try something out in the project storyboard but you're not sure you want to leave your trailer behind, then go to your Projects list, select your trailer, and then choose File→Duplicate Project. This creates a copy of your trailer that you can convert to a project, ready for experimentation.

Advanced Editing

Stumble around in iMovie long enough, and you'll be able to figure out most of its inner workings. But in this chapter, you'll read about another level of capability, another realm of power and professionalism, that would never occur to most people.

This brief chapter covers *advanced editing theory*. Where the preceding chapters covered the *technical* aspects of editing video in iMovie—what keys to press, where to click, and so on—this chapter is about the *artistic* aspects of video editing. It covers when to cut, what to cut to, and how to create the emotional impact you want.

■ The Power of Editing

The editing process is crucial to any kind of movie, from home videos to Hollywood thrillers. Clever editing can turn a troubled movie into a successful one, or a boring home movie into one that, for the first time, family members don't interrupt every 3 minutes by lapsing into conversation.

You, the editor, are free to jump from camera to camera, angle to angle, from one location or time to another, and so on. Today's audiences accept that you're telling a story. They don't stomp out in confusion because one minute James Bond is in his London office, and then shows up in Venice a split second later.

You can also compress time, which is one of editing's most common duties. (That's fortunate, because most movies tell stories that, in real life, would take days, weeks, or years to unfold.) You can also *expand* time, making 10 seconds stretch out to 6 minutes—a technique familiar to anyone who's ever watched a bomb's digital timer tick down the seconds as the hero races to defuse it.

Editing boils down to choosing which shots you want to include, how long each shot lasts, and in what order they should play.

Modern Film Theory

If you're creating a rock video or an experimental film, you can safely chuck all the advice in this chapter—and in this book. But if you aspire to make good "normal" movies, designed to engage or delight your viewers rather than to shock or mystify them, you should become familiar with the fundamental principles of film editing that have shaped virtually every Hollywood movie (and even most student and independent films) over the last 75 years. For example:

■ TELL THE STORY CHRONOLOGICALLY

Most movies tell a story from beginning to end. This part is probably instinct, even if you're making home movies. Arrange your clips roughly in chronological order, except when you want to represent your characters' flashbacks and memories, or when you deliberately want to play a chronology game, as in *Pulp Fiction*.

■ TRY TO BE INVISIBLE

These days, an expertly edited movie is one where the audience isn't even aware of the editing. This principle has wide-ranging ramifications. For example, the simple cut is by far the most common joint between film clips because it's so unobtrusive. Using, say, the Circle Open transition between alternate lines of the vows at somebody's wedding would hardly qualify as invisible editing.

Within a single scene, use simple cuts, not transitions. Try to create the effect of seamless real time, making the audience feel as though it's witnessing the scene in its entirety, from beginning to end. This kind of editing is more likely to make your viewers less aware that they're watching a movie.

■ DEVELOP A SHOT RHYTHM

Every movie has an editing *rhythm* that's established by the lengths of its shots. The prevailing rhythm of *Lincoln*, for example, is extremely different from that of *The Bourne Identity*. Every *scene* in a movie has its own rhythm, too.

As a general rule, linger less on closeup shots, but give more time to establishing wide shots. (After all, in an establishing shot, there are many more elements for the audience to study and notice.) Similarly, change the pacing of the shots according to the nature of the scene. Most action scenes feature very short clips and fast edits. Most love scenes include longer clips and fewer changes of camera angle.

Maintain Continuity

As a corollary to the notion that the audience should feel that they're part of the story, professional editors strive to maintain *continuity* during the editing process. This continuity business applies mostly to scripted films, not home movies. Still, knowing what the pros worry about makes you a better editor, no matter what kind of footage you work with.

Continuity refers to consistency in the following:

- **The picture.** Suppose we watch a guy with wet hair say, "I'm going to have to break up with you." We cut to his girlfriend's horrified reaction, but when we cut back to the guy, his hair is dry. That's a continuity error, a frequent by-product of having spliced together footage that was filmed at different times. Every Hollywood movie, in fact, has a person whose sole job is to watch out for errors like this during the editing process.

- **Direction of travel.** To make edits as seamless as possible, film editors and directors try to maintain continuity of direction from shot to shot. That is, if the hero sets out crawling across the Sahara from right to left to be with his true love, you better believe that when we see him next, hours later, he'll still be crawling from right to left. This general rule even applies to much less dramatic circumstances, such as car chases, plane flights, and even people walking to the corner store. If you see a character walk out of the frame from left to right in Shot A, you'll see her approach the corner store's doorway from left to right in Shot B.

- **The sound.** In an establishing shot, suppose we see hundreds of men in a battlefield trench, huddled for safety as bullets fly and bombs explode all around them. Now we cut to a closeup of two of these men talking, but the sounds of the explosions are missing. That's a sound continuity error. The audience is certain to notice that hundreds of soldiers were issued a cease-fire just as these two guys started talking.

- **The camera setup.** In scenes of conversations between two people, it would look really bizarre to show one person speaking only in closeup, and his conversation partner filmed in a medium shot. (Unless, of course, the first person were filmed in *extreme* closeup—just the lips filling the screen—because the filmmaker is trying to protect his identity.)

- **Gesture and motion.** If one shot begins with a character reaching down to pick up the newspaper from her doorstep, the next shot—a closeup of her hand closing around the rolled-up paper, for example—should pick up from the exact moment where the previous shot ended. And as the rolled-up paper leaves our closeup field of view, the following shot should show her straightening into an upright position. Unless you've made the deliberate editing decision to skip over some time from one shot to the next (which should be clear to the audience), the action should seem continuous from one shot to the next.

> **TIP** When filming scripted movies, directors always instruct their actors to begin each new scene's action with the same gesture or motion that *ended* the last shot. Having two copies of this gesture, action, or motion—one on each end of each take—gives the editor a lot of flexibility when it comes time to piece the movie together.

This principle explains why it's extremely rare for an editor to cut from one shot of two people to another shot of the *same* two people (without inserting some other shot between them, such as a reaction shot or a closeup of one person or the other). The odds are small that, as the new shot begins, both actors will be in precisely the same body positions they were in when the previous shot ended.

When to Cut

Some Hollywood directors may tell their editors to make cuts just for the sake of making the cuts come faster, in an effort to pick up the movie's pace. More seasoned directors and editors, however, usually adopt a more classical view of editing: Cut to a different shot when it's *motivated*. That is, cut when you *need* to cut, so that you can convey new visual information by taking advantage of a different camera angle, switching to a different character, providing a reaction shot, and so on.

Editors look for a motivating event that suggests *where* they should make the cut, too, such as a movement, a look, the end of the sentence, or the intrusion of an off-camera sound that makes us *want* to look somewhere else in the scene.

Choose the Next Shot

As you read elsewhere in this book, the final piece of advice when it comes to choosing when and how to make a cut is this: Cut to a *different* shot. If you've been filming the husband, cut to the wife; if you've been in a closeup, cut to a medium or wide shot; if you've been showing someone looking off-camera, cut to what she's looking at.

Avoid cutting from one shot of somebody to a similar shot of the same person. Doing so creates a *jump cut*, a disturbing and seemingly unmotivated splice between shots of the same subject from the same angle.

Video editors sometimes have to swallow hard and perform jump cuts for the sake of compressing a long interview into a much shorter sound bite. Customer testimonials on TV commercials frequently illustrate this point. You'll see a woman saying, "Wonderglove changed...[cut] our lives, it really did...[cut] My husband used to be a drunk and a slob...[cut] but now we have Wonderglove." (Often, directors apply a fast cross dissolve to the cuts in a futile attempt to make them less noticeable.)

However, as you can probably attest if you've ever seen such an ad, that kind of editing is rarely convincing. As you watch it, you can't help wondering exactly *what* was cut and why. (The editors of *60 Minutes* and other documentary-style shows edit the comments of their interview subjects just as heavily but conceal it better by cutting away to reaction shots—of the interviewer, for example—between edited shots.)

■ Popular Editing Techniques

Variety and pacing play a role in every decision a video editor makes. The following sections explain some common tricks of professional editors that you can use in iMovie.

Tight Editing

One of the first tasks you'll encounter when editing your footage is choosing how to trim and chop up your clips, as described in Chapter 5. Even when you edit home movies, consider the Hollywood guideline for tight editing: Begin every scene as *late* as possible, and end it as *soon* as possible.

In other words, suppose the audience sees the heroine receiving the call that her husband has been in an accident, and then hanging up the phone in shock. We don't really need to see her putting on her coat, opening the apartment door, locking it behind her, taking the elevator to the ground floor, hailing a cab, driving frantically through the city, screeching to a stop in front of the hospital, and finally leaping out of the cab. In a tightly edited movie, she would hang up the phone and then we'd see her leaping out of the cab (or even walking into her husband's hospital room).

Keep this principle in mind even when editing your own, slice-of-life videos. For example, a very engaging account of your ski trip could begin with only three shots: an establishing shot of the airport; a shot of the kids piling into the plane; and then the tumultuous, noisy, trying-on-ski-boots shot the next morning. You get less reality with this kind of tight editing, but much more watchability.

Variety of Shots

Variety is important in every aspect of filmmaking—variety of shots, locations, angles, and so on. Consider the lengths of your shots, too. In action sequences, you may prefer quick cutting, where each clip in your movie track is only a second or two long. In softer, more peaceful scenes, longer shots may set the mood more effectively.

■ ESTABLISHING SHOTS

Almost every scene of every movie and every TV show—even the nightly news—begins with an *establishing shot*: a long-range, zoomed-out shot that shows the audience where the action is about to take place.

Now that you know something about film theory, you'll begin to notice how often TV and movie scenes begin with an establishing shot. It gives the audience a feeling of being there and helps them understand the context for the medium shots or closeups that follow. Furthermore, after a long series of closeups, consider showing *another* wide shot, to remind the audience of where the characters are and what the world around them looks like.

As with every film-editing guideline, this one is occasionally worth violating. For example, in comedies, a new scene may begin with a closeup instead of an establishing shot, so that the camera can then pull back to *make* the establishing shot the joke. (For example: Closeup on main character looking uncomfortable; camera pulls back to reveal that we were looking at him upside down as he hangs, tied by his feet, over a pit of alligators.) In general, however, setting up any new scene with an establishing shot is the smart—and polite—thing to do for your audience's benefit.

■ CUTAWAYS AND CUT-INS

Cutaways and *cut-ins* are extremely common and effective editing techniques. Not only do they add some variety to a movie, but they let you conceal enormous editing shenanigans. By the time your movie resumes after the cutaway shot, you can have deleted enormous amounts of material, switched to a different take of the same scene, and so on. Figure 14-1 shows the idea.

The *cut-in* is similar, but instead of showing a different person or a reaction shot, it usually features a closeup of what the speaker is holding or talking about—a very common technique in training tapes and cooking shows.

■ REACTION SHOTS

One of the most common sequences in Hollywood history is a three-shot sequence that goes like this: First, we see the character looking offscreen; then we see what he's looking at (a cutaway shot); and finally, we see him again so that we can read his reaction. This sequence is repeated so frequently in commercial movies that you can feel it coming the moment the performer looks off the screen.

From the editor's standpoint, of course, the beauty of the three-shot reaction is that the middle shot can be anything from anywhere. That is, it can be footage shot on another day in another part of the world, or even from a different movie entirely. The ritual of character/action/reaction is so ingrained in our brains that the audience believes the actor was looking at the action, no matter what it is.

In home-movie footage, you may have been creating reaction shots without even knowing it. But you've probably been capturing them by panning from your kid's beaming face to the petting-zoo sheep and then back to the face. You can make this sequence look great in iMovie by just snipping out the pans, leaving you with crisp, professional-looking cuts.

■ PARALLEL CUTTING

When you make a movie that tells a story, it's sometimes fun to use *parallel editing* or *intercutting*. That's when you show two trains of action simultaneously and you keep cutting back and forth to show the parallel simultaneous action. In *Fatal Attraction*, for example, the intercut climax shows main character Dan Gallagher (Michael Douglas) downstairs in the kitchen, trying to figure out why the ceiling is dripping, even as his psychotic mistress Alex (Glenn Close) is upstairs attempting to murder his wife in the bathtub. If you're making movies that tell a story, you'll find this technique an exciting one when you're trying to build suspense.

FIGURE 14-1

Top: You've got a shot of your main character in action.

Middle: We cut away to a shot of what he's looking at or reacting to.

Bottom: When you cut back to the main character, you could use a different take on a different day, or dialog from a much later part of the scene (due to some cuts suggested by the editor). The audience will never know that the action wasn't continuous. The cutaway masks the fact that there was a discontinuity between the first and third shots.

Share Your Movies

Share via Email and the Web

I f you ask Apple, the DVD has had its day in the sun. Today, the real action is on the Web, that billion-seat megaplex where unknown independent filmmakers get noticed, and where it doesn't cost a penny to distribute your work.

Email is a distribution option for short movies, but hardly a way to showcase your 1080p feature-length film. For that, you need to turn to online video-sharing services like YouTube. People watch six *billion* hours of YouTube videos every *month*. Facebook is no slouch, either. Its video-hosting tools help you quickly share your movie with your closest (or remotest) friends. And for projects that need a certain sophistication, try the classy site Vimeo. Even professional filmmakers use it as a video outlet, so you'd be in good company.

Fancy yourself a witness to history? Do some citizen reporting and post your movies to CNN's iReport website, where one of the CNN networks might pick up your footage and broadcast it to the world. Or, what the heck: Post videos to your own website and share it there.

This chapter covers all the ways to distribute your opus via the Web. And if you disagree with Apple's take on DVDs and prefer the ease and simplicity of sharing that way, take a trip to Chapter 16.

First, a Word About Sharing Raw Footage

If you've ever dusted off a tape camcorder or a DVD video camera full of raw footage from old home movies, you've probably had a lot of fun reveling in the memories—seeing, for example, what the kids used to look and sound like. Odds are that other people—like your grown kids and their grandparents—would enjoy seeing those clips, too. In short, you want to be able to share old footage.

Since iMovie debuted, the only way to do that was by creating a movie—you couldn't share clips straight from the Event browser. Unfortunately, the only way to distribute old footage is by creating a movie project. You can't share raw, unedited clips straight from the Event browser. Luckily, the process takes just a few steps, as described in Chapter 5.

TIP Be considerate when you share old footage. Even simple edits, like deleting shaky shots, can make a world of difference in watchability. Whatever you do, don't be *that* guy, the one who makes people sit through hours of boring shots of your vacation. Read up on the advice in Chapter 9 for simple tricks to improve your movies.

■ Share via Email

As noted, email isn't the ideal way to send movies, because they tend to be big, and your Internet service provider can limit the size of email attachments (in which case it won't deliver your file). The exception is small movies, though even there you'll have to dial down the dimensions—what you gain in convenience, you give up in quality.

To send a movie by email, click the Share icon in the iMovie toolbar, and then choose Email from the drop-down menu (or choose File→Share→Email). iMovie displays a dialog box like the one in Figure 15-1, top. It includes a thumbnail of your movie, and, underneath that, the movie's duration (2:54, for example, for 2 minutes, 54 seconds). You can edit your movie's title, description, and tags by clicking once in the text boxes. (Oddly, the original title shows up in your email's subject line when you send the file.)

You can change the video's dimensions, too, and therefore its file size, using the drop-down Size menu. iMovie offers three less-than-hi-def options for movies you want to email:

- Small (428 × 240 pixels)
- Medium (854 × 480)
- Large (960 × 540)

When you select a dimension, iMovie displays the resulting file size under the thumbnail. Notice that when you choose a size that results in a file larger than 10 MB, iMovie warns you to reconsider. That's because the file will take a long time to transmit, and your email system may not let you send that big an attachment.

Once iMovie generates an email version of your project, it automatically opens your Mac's Mail application and attaches the video to a message (Figure 15-1), though the description and tags are nowhere to be found. Enter the recipients' addresses, type a personal word or two, and send away.

NOTE If you use a Web-based email service like Gmail, the Share→Email option doesn't work. For Web-based email accounts, you have to save your movie as a file (see page 263) and then attach it to a mail message yourself.

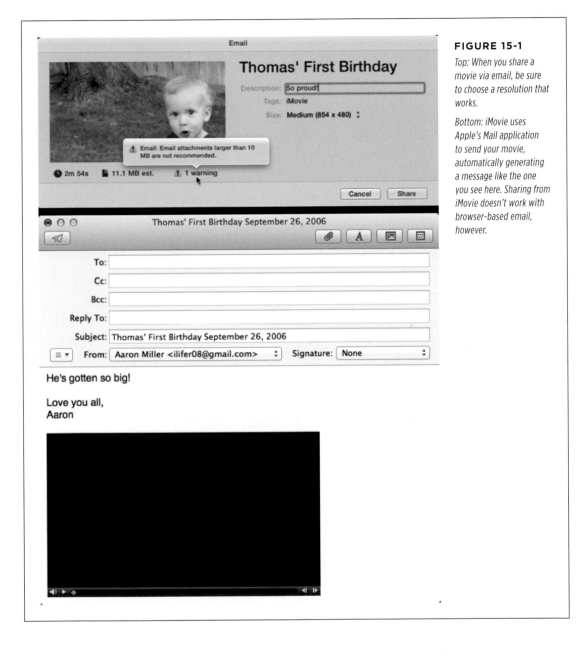

FIGURE 15-1

Top: When you share a movie via email, be sure to choose a resolution that works.

Bottom: iMovie uses Apple's Mail application to send your movie, automatically generating a message like the one you see here. Sharing from iMovie doesn't work with browser-based email, however.

◼ Share to YouTube

By far the easiest way to share your movies on the Internet is through YouTube.

YouTube is, of course, the insanely popular video-sharing website, filled to the brim with hundreds of millions of funny home videos, TV excerpts, amateur short films, memorable bloopers—and now your iMovie projects. Once you post a movie, other people can find it in many ways: by typing in its web address, by searching for your name, or by searching for keywords (called *tags*) you list in the video's description.

The first thing you need in order to post to YouTube is a YouTube account (it's free). To get one, visit *www.youtube.com/signup* and fill in the blanks. If you have a Gmail account, you can use that login information to sign in to YouTube. One signed into YouTube, be sure to click the Upload button at the top of the page and follow the brief instructions to create a channel for all your videos.

Post to YouTube

Once your movie is ready for the masses:

1. **Choose the Share icon from iMovie's toolbar, and then select YouTube.**

   A dialog box appears. The first time you post, it looks like the one in Figure 15-2.

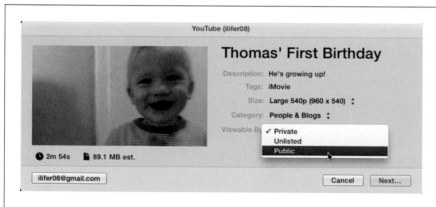

FIGURE 15-2

Sign into your YouTube account and then add information about your film to this dialog box. iMovie uploads the info along with your movie.

2. **Click Sign In and, in the box that pops up, enter your YouTube username and password. Then click OK.**

   You need to sign into your account so the edits you make in the dialog box get transferred over to YouTube. Turn on the "Remember this password in my keychain" checkbox so you don't have to type in your username and password the next time you share.

3. **Edit the placeholder text for your movie's name, description, and tags (keywords) (see Figure 15-2).**

   Click the text once to edit it. iMovie transfers this info when you post your movie to YouTube—it appears right under your posted movie.

4. **Specify what size you want the movie to be.**

   You can upload any of the four size movies iMovie offers: SD 480p, Large 540p, HD 720p, or HD 1080p (assuming your source video even has that much resolution). Generally, you should go big. YouTube automatically scales down your video for people with slower Internet connections. In fact, the only reason *not* to go big is if *your* Internet connection is too slow to upload a large movie.

5. **Choose who can see the movie.**

   Most people make their YouTube movies available to the entire Internet, but you have three options: Private, Unlisted, and Public. If you make a movie private, *nobody* will see it unless you invite them from YouTube's video settings page. If you make it unlisted, people can see it only if you send them the movie's web address (which YouTube gives you). If you don't care who sees your video and you want to invite the whole world to the party, choose Public.

6. **Click Next.**

   A dialog box appears reminding you that it's naughty to upload TV shows, movies, or anything else that's copyrighted.

7. **Click Publish.**

   iMovie springs into action, compressing and uploading your video. This part can take awhile. You can check its progress by clicking the blue circle in the top-right corner of the iMovie window. Feel free to check your email while iMovie crunches away.

   Once iMovie finishes, you'll see a message like the one in Figure 15-3.

FIGURE 15-3

iMovie uses OS X's built-in notification system to let you know you've successfully shared a movie.

8. **Click Visit to watch and share your movie.**

   Your uploaded video isn't available right away. YouTube needs a little time to process it. (You'll see a message like the one in Figure 15-4.) Before long, though, your movie will join the millions of others. If you close your browser and want to see the movie later, visit *http://www.youtube.com/my_videos*.

After the YouTube Movie Is Up

Once you post a video to YouTube, you can tell others about it simply by sharing the web address, which you find in the Video URL box beside your movie.

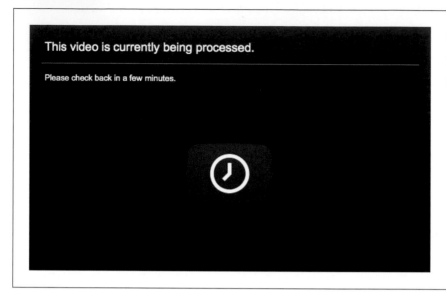

FIGURE 15-4

Newly posted YouTube videos aren't available to the masses immediately.

You can manage your videos—rename, annotate, or remove them—by visiting the Video Manager page at *http://www.youtube.com/my_videos* (Figure 15-5).

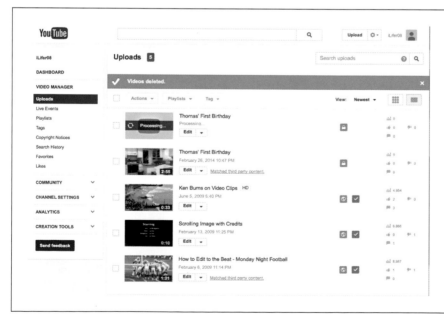

FIGURE 15-5

The YouTube Video Manager is where you organize all your movies. You can change their privacy settings, edit their descriptions and tags, and even enhance them.

If you realize you made a mistake in an uploaded movie, you can delete it from You-Tube and upload a new one. You can even upload the same movie multiple times, so don't count on iMovie or YouTube to detect duplicates for you.

Share to Facebook

More than a billion people use Facebook every month. With that many members, the odds are pretty good that someone (everyone) you know has a Facebook account—probably one that's checked frequently. For that reason, Facebook is a no-brainer when you want to share your videos with friends and family. It even plays HD videos, so your work can look its best.

Post to Facebook

When you choose Share→Facebook for your project, iMovie displays the screen in Figure 15-6. The steps for uploading to Facebook are basically the same as they are for YouTube and the sites mentioned on the following pages: Enter your account information, type in a movie title, description, and tags, and then choose a video quality.

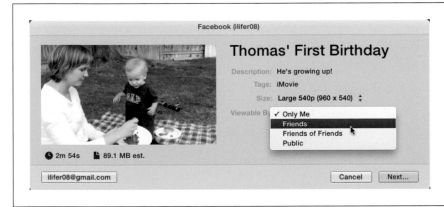

FIGURE 15-6

Publishing your video to Facebook is basically the same as publishing to YouTube. The biggest difference is the privacy settings you have available. You can keep your movie to yourself or share it with friends, friends of friends, or all 500 million Facebook users.

Facebook lets you choose who can see your movie, too (Figure 15-6). You can make it an entirely private affair (click Only Me), share it with friends, friends of friends, or the whole world (Public). If you change your mind later, go to your Facebook timeline to find your video and then edit the sharing settings that appear when you click Edit This Video.

Facebook takes a few minutes to process your video before you can view it. As you're probably aware, Facebook offers plenty of other ways to spend your time while you wait.

After the Facebook Movie Is Up

Publishing your video creates a copy of it on Facebook. To delete it, go to your Facebook video page (see the previous instructions) and click Delete Video.

▇ Share to Vimeo

If YouTube is the McDonald's of online video—ubiquitous, but full of "fast-food" movies—Vimeo is the Whole Foods, directed at those with a more refined palate. It's still a video-sharing website, but the videos posted there tend to be of higher production values. The site also shies away from the cluttered look you find on YouTube. For this reason, people who are picky about how their videos look online tend to turn to Vimeo.

If you're the Vimeo type, you can create a free account at *http://vimeo.com/join*. (You can also sign up for a Plus account, which, for $10 a month, gives you a bunch of additional benefits, like higher upload limits and more control over how your videos appear to viewers.)

Upload to Vimeo

Choose Share→Vimeo to upload your video. The Vimeo publishing screen (Figure 15-7) has the same Sign In button you saw on the YouTube screen.

As usual, be sure to enter a good description and tags so people searching the Internet will have more luck finding your video, and you can upload movies with resolutions of up to 1080p.

Vimeo offers several ways to limit who sees your movie, the most interesting being "Anyone with Password." Enter a password in the box provided, and only the people you send the code to can watch your movie.

FIGURE 15-7

Uploading to Vimeo works almost identically to sharing to YouTube. The privacy settings are unique, however, since you can limit viewing to those with a password you choose.

When you finish filling in the dialog box, click Next to get the same copyright warning/scolding you see when you upload to YouTube. iMovie processes and uploads your video, displaying a confirmation message when it's done.

After Your Vimeo Movie Is Up

To delete a movie, log into Vimeo, go to your video's page, and then click the big Delete button at the top-right corner. Once again, if you share the video to Vimeo once and then share it again, you'll post two versions of it on the Vimeo website.

◼ Share to CNN iReport

Now that almost everyone carries around a smartphone, laptop, or camera, the big news agencies are wising up to the power of citizen journalism. These days, the first video you see of a natural or celebrity disaster usually comes from the Man on the Street™.

If the idea of citizen reporting excites you, make sure to take advantage of the convenience iMovie offers in sending your reports straight to CNN's iReport website (*http://ireport.cnn.com/*).

iReport is CNN's system of publishing video news from ordinary people like you. (Some of the photos and videos even make it onto CNN's TV broadcasts.) The first time you visit the site, it gives you a brief explanation of how it all works (Figure 15-8). Follow the link in the top-right corner to create an account and get started.

CNN iReport
Hi! You're new here, right?

Welcome to iReport, where people take part in the news with CNN. Your voice, together with other iReporters, helps shape how and what CNN covers every day.

So you know: iReport is the way people like you report the news. The stories in this section are not edited, fact-checked or screened before they post. Only ones marked 'CNN iReport' have been vetted by CNN.

Learn more »   ☐ I get it. Don't show me this again.   CLOSE

FIGURE 15-8

Your first visit to CNN's iReport website (http:// ireport.cnn.com/) greets you with this message. Basically, CNN loves to take the great stuff you create, but it won't take the blame for the bad stuff.

TIP Once you create a CNN account, you'll notice that CNN regularly sends out "assignments" to you, the citizen reporter. Obviously, if your goal is to be seen on TV, your chances of success go up if you file reports meeting these assignments.

Upload to iReport

When you have your Pulitzer Prize–worthy report ready to go, choose Share→CNN iReport in iMovie and then select a resolution from the Size menu (Figure 15-9). CNN doesn't offer any tag or description fields, but you can add that info on the iReport website. Click the Sign In button and enter your iReport account vitals (email address and password).

Unlike YouTube, Vimeo, and Facebook, iReport doesn't let you limit who can see your video. Everything you upload is public, viewable by *anyone*. (iReport is for public reporting, after all, not private video sharing among friends.)

Once you upload your report, you can see it online and tell friends about it. If you try to watch your report right away, you might see a message telling you that CNN's servers are still processing the video.

FIGURE 15-9

The publish screen for CNN's iReport has the basic options, except for the one to keep it private. This is news, people! (Your 1-year-old's birthday doesn't happen every day, right?) Be sure that what you upload is exactly what you want, because there's no simple way to remove or update an iReport.

After the iReport Is Up

You manage your uploaded videos—including editing their names and descriptions—from the iReport website. Uploading your video again just makes a duplicate.

> **TIP** There's no easy way to delete your iReport, short of contacting CNN and asking them to take it down. Be sure you know exactly what you're uploading beforehand, particularly with regard to copyright issues.

■ Share to Your Own Web Page

If you're a savvy, webmastery kind of person, you can design a website and then post your videos without any help from iMovie.

Post a Movie on Your Own Site

To post a movie to your site, export a file version of it from iMovie (page 263) and then upload it to your site's hosting service. You can embed *any* movie into your web page by writing the necessary HTML, and every modern browser can play back your movie natively.

This isn't really a book about building websites, but to get you started, you can download a free PDF appendix to this chapter called "Movies on Custom Websites." You can find it on this book's Missing CD page at *http://oreilly.com/missingmanuals/cds/imovie2014/*. It provides the HTML code you need to post a movie on your web page, make it pop up in a window or play embedded in the page, and other advanced topics.

Post to Blogging Services

Every major blogging service (Tumblr, Blogger, and the like) offers a simple way to embed YouTube videos in your blog. It's easy and requires no knowledge of web programming. You can get the code you need to add to your blog from your video's page on YouTube.

Vimeo also offers the custom code you need to embed a movie you uploaded there in your blog.

Share to the iPhone, iPad, iPod Touch, Apple TV, and iDVD

I n case you haven't noticed, Apple thinks that one of the classic destinations for your home movies—DVDs—is ancient history. What Apple *really* wants you to do with your videos is post them to the Web (see Chapter 15) or transfer them to another Apple device, like an iPad, iPhone, iPod Touch, or Apple TV.

The bulk of this chapter covers those latter options: sending your finished masterpiece to another fine piece of Apple merchandise.

But if you're a DVD holdout—*and* you have iDVD on your Mac from an earlier version of iMovie (see page 264)—you'll learn how to save your movies old school, out of iMovie, into iDVD, and, finally, onto DVD.

Sharing Basics

To share a video in iMovie, click the Share icon in iMovie's toolbar, or choose File→ Share. iMovie displays a list of destinations (iMovie Theater, Email, iTunes, and so on). When you select one, iMovie gets to work sewing up your film in a format suited to its eventual home. The details of sharing for each destination are in the following sections.

iMovie Theater

Until this version of iMovie, sharing your project to an iDevice required a trip to iTunes, which added an extra and cumbersome step to the whole sharing process. In recent years, however, Apple has replaced iTunes as the interim medium with one that's much more convenient—iCloud, Apple's online storage locker. You can wirelessly tap into files saved "in the cloud" from any Apple gadget. For example, with an iCloud account, you can add a friend to your Contacts list on your iPhone and she will show up on your iPad's Contacts list, too.

Now iMovie is up with the times. With the iMovie app installed on your iDevice, a movie you share to iMovie Theater (iMovie's full-size playback screen) gets synced with your iCloud account and shows up on all your Apple devices. iMovie Theater is the simplest way to share a movie with people who have an Apple gadget, whether that device is an iPad, iPhone, iPod Touch, or Apple TV.

iCloud

For iMovie Theater to work, you need two things: the iMovie app installed on your device and an iCloud account.

To get iMovie for an iPhone, iPad, or iPod Touch, head over to the App Store, type "iMovie" into the search box, and get ready to shell out $4.99, unless you bought your iDevice after September 2013, in which case it's free. Once you have the app installed, you watch your movies through iMovie Theater, the playback portion of the iMovie app. If you own an Apple TV, iMovie Theater is already installed.

iCloud accounts are free, and you're invited to create one anytime you set up a new piece of Apple hardware. (This same account gives you cool features like the Find My iPhone device-location app, an iCloud email account, and the PhotoStream image-sharing service.) Point is, you probably already have an iCloud account.

If not, or if you're not sure, go to the Apple menu on your Mac and choose System Preferences (⌘→System Preferences). In the window that appears, choose iCloud.

If you see a window like the one in Figure 16-1 (top), you're good to go. If not, you need to create an iCloud account by signing in with your Apple ID and password, which you probably established when you set up your Apple device for the first time. (If you skipped that step during setup, click "Create new Apple ID" and follow the instructions.)

Because iMovie Theater stores your videos in iCloud, you need to be able to tap into the cloud from your iDevice, too. To set up iCloud there, open Settings→iCloud. If you see a screen like the one in Figure 16-1 (bottom), you have everything you need. If not, you either need to log in with your Apple ID and password, or you have to click "Create new Apple ID" and follow the instructions. When you finish, you'll have iCloud up and running on your gadget.

Share to iMovie Theater

With your iCloud account sorted out, sharing to iMovie Theater, and then to iCloud itself, couldn't be easier. First, make sure iMovie automatically uploads your movies to iCloud. Go to iMovie→Preferences in iMovie's menu bar and make sure "Automatically upload content to iCloud" is turned on. Then, with a project open in iMovie, click Share→Theater in iMovie's toolbar (or press ⌘-E, or choose File→Share→Theater). iMovie opens the iMovie Theater window (Figure 16-2) and exports your movie. (If you don't have "Automatically upload content to iCloud" turned on, you can export movies to iCloud individually by clicking the cloud icon in the top-right corner of an exported movie.)

FIGURE 16-1

Top: To share movies through iMovie Theater, you need to have iCloud set up on your Mac.

Bottom: If you see this screen when you select iCloud from the Settings menu, either sign in with your Apple ID and password or click Create New Apple ID and follow the instructions.

To view your movie on an iPad, iPhone, or iPod Touch, open the iMovie app and choose Theater from the menu bar at the top of the screen. The movie you shared to iCloud appears as a thumbnail on the next screen.

Tapping the > button on the thumbnail gives you options for managing your video (Figure 16-2); they include a way to preview the movie now, and to download it now from iCloud so you can share or watch it when your device is offline.

If you have an Apple TV, select the iMovie Theater icon from the menu, and you'll see thumbnails for all the movies you shared to iCloud.

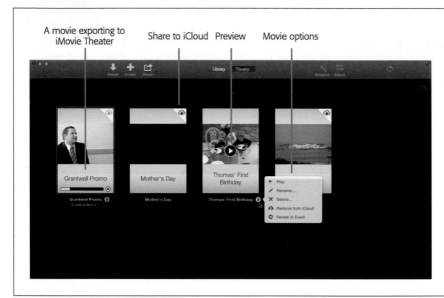

A movie exporting to
iMovie Theater

Share to iCloud   Preview   Movie options

FIGURE 16-2

*iMovie Theater is the
easiest way to share your
projects to other Apple
devices. Once you export a
movie to the Theater, you
can manage it using the
options shown here.*

NOTE Apple TV requires you to be logged in with an Apple ID to do, well, just about anything, so your account information is likely already set up.

■ Share to iTunes

If you don't use iMovie Theater to share your films on Apple gadgets, iTunes is the next-best option. iTunes, like iCloud, lets you sync information to an iDevice, but this time you share files stored in iTunes' libraries (Music, Movies, Books, and so on), and you share them one at a time to a single, connected device.

Just as with iMovie Theater, the first step in sharing a movie is to export it. This time, however, you share to iTunes.

1. **When your project is ready for prime time, click Share→iTunes in the iMovie toolbar.**

    iMovie launches the iTunes dialog box (Figure 16-3). You can skim your mouse over the preview window to make sure your movie looks right. Although you'll see an active Share button, don't click it just yet.

2. **Mouse over the ✓ button below the movie thumbnail.**

You've probably never seen an information box quite like this. Since different Apple gadgets have different maximum screen sizes, iMovie offers to export your movie at a size tailored to your device (Figure 16-3, bottom).

> **TIP** In any of the various Share windows that appear when sharing from iMovie, the little preview is not a mere static image, but a skimmable version of your movie.

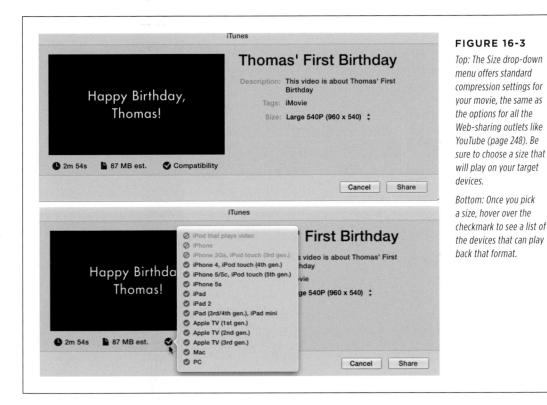

FIGURE 16-3

Top: The Size drop-down menu offers standard compression settings for your movie, the same as the options for all the Web-sharing outlets like YouTube (page 248). Be sure to choose a size that will play on your target devices.

Bottom: Once you pick a size, hover over the checkmark to see a list of the devices that can play back that format.

For example, the iPhone 4 can handle an HD 720p movie, while the iPhone 5s can manage an HD 1080p film. The same difference applies to second- and third-generation Apple TVs. Point to the checkmark without clicking to see the devices compatible with the format you chose (Figure 16-3, bottom).

3. **Click Share.**

iMovie begins the time-consuming process of compressing and exporting your video. If your movie is long, feel free to switch to other programs—check your email or surf the Web, for example—while iMovie crunches away. A blue "progress" circle in the top-right corner of the iMovie window gives you an idea of how long the export will take. Click it to get a specific amount of time or to cancel the export.

When it's all over, iTunes opens by itself. If you click the Movies folder, you'll see your newly exported movies in the Home Videos section (Figure 16-4).

FIGURE 16-4

Movies you share to iTunes show up in the Home Videos library. To watch a movie, double-click it.

From iTunes to iPad, iPhone, iPod Touch, or Apple TV

Once you have your movie in iTunes, getting it onto your iPad, iPhone, iPod Touch, or Apple TV works just like it always does:

- **iPad, iPhone, iPod Touch.** Connect the gadget to your Mac. Its icon shows up under Devices in the left column of the iTunes window. Select your device, click the Movies tab, select the movie you want iTunes to copy over to your gadget, and then click Apply or Sync (Figure 16-5).

- **Apple TV.** To play your exported movie on an Apple TV, you need to turn on Home Sharing in iTunes. That lets your Apple TV play items from your iTunes library (which sits on your Mac, hence the need for Home Sharing).

  In iTunes, choose File→Home Sharing→Turn On Home Sharing. On the Apple TV, choose Settings→Computers and then turn on the feature there.

  With Home Sharing turned on, choose Computers from the Apple TV app icons and you'll see your Mac's iTunes libraries listed. (Be sure that iTunes is running on your Mac.) There you can browse everything in iTunes, including the Home Videos folder, where your exported movie lives.

FIGURE 16-5

When you connect an iPad, iPhone, or iPod Touch to iTunes, it shows up in the Devices list in the left-hand column. Click the gadget's name to sync music, movies, and other files using the tabs at the top of the screen. You'll find all your iMovie exports in the Movies tab.

File Exports

There are plenty of non-Apple devices in the world, and sharing your movies to them requires you to export your movie as a file. You end up with a movie file on your Mac that you can copy to your destination.

NOTE The files you export will probably be big, so copying them will probably take some time. It also requires you to connect the destination device to your Mac somehow. If either of these is a problem, consider just sharing your movie to the Web using any of the options explained in Chapter 15.

Choose Share→File to see an export box like the one in Figure 16-3. Use the size menu to change the quality of your movie (which also affects its file size and conversion time). iMovie displays how big the resulting file will be under the skimmable preview of your movie.

When you click Next, iMovie asks you to name the file and pick a destination. Once you do, click Save and iMovie goes to work. The top-right corner of the iMovie window displays a blue progress circle; click it to see exactly how much longer the export will take. Eventually, iMovie notifies you that it's finished and you'll find the movie file in your selected destination. As an added touch, QuickTime opens the file automatically so you can play your movie right away.

iDVD

As a company, Apple has always been forward-thinking, but that also means that it usually abandons the status quo before everyone else does. So even though Apple has moved on from the DVD player, not everyone has. After all, players are inexpensive and Red Box rental kiosks are widespread. In fact, DVDs are still the most common way people watch movies. More importantly, many of your loved ones probably still use DVD players.

Once upon a time, iMovie came with a companion program called iDVD that let you save your movies to DVD. That option is long gone now, but that doesn't mean you can't use iDVD with your current iMovie projects. In fact, it's still pretty simple to burn your movies to DVD and then share them.

To do that, you have to have iDVD on your Mac. You may, if you've used an older version of iMovie. But you can't download iDVD from the App Store: Apple simply doesn't offer it.

But you *can* still get iDVD, by buying an older version of iLife, the software suite that included iMovie and iDVD. Look for iLife on sites like Amazon.com and eBay. Any version from '08 to '11 includes the most recent version of iDVD.

Of course, you also need a DVD burner in your Mac. Newer laptop models, like the Retina MacBook Pros and the MacBook Air, don't have one. If that's the case for you, you need to buy an external burner. Apple sells one for $79 that works just fine.

To burn your iMovie project to DVD, follow these steps:

1. **Export your movie as a file.**

   Follow the instructions in the previous section. Be sure to remember where you saved the file, because you'll need to drag it into iDVD.

2. **Open iDVD and create a new project (File→New or ⌘-N).**

   When you start a new project, iDVD asks you to choose a name and destination for it. You also need to choose between the Standard and Widescreen DVD format. That setting won't change the format of your actual movie, it just changes the look of the DVD menus. Choose a format that matches the dimensions of your TV.

3. **Drag your movie file from the Finder into the iDVD window.**

   iDVD creates a menu with a single item on it, labeled with your movie's file name. After you burn the DVD, this will be the menu item people choose to play the movie (Figure 16-6).

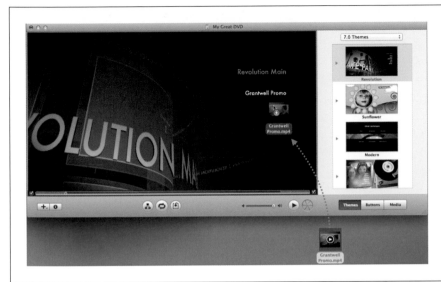

FIGURE 16-6

When you drag a movie file into iDVD, the software creates a new menu item. Feel free to change the menu's labels and appearance. Just be sure not to delete the menu item representing your movie, or you won't be able to play it after you burn the disc.

4. **Customize your menu and then burn the DVD.**

   You can change all kinds of things about your DVD menus and settings. The most popular edit is to choose a theme from among the dozens Apple offers. Once your DVD menu looks right, choose File→Burn DVD (⌘-R) and then follow the instructions iDVD gives you. Behind the scenes, iDVD converts your movie file to DVD format. Wait until iDVD burns the disc, and your DVD is ready to go.

NOTE If you'd like to dive into your old copy of iDVD in more detail, a free PDF appendix to this chapter called "iDVD: The Missing Manual" awaits you on this book's Missing CD page at *http://oreilly.com/missingmanuals/cds/imovie2014/*.

QuickTime Player

QuickTime Player is a small, free program that comes with every Macintosh (it's in your Applications folder). While you can use it to play back movies (duh), you can also use it to upload them to video-sharing sites, to record what happens on your Mac desktop as you mouse around, and to video your own antics using the iSight camera.

There are two reasons QuickTime Player is worth knowing about. First, if you save your iMovie projects as files (Chapter 15), you can use QuickTime as the playback program, and, second, the software serves as a mini-iMovie for quick-and-dirty edits.

This chapter covers QuickTime Player version 10.3, the one that comes with any Mac capable of running the newest iMovie.

NOTE You may remember an older version of QuickTime called QuickTime Pro. That was a much more sophisticated (and complicated) piece of software, one that Apple stopped updating a few years ago. If you have it and want to put it to good use, previous editions of this book cover it in great detail.

■ QuickTime Basics

You can open a movie file in QuickTime by double-clicking its file name, by dragging it onto QuickTime's icon in the Dock, or by opening the QuickTime Player and then choosing File→Open File.

Once your movie is open, you see QuickTime's streamlined, minimalist playback window (Figure 17-1). This design works great when all you want to see is your movie. In fact, if you move your mouse away as the movie plays, the title bar and controls go away, leaving nothing but your movie. When you move your cursor back over the screen, the controls reappear. (You'll find all the controls explained in Figure 17-1.)

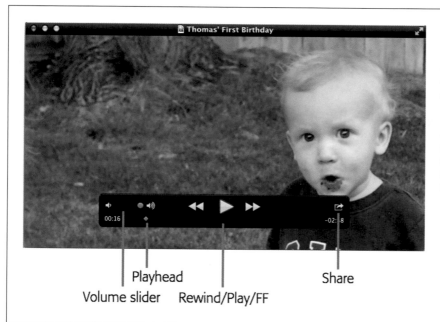

Playhead

Volume slider   Rewind/Play/FF

Share

FIGURE 17-1

In this typical QuickTime screen, you see the usual Play/Pause, Fast-Forward, and Rewind buttons. The volume slider controls your movie's sound. Drag the playhead to a specific part of your movie to play it from that point forward. Click the Share button to see your export options.

Share Using QuickTime

You can export any movie file that QuickTime can play. To see your options, click the share icon in the QuickTime toolbar (Figure 17-1) or choose File→Share from the menu bar. Here's what you'll find:

- **Email.** When you choose Share→Email, QuickTime opens a new Apple Mail message with your movie already attached. The same thing happens when you share by email from iMovie (page 246), but the QuickTime player doesn't resize the file for you—you need to manually verify that the file isn't too big to send as an attachment. To check, choose Window→Show Movie Inspector (⌘-I).

- **Messages.** Apple offers a free texting service, called Messages, with every iCloud account, but it works only on Macs, iPads, iPhones, and iPod Touches. When you choose Messages from the share menu, QuickTime opens a new message with the movie file already in the text window. Type in another Messages user's name, and then click Send. Like email, Messages has a maximum file size limit, 100 MB, which is much more generous than most email services.

- **AirDrop.** Apple's AirDrop lets you wirelessly share files with any other AirDrop-capable Mac nearby. The coolest part is that you don't need to be on a network to share. When you choose AirDrop, QuickTime launches a small window with your movie "paper-clipped" to it. On the other Mac, open the Finder and choose AirDrop from the left-hand column. When you do, that computer shows up in QuickTime's AirDrop window. Choose that computer and then click Send. On the other Mac, accept the transfer, and the file shoots from your Mac to the other one.

- **Vimeo/Facebook/YouTube/Flickr.** You can upload to all four of these services from QuickTime, just as you can from iMovie. When you choose a service by selecting File→Share, QuickTime asks you to sign into your account (or to create one—it handily launches the System Preferences' Internet Accounts window for that purpose). Once you select a service, QuickTime launches a window that lets you add the information unique to that service (like YouTube's keyword tags or Facebook's limits on who can see your video). A Share window shows you the progress as QuickTime exports and uploads the file.

  If you want to remove a shared movie, you have to go to each site and delete them manually.

Export from QuickTime

QuickTime can export into multiple formats any movie it can play. So if you have, say, a big movie that you need to make smaller so you can email it, go to the File→Export menu. There you'll see several options. When you choose 1080p, 720p, or 480p, QuickTime opens the Finder so you can save the video somewhere on your Mac. It starts the export when you click Save.

You can export just the audio portion of a film, too (choose File→Export→Audio Only). QuickTime saves the soundtrack as an .m4a file, which plays back in pretty much any modern device.

Of course, once you have the movie file, you may want to get it onto your other Apple gadgets. Syncing through iTunes is the easiest way, so consider just choosing that last export option, File→Export→iTunes.

When you do, QuickTime shows you a window like the one in Figure 17-2. Choose a quality to match your device and then click Share. QuickTime exports the movie to iTunes' Home Videos library. Then all you have to do is sync from iTunes to your device (read how on page 262).

But you might be exporting a file you'll copy to another computer for syncing through a different iTunes library. For that, choose File→Export→"iPad, iPhone, iPod Touch, & AppleTV." QuickTime lists three sets of destination iDevices (similar to what you see in Figure 17-2). Choose one by turning on the radio button for your device. When you do, QuickTime displays more details about compatible devices at the bottom of the screen. Click Save and then choose a file location.

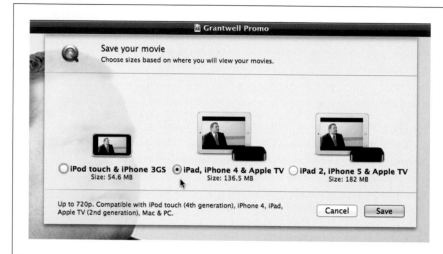

FIGURE 17-2

Here's where you export your movie from Quick-Time to iTunes. Choose any option and QuickTime gives you more detail on compatible devices.

Trim a Movie

If you need to make a quick trim to a movie, you can save loads of time by using QuickTime instead of iMovie. That's because iMovie requires you to add the movie to the Event library, create a project with it, edit the movie, and then export the result. QuickTime lets you trim the movie on the spot, with one limitation: You can edit only the ends of your movie; you can't make any cuts in the middle of it.

To trim your movie from either end, open it in QuickTime, and then choose Edit→Trim (⌘-T.) QuickTime displays a filmstrip of your movie enclosed by the same yellow editing border you see in iMovie (see Figure 17-3). It works the same way, too (page 54).

Drag the handles on either end of the yellow border inward to trim your movie. (Make sure everything you *don't* want is outside the yellow border.) As you drag the handles, the playback window shows you exactly where you'll be making the cut. Once you isolate the part of the movie you want to keep, click the yellow Trim button and QuickTime deletes all the unwanted footage.

Click File→Save. You can't save your edited movie with the same name as the original, so choose a new file name and a location for your edited movie.

Combine Videos

Another trick that works faster in QuickTime than in iMovie is combining clips. In iMovie, you'd have to import the videos, start a new project, add the clips, and then export the combined movie. In QuickTime, you can do all that in a couple of steps.

FIGURE 17-3

Trimming a movie in QuickTime couldn't be easier. Just drag the yellow handles so that everything you want to keep sits inside the yellow border, and then click Trim to cut your movie down to size.

In QuickTime, open a movie and then choose Edit→"Add Clip to End." QuickTime opens the Finder. Pick a second video file, and then click "Choose media." QuickTime combines the videos in a new file, which you can name and save wherever you like.

If you want to insert another clip into the middle of a movie, you need to split the movie first. Position the playhead on the spot where you want to insert the clip, and then choose Edit→Split Clip. QuickTime lops your movie into two pieces. Click the first clip to select it and then choose Edit→Insert Clip After Selection. Choose the clip you want to insert from the Finder, and QuickTime puts it between the two pieces.

Record with QuickTime Player

If you ever need to record a quick webcam video wishing your mom a happy birthday, record a track of audio only, or record what happens on your screen (to show a colleague how to use a program, for example), QuickTime Player makes the process easy.

Under the File menu, choose from one of three options:

- **New Movie Recording (Option-⌘-N).** This records a movie using your built-in iSight camera.

- **New Audio Recording (Control-Option-⌘-N).** This records an audio "movie" using the sound input source you select from the drop-down menu in the record window (Figure 17-4).

- **New Screen Recording (Control-⌘-N).** This records all the action on your screen as you mouse around it, including what happens as you use an application. It also records audio from the sound source you choose in the drop-down menu (click the down-arrow button in the Screen Recording window).

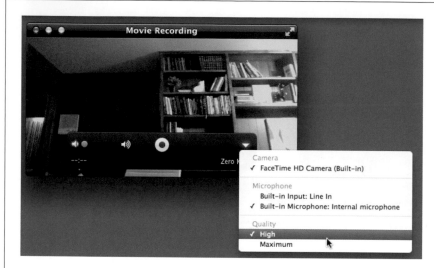

FIGURE 17-4

Recording a movie in QuickTime is easy. To change the sound source, the quality of the recording, or the save location for your movie, click ▼ in the Recording window.

TIP If you ever need to teach someone how to do something on a computer, like run Software Update, QuickTime Player's screen-recording feature is an awesome way to *show* rather than simply tell. Just record the steps, narrating as you go, and then export an email-sized version of your movie and send it on.

To start and stop recording, click the big red button in the Screen Recording window. (If you're recording your computer screen, the Stop button appears in the menu bar.) Once you stop, QuickTime automatically creates a new, untitled movie that you can save by typing in a file name and destination.

Once your movie file is ready to go, use one of the sharing options listed on page 268 to send it off to the world.

iMovie for iOS

iMovie for iOS: The Lay of the Land

Twenty years ago, editing video on a computer was a very big deal. Of course, those computers were incredibly expensive and required lots of training. But with the advent of iMovie, video editing came to the masses. Normal people could edit video on computers they could actually afford. iMovie was, historically speaking, a major breakthrough.

Today, you don't even need a *computer* to edit video. Thanks to an app called iMovie for iOS, you can cut clips on an iPhone, iPad, or iPod Touch. This is real video editing, too, not just clip-trimming. You can add titles, slo-mo effects, soundtracks, and transitions. If that doesn't blow you away, consider that you can do all of this on the same device you used to *film* your movie.

There are some limits. You won't find as many tools in iMovie for iOS as you will in the Mac version. (Notice how this section of the book is decidedly thinner?) You get fewer options for titles, transitions, sound and video effects, and themes. But in exchange for those sacrifices, you get a video editor that's easy to use *and* that fits in your pocket. (Unless you use an iPad or have small pockets.)

■ Download iMovie

iMovie for iOS, like other iPhone and iPad apps, comes from the App Store. Tap the App Store icon on your touchscreen gadget and type "iMovie" into the store's search box (or scroll to the bottom of the Featured page and tap the link "Apps Made by Apple." You'll see a list that includes iMovie.)

For any iDevice bought after September 2013, iMovie is free. If you bought your iPhone or iPad before then, the app will set you back $4.99. In either case, tap the "Free" or "$4.99" button, and then type in your Apple ID and password to start the download (Figure 18-1). iMovie shows up on your home screen, nestled in with your other apps.

NOTE iMovie is big: over 500 MB in size. Downloading and installing it takes a while, depending on the speed of your Internet connection. And you need a WiFi connection—Apple doesn't let you download apps bigger than 100 MB using a cellular network.

FIGURE 18-1

As you download iMovie from the App Store, the blue progress circle shows you how far along you are. iMovie is big, so settle in if your Internet connection is slow.

If you have, for example, both an iPhone *and* an iPad, you only have to buy iMovie once (though you have to *download* it twice). Pay once, use it on all iDevices that use the same App Store account. And iMovie is a "universal" app, which means it works great on Apple gear of all sizes.

NOTE This book uses illustrations from the iPad version of iMovie, but all the same buttons, features, and functions appear in the iPhone and iPod Touch version, too.

This book covers the latest version of iMovie for iOS (version 2.0). If you're using an older version, update it. (That means you need to be running iOS 7, too.)

NOTE Occasionally, Apple updates iMovie to squash bugs or add new features. To make sure you always have the latest and greatest version of iMovie on your device, turn on the auto-update feature (explained in Figure 18-2).

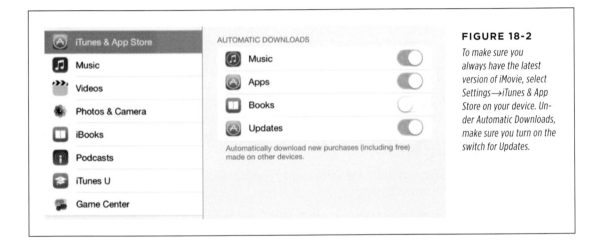

FIGURE 18-2

To make sure you always have the latest version of iMovie, select Settings→iTunes & App Store on your device. Under Automatic Downloads, make sure you turn on the switch for Updates.

The Changing Face of iMovie for iOS

Up to this point in the book, showing you how something will look on your screen hasn't been very complicated. That's because iMovie for the Mac looks pretty much the same no matter what screen it's on.

iMovie for iOS has the unique duty of working on tablets and smartphones. Like any other app, iMovie fills up these screens with its buttons and features. But because these screens come in different shapes and sizes, iMovie has to adapt its appearance. To make matters more complicated, it also has to change depending on how you're holding your device, upright or on its side.

The software gurus behind iMovie for iOS accommodated all of these scenarios, adjusting iMovie's appearance to work best on any iOS screen. But to do that, they had to move some things around.

There's a decent chance that the screenshots displayed in this book won't match what you see on your device. The button or slider in question will still be there, just maybe in a different spot on the screen. To minimize further chopping down of the Brazilian rainforest, this book generally just shows one of them and points out the particular target of your attention.

■ The Video Browser

When you open iMovie for the first time, you see the Welcome screen (Figure 18-3, top). Tapping Continue takes you to iMovie's Video Browser (Figure 18-3, bottom). If you haven't shot any movies with your device, this screen is bare, but it fills up as you capture video.

If you *have* used iMovie before, open it and select Video at the top of the screen to see the Video Browser.

The Video Browser looks much like the Event browser in iMovie for the Mac (Chapter 2). It shows you all the clips in your device's photo library, sorted by date (Figure 18-4). Each clip's duration appears on the left.

You can browse all your footage from this screen and even mark clips as Favorites (page 281). You can also share a video clip from here (page 345).

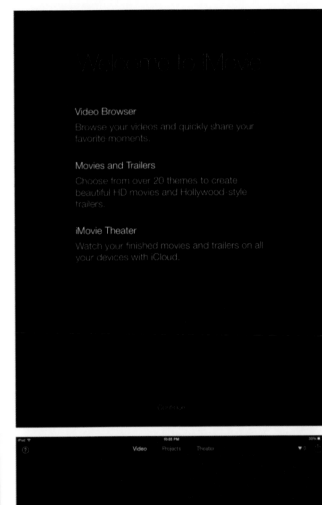

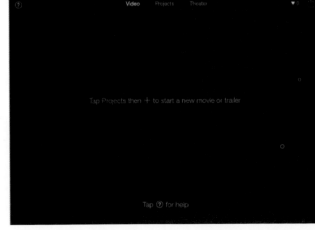

FIGURE 18-3

Top: iMovie's Welcome screen gives you an overview of the app.

Bottom: If the Video Browser is empty, it looks forlorn. Start shooting video, though, and it fills up with footage.

FIGURE 18-4

With lots of footage in the Video Browser, it looks much more exciting. Notice how iMovie automatically groups and sorts the clips by date, and displays their durations on the left.

Playback

To play a clip, tap it in the Video Browser. iMovie displays a playback screen showing the first frame of the clip and a filmstrip of the complete clip underneath (Figure 18-5).

Tap the Play button to play back the clip. (Make sure you hit the button head-on—tapping anywhere else closes the screen.) Once playback begins, tap anywhere on the screen to stop it.

FIGURE 18-5

Use the Play button to preview a video clip. The rabbit button plays back the clip at twice the speed, and the tortoise button slows it down to half speed.

If the normal playback speed doesn't suit you, use the rabbit and tortoise buttons (Figure 18-5) to quickly move through long, boring bits, or to slow down scenes with a lot of action. Neither button permanently changes the speed of your clip. (To do that, see page 298.)

Tap-Hold Scrubbing

iMovie just wouldn't be iMovie without the ability to scrub video. To scrub through a clip, drag your finger on the filmstrip; the playhead follows your finger. You can scrub forward or backward.

Scrubbing is a fast way to move around a clip at random, previewing the interesting bits as you go: Scrub to the part of a clip you want to see, tap Play in the preview screen, and then, if you like what you see, mark that passage as a Favorite (see the next section). Tap the screen again to stop playback and scrub to a different spot. This approach makes quick work of long clips.

Favorites

Scrubbing is most useful when you have a lot of footage to review. You're looking for moments that you actually want to include in your movie. Once you find them, you can save yourself mountains of time by marking them as Favorites. You'll thank yourself later, when you assemble your movie from a slew of clips.

Marking a selection as a Favorite is a two-part process. First, you isolate the part of the clip you want by adjusting the yellow border around it, and then you tap the Favorite button.

To make part of a clip a Favorite, first select the clip to call up the yellow editing border. Then, drag either end of the border until you isolate the juicy center of your footage. As you drag, the preview window displays a closeup of the current frame so you can make sure you're "cutting" the clip where you want.

Once you select the right spot—like the moment when little Petey steps up to the plate and knocks that tee ball to Timbuktu—tap the ♥ button to the right of the preview screen (Figure 18-6). A green strip along the bottom of the selection confirms that you marked it as a Favorite.

FIGURE 18-6

Marking favorite footage saves lots of time later, when you're editing. Drag the ends of the yellow selection border to match the best part of a clip, and then tap the ♥ button to mark it as a Favorite. A green stripe at the bottom of a clip shows you that that part has been favorited.

To unmark a Favorite, select the entire clip (you don't have to zero in on the segment you chose) and then hit ♥.

Sort Clips

As you shoot footage, it won't take much time before your Video Browser fills up with clips, making finding the ones you want to add to your movie tricky. You can aid your search two ways:

- **Sort by Date.** iMovie helps you find clips by sorting your footage by date. At the outset, the newest clips appear at the top. (After all, these are the ones you'll most likely need when you go into iMovie.) You can reverse the order and put older clips at the top by tapping ▼ in the toolbar (Figure 18-7) and choosing Oldest First. If you change your mind, tap the same button and then choose Newest First.

- **Only Show Favorites.** If you've invested time in marking favorite footage, you can see just your "best of" clips by tapping ▼ in the toolbar and then choosing Favorites. To see all your clips again, choose All.

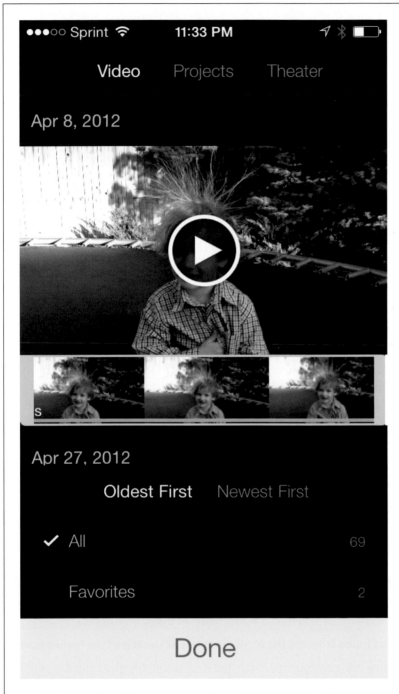

FIGURE 18-7

*When you click the ▼ button in
the toolbar, you can reverse the
chronological order in which your
clips appear by selecting Oldest
First. You can also select All to see
your entire clip library, or Favorites
to see only the clips you like.*

■ Import Video

Eventually you may want to edit some footage on your iDevice that isn't already *on* your device. For example, your brother may have been the only one brave enough to film your dad lighting the charcoal grill while everyone else ducked for cover. You can get that footage on your gadget two ways: Import it from your computer, or pull it in from another iDevice. Follow either approach and you can end the family reunion video with a—literal—bang.

> **NOTE** Video comes in all different file formats, but iMovie iOS can edit only video that will actually *play* on an iDevice. In general, that means video files whose names end in either .mov or .mp4.

Import Video from Your Computer

To get a video file from your computer onto an iPad, iPhone, or iPod Touch, use iTunes. (To get the video on your computer in the first place, see the options in Chapter 2.)

1. **The easiest way to transfer a video file from your computer to an iDevice is to save the file in a folder on your desktop.**

   On your Mac, open the Finder and select File→New Folder to create a folder where you can store your video file(s). Name it something like "Video File Transfers."

2. **Save your movie as a file in the folder you just created.**

   You can get the video as a file by importing it from a camcorder (see Chapter 2), or importing it into iMovie and then saving it as a file (click the Share icon in the iMovie toolbar and then select File). If you saved the video in iPhoto or Aperture, just drag it from those applications and drop it in the folder. The same is true for video files you get from other sources, like an email message or an iMessage. For other applications, look for a Save As or Export function in the file menu.

   The goal is to get your video file in the desktop folder you just made.

3. **Connect your iDevice to your computer via USB cable, and then open iTunes.**

   If you sync by WiFi, you don't have to connect your device first—proceed to step 4. If you don't know what WiFi syncing is, plug your gadget into your computer with the USB cable that came with it.

4. **Look for the name of your gadget under "Devices" in the left-hand column of iTunes.**

   It might appear as iPhone, iPad, iPod Touch, or, if you named your device, something like "Seth's iPad." Click its name to select the device.

5. **Choose Photos from the list of media types at the top of the iTunes screen.**

   It's not the most obvious approach, but clicking Photos gives you the option to sync video files to your iDevice, too.

6. **Tell iTunes where your video is.**

   Turn on "Sync Photos from" and then turn on "Include videos." In the drop-down menu to the right of "Sync photos from," select "Choose folder" (see Figure 18-8).

FIGURE 18-8

Syncing video files to your iDevice means using the Photo syncing feature in iTunes. Choose the folder where you stored the clips you want to sync to your iPhone, iPad, or iPod Touch, and then turn on the "Include videos" checkbox. iTunes syncs the video files in that location to your iDevice when you click Sync or Apply.

7. **When the navigation window opens, browse to the folder you created in step 1 and then click Open.**

   iTunes transfers the videos in that folder to your iDevice; it displays how many files it'll sync beside the drop-down menu.

8. **In the bottom-right corner of iTunes, click the Apply or Sync button.**

   Depending on the last time you synced your iDevice, it might take awhile to run the backup and sync new media. Once that's done, the video file will be on your iOS device.

Open iMovie on your device, and the clip should appear in the Video Browser, available for any movie project as well.

Transfer Video from One iDevice to Another

You can share video files between Apple devices in several ways. Here are the most useful, from the most to the least simple:

> **NOTE** Most of these choices involve tapping the ubiquitous Share button on your iDevice (⬆️). Sometimes it means "Share with someone else," and other times it means "Share with another app on my device."

- **AirDrop.** If both the sending and receiving devices offer AirDrop—a super-easy way to wirelessly transfer files between Apple devices—this is probably the best way to go.

NOTE To use AirDrop, you need an iPhone 5 or later, a fourth-generation iPad or later, any iPad Mini, or at least a fifth-generation iPod Touch. And both devices need to be running iOS 7 or later.

On the destination device, slide your finger up from the bottom of the screen to call up the Command Center. Tap the AirDrop button and make sure it's set to be seen by the other device. (The easiest way to do that is to set AirDrop to "Everyone"—see Figure 18-9.) That device name should appear in the list iMovie displays when you choose the Share button. Tap it and the other device is asked to confirm the transfer. Click Accept on the destination device; the video clip copies itself over into the Camera Roll.

- **iMessages.** If your device doesn't offer AirDrop, Apple's iMessages service works great, too, with one caveat: You can send files up to only 100 MB in size—about a minute of video shot on an iPhone or iPad.

  On the device with the video clip, select the file and then tap the Share button. If your clip is small enough, choose Messages, and then enter the iMessage contact information for the other device (usually an email address or a phone number). Click Send and the clip shows up on the other device. Press the Play button. In the screen that plays the video, find and tap the Share button again. Choose Save Video, and the clip will appear in iMovie the next time you open it.

TIP You can even send a message to yourself if you want to send clips between two of your own iOS devices. This also works for sending clips from a Mac with the Messages application installed.

- **Dropbox, or some other third-party file-sharing service.** All kinds of companies let you easily share files between devices by way of a free storage locker on the Web. Dropbox is one of the most popular, there's an iOS app for it, and it offers storage large enough (2 GB) so you can share at least some video files. All the services provide simple instructions for transferring files to and importing them from the online locker. Once you have the clip on your iDevice, use the Share button to save it.

- **Email.** Remember email? You can always email a file between iPhones, iPads, or iPod Touches, and then use the Share button to save it to the destination device. The only drawback to email—and it's a big one for video files—is that most Internet service providers limit the size of file attachments. If you're sharing an HD-quality clip, you'll have room for only a few seconds' worth of footage.

- **Save the file to your computer, and then sync it to your iOS device.** If all else fails, you can sync video files from an iDevice to your computer and then to another iOS device using the steps described on page 262. Either save to and import from the same folder on your computer, or use different folders. If you do the latter, you need to manually copy the video file from one folder to the other.

1:41 ———————————— -1:57

You can make yourself discoverable to everyone or only people in your contacts.

Off

Contacts Only

Everyone

Cancel

FIGURE 18-9

AirDrop is an easy and powerful way to share clips or projects from iMovie. To use it, open the Control Center (slide your finger up from the bottom of your iOS screen), and then choose AirDrop. Select Everyone from the menu that opens, shown here. Now any nearby iOS device will be able to see yours.

iMovie for iOS Projects

Now that you have some video to work with, you can start a new movie project or trailer. This chapter deals with the basics of editing a movie, though many of the same processes apply to trailers, too. If you're set on making a trailer as your first project, review this chapter and then head over to Chapter 23.

◼ Create a New Movie

When you open iMovie, you see a toolbar with three options: Video, Projects, and Theater. Chapter 18 describes the Video Browser; Chapter 24 covers iMovie Theater. For now, pay attention to the Projects link (Figure 19-1).

To create your first movie, click Projects. That takes you to a screen that says "Tap + to start a new movie or trailer." Do that and then choose Movie from the next screen.

Pick a Theme

Once you choose Movie, iMovie opens a theme screen so you can choose from the eight offered. The theme you choose will determine which titles, transitions, and other elements your movie uses.

> **TIP** Themes in iMovie for iOS work just like they do in iMovie for the Mac, except that there's no No Theme option. Don't sweat it, though. If you want your movie to be clean and simple, without excessive animations or colors, choose the Simple theme to keep things, well, simple.

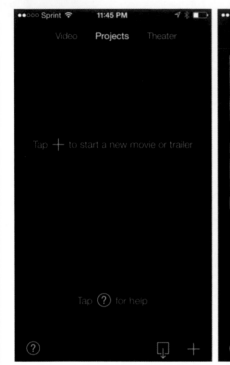 

FIGURE 19-1

Left: The Projects view will be empty when you first get started. Tap the + button to create your first movie.

Right: Once you have a few projects and trailers under your belt, you can tap one of the thumbnails to preview it or to do more editing.

All eight of the themes found in iMovie for iOS match ones found in iMovie for the Mac. That's a good thing. If you want to edit a single project both at home and on the fly—between your desktop Mac and an iDevice, in other words, just choose a theme common to both machines.

Don't stress out when you choose a theme; you can always change it later. To do that, tap ✿ as you edit a project; iMovie displays all eight themes again. Pick a new one. iMovie automatically updates all the theme-specific elements in your film, like the titles and background music.

■ Find Clips

Once you select a theme and click Create Movie, iMovie takes you to the Timeline screen so you can start building your movie. Since you haven't selected any clips yet, the screen is pretty barren, with a few tools and silhouette placeholders for your clips (see Figure 19-2).

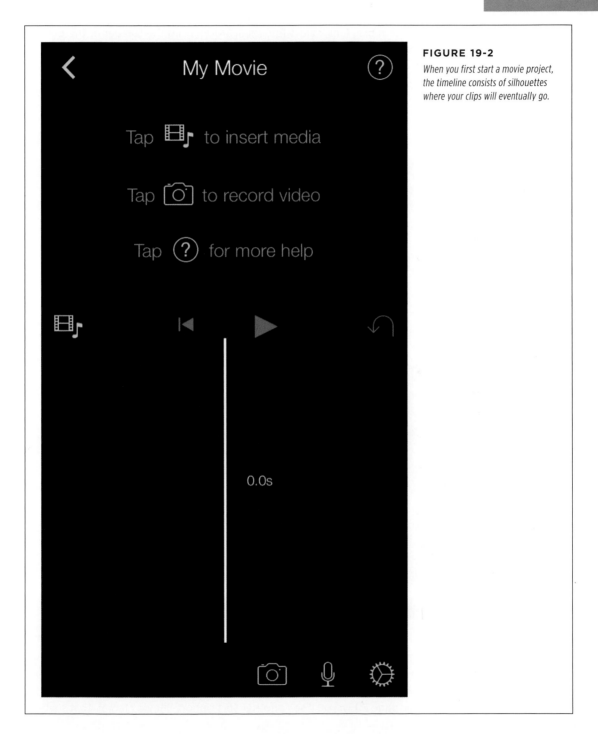

FIGURE 19-2

When you first start a movie project, the timeline consists of silhouettes where your clips will eventually go.

To add clips, tap the Add Media button—the tiny film strip/musical note icon circled in Figure 19-3. That opens the Media screen, where you see all the videos, photos, and music stored on your iDevice. You generally see your video clips first. To see your photos or music files, select Photos or Audio from the toolbar at the bottom of the screen.

NOTE If you're using an iPad in landscape mode, you don't need to tap Add Media. You can browse your clips from the top-right corner of the screen.

FIGURE 19-3

The Add Media button (top, circled) gives you access to all your clips, photos, and music files (bottom).

To sort your footage, tap < on the Media screen. You can choose to see all your clips (select All), your best-of clips (choose Favorites), or footage shot with your device's camera app (choose Camera Roll). If you use the camera app *within* iMovie to shoot footage (see page 295), you'll see another sort option, iMovie Media—that's where iMovie-shot clips live (yes, in iMovie for iOS, you can shoot video from both the camera app and from within iMovie itself. The clips show up in different places).

Once you choose a sort option, all the clips in that group show up as filmstrips. You can scrub each one by drawing your finger across it.

Rename a Project

As soon as you add a clip to a movie project, iMovie automatically saves the project with the uninspiring name "My Movie 1." If you keep creating projects without renaming them, iMovie names each new one in sequence, so your second opus will be "My Movie 2." If you want something catchier, like "My Movie 2: The Return of My Movie," you need to rename the project.

You do that from a movie's Project Info page (Figure 19-4), which you can get to two ways. One is by opening iMovie and then selecting Projects in the toolbar, which shows you all your movies-in-progress. Tap the thumbnail of a movie to open its Project Info page. The other way is from the timeline, when you're in the process of editing a movie. From there, tap < in the top-left corner.

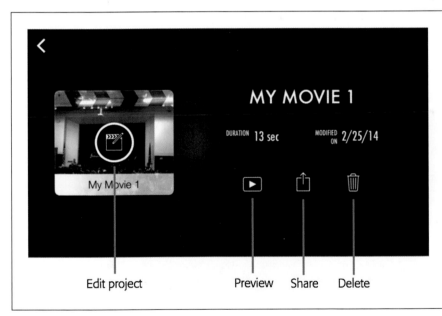

FIGURE 19-4

The Project Info screen offers all kinds of useful information related to your project, like its duration, the date it was last edited, and playback and sharing buttons. To rename your project, tap the name and type in a new one.

Either way, iMovie opens the Project Info screen, which includes your movie's name, duration, and the date you last edited it. Tap the placeholder movie name, and iMovie calls up the iOS keyboard and places your cursor at the end of the text box. Tap the X there to delete the current moniker and type in a new one.

Find Audio and Photos

You'll probably want to add photos and music or sound effects to your movie, too. This chapter focuses on video, while two other chapters discuss audio (Chapter 21) and photos (Chapter 22).

Build Your Movie

If you're accustomed to iMovie on the Mac, you might assume that you can drag a clip from the Media screen into your timeline, but it doesn't work that way in iMovie for iOS. You first have to select the clip, which calls up the yellow editing border and floating menu shown in Figure 19-5.

You can use all or part of the clip in your movie. To use just part of it, drag either end of the yellow border. When you finish, tap the swirling down-arrow button to add the clip or a clip section to your movie.

> **TIP** You can add a clip to the timeline one other way: If you're in the Video Browser (page 278) and find a clip you want to use, select it and then tap the Share button (⬆). From there, choose Create Movie. iMovie gives you the option to start a new project or add the clip to an existing project. If you choose the latter, iMovie adds it to the end of that project's timeline.

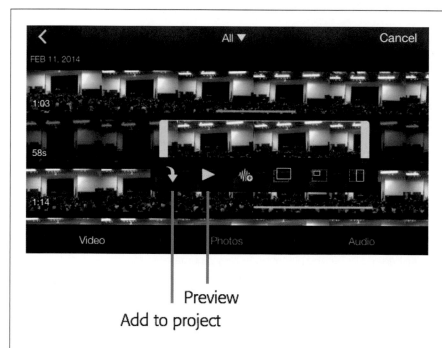

FIGURE 19-5

Use this floating menu to add footage from the Media screen to your project. Drag the ends of the yellow border to select just part of a clip. Press ▶ to preview what you've selected. Press the down arrow to add the selection to your project.

Preview

Add to project

As you add clips to your movie, your timeline starts to fill in nicely. To see different parts of your movie, drag the clips in the timeline (in iMovie for iOS, the playhead remains stationary, and you move the clips themselves to scrub through your project). The white playhead line marks the frame you see in the preview screen above. The position of that line matters when you add clips—each time you add a new clip, iMovie slips it in *after* the clip that's currently under the playhead.

Add Favorites

Remember all that work you did marking favorite footage in Chapter 18? (Page 282 explains the process.) Now your hard work pays off. In the Media screen, choose ▼→Favorites so iMovie shows you only the good stuff. Select and add footage as described in Figure 19-5.

If you didn't mark favorite clips earlier, you don't have to go back out to the Video Browser. You can flag them right from the Media screen. Tap ▼ at the top of the screen and then choose "Find more favorites" from the menu that opens. iMovie displays your clips in a new screen. Select one, trim it by dragging the yellow borders, and then hit the ♥ button to mark it as a Favorite. Tap Done when you finish.

Shoot New Video

You can film footage or shoot photos from within iMovie itself; those recordings appear right on your timeline.

Find the camera icon in the iMovie toolbar (Figure 19-6) and tap it to open the Camera app you know and love. Once you shoot some footage or take a photo, preview it and then choose to reshoot it or save it to the timeline.

FIGURE 19-6

Left, top: The Camera button lets you film video or shoot photos and save them right in your timeline.

Left, bottom: The camera appears and works just as it normally does.

Right: Once you finish shooting, you can reshoot the clip or video, preview it, or add it to your timeline (by tapping Use Video).

This is a great strategy to use if you have your movie planned out in your head and you just need to shoot the footage. Go from one shot to the next, adding each to the timeline as you shoot. If a take doesn't work, tap Retake instead of Use Video. Get good at this and you'll be cranking out blockbusters in record time.

iMovie Media vs. Camera Roll

iMovie automatically gives you access to any videos or photos stored on your iDevice. It also lets you shoot and then save videos and photos straight to the timeline (see page 295). But iMovie will be stingy with that media unless you tell it to play nice and share.

At the heart of every iDevice is the Camera Roll, a central repository for photos and video, available to any and all installed apps. iMovie taps into the Camera Roll to find stuff to use in your projects.

But when you shoot footage and images through iMovie, it keeps those files in iMovie alone. Other apps can't access them until you tell iMovie to share them to the Camera Roll.

To do that, tap ▼ on the Media screen (page 280) and then tap "Manage local media." From there, you can see how iMovie highlights locally stored clips with a gray Import button (⬇) and a red trash can. The Import button saves the clip to your Camera Roll, making it available to other apps.

Be careful with the trash can button. Tap it once and your clip goes away forever, without so much as a warning screen.

Add Clips as Overlays

Like iMovie for the Mac, iMovie for iOS lets you insert clips as cutaway, picture-in-picture, or side-by-side shots (explained starting on page 140). iMovie for iOS calls these overlays. (In the Mac version, they're called connected clips.)

To add an overlay clip, first position the playhead where you want the overlay to appear. Now select a clip in the Add Media screen, and then tap the ••• button. You see three buttons for creating a cutaway, picture-in-picture, or side-by-side overlay (see Figure 19-7). Tap the desired button, and iMovie inserts the clip as the chosen type of overlay. It shows up as a small filmstrip hovering above your main one.

Tap the overlay filmstrip in your storyboard to make these custom edits:

- For a cutaway, you can zoom the video (page 299).

- For a picture in picture clip, you can tap the compass button in the Viewer and resize or reposition the inset window.

- For a side by side clip you can position it to the left, right, top, or bottom using the buttons in the toolbar.

- You can change the type of overlay you inserted using the toolbar buttons that mimic the ones in Figure 19-7.

- Finally, you can make audio adjustments in the toolbar (page 323).

If you change your mind, you can delete an overlay clip by selecting it and tapping 🗑.

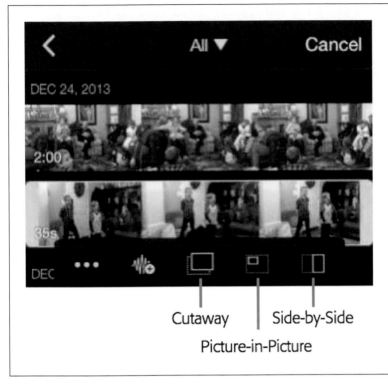

FIGURE 19-7

Add an overlay clip (a cutaway, picture in picture, or side by side clip) using one of these three buttons on the Add Media screen.

Reposition Clips

To reorder a clip in the timeline, press down on it (lightly) until it attaches itself to your finger. Then drag it to its new position and let go. The clips underneath slide around to make space for the one you just dropped in.

Edit Clips in the Timeline

Once you have your clips assembled in the timeline, you can edit them by selecting them and using the tools iMovie provides.

You can adjust a clip's final edit, change its theme titles, speed it up or slow it down, split it so you can insert a new clip in between, freeze a frame, duplicate the clip, zoom in on an area of it, and rotate the clip.

You see options to do all this when you select an individual clip in the timeline. On iPhones, you find these tools spread across two "pages" of options (see Figure 19-8).

Tap the second, small dot beside Title and Speed to get to the second page. On iPads, all the tools fit on a single toolbar.

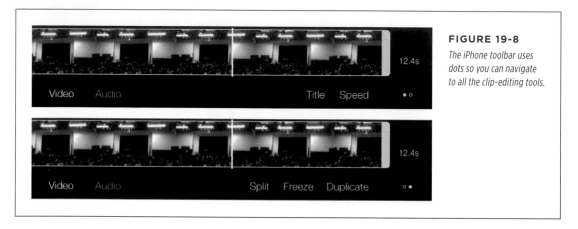

FIGURE 19-8

The iPhone toolbar uses dots so you can navigate to all the clip-editing tools.

If you don't see the tools, make sure you have a clip selected in the timeline and that you have Video (not Audio) selected in the toolbar.

Re-Edit a Clip

You may find that a clip starts too late or ends too soon, or just goes on too long. Don't waste time deleting it and adding a newly edited version back in. Make the adjustments right in the timeline.

Tap the clip to call up the yellow border, and then drag either end to shorten or lengthen it. Then tap anywhere outside the yellow border to unselect the clip and move on.

Shortening clips is neat, but adding to them is pretty advanced. iMovie for iOS can do this because it edits by reference, just as iMovie for the Mac does. (See page 35 for an explanation of reference editing.)

Edit Movie Titles

Most movies have titles (text) that include things like the name of the movie, the actors' names, subtitles, and so forth. iMovie for iOS's titling feature is explained in detail in the next chapter.

Change a Clip's Speed

Sometimes the normal pace of life just doesn't do a moment justice. iMovie for iOS can change the speed of a clip. You can recreate a frenzied Benny Hill shtick or the slo-mo finish-line victory in *Chariots of Fire*.

Select a clip and then choose Speed in the toolbar. iMovie displays a timing slider (Figure 19-9). Drag it to the left to slow a clip down to as little as one-quarter the normal speed. When you do, a little tortoise appears in the top-left corner of the clip. Drag the slider to the right to speed up the clip by as much as twice the normal speed. A rabbit appears in the corner of the clip.

TIP Normally, slowed-down footage looks a little jumpy, because it's shot at 30 frames per second, and slowing it down makes the individual frames more obvious to the human eye. But if you have an iPhone 5s and you know you want to play back footage in slow motion, you can shoot that footage at 120 frames per second (with your Camera app open, just swipe to the Slo-Mo setting). That way, it'll look smooth when you slow it down.

Split Clips

To break up a clip so you can put another one in the middle, first drag the filmstrip so the playhead sits over the spot where you want the split. Tap the clip to select it and then choose Split in the toolbar. iMovie dutifully cuts the clip in two.

NOTE If you don't want a clip split anymore, tap the Undo button (page 303) immediately after you split the clip (though a split clip doesn't affect playback). Or, if it's too late for that, you can always delete the two parts (🗑) and then add the whole clip back in from the Media screen.

FIGURE 19-9

Use the speed tool to change the pace of your clip. Drag the slider left to go slower and right to speed up.

Freeze a Frame

In iMovie, you can turn a frame of video into a still image that you can use in your project. Page 329 explains how.

Duplicate a Clip

You can use more than one copy of a clip in the timeline without having to find it in the Media screen and add a second copy. Select the clip in the timeline, and then choose Duplicate in the toolbar. Now you have two copies to work with.

Don't worry about taking up extra storage on your device—remember, iMovie edits by reference, not by making multiple copies of clips (see page 35).

Zoom in on a Clip

Shooting on an iPhone or an iPad has one big drawback: It doesn't have a zoom lens. The best way to get a closeup while you shoot is to use your feet, but that won't help you with footage you've already shot.

To zoom in on a clip after the fact, tap it in the timeline and then tap the small magnifying glass in the preview window. Once tapped, the glass turns blue, indicating that you turned on the zoom tool.

Now you spread two fingers on the glass to zoom in, as though you were stretching a sheet of rubber to make it bigger. Then, if necessary, use one finger to drag the zoomed clip until the part you want fills the frame.

You can zoom out on a clip by pinching with two fingers. That can come in handy when you rotate a clip (see the next section), so that the whole thing fits your screen. Doing this creates big black bars on either side of the image, but at least you'll be able to see everything in the frame.

Rotate a Clip

Without repeating the tirade against smartphone footage shot in the vertical orientation, suffice it to say that filming with your iPhone upright (instead of on its side) is a bad idea (see page 73). Knowing that now doesn't fix the footage after the fact, however. Lucky for you, iMovie offers a way to rotate a clip in your timeline.

This trick requires some finger dexterity. Select a clip in the timeline, and then put two fingers on the preview screen. Now twist your fingers in a circle right or left, dragging the clip with you. iMovie rotates the clip a quarter-turn in that direction. Repeat as necessary. A quarter-turn takes vertical footage and crops it to fill the screen.

If you want to see more of the image, zoom in on the clip so the whole thing fills the screen. Doing this creates big black bars on either side of the image, but at least you'll be able to see everything in the frame. If you end up with the wrong part of the rotated clip showing, drag the clip with your finger until you get the framing you want.

TIP Rotating footage can have artistic value, too. For example, you might want part of your movie upside-down to make the audience feel unbalanced. Two quarter-turns will make a clip play upside-down.

■ Play Back Your Movie

As you work on your project, you'll want to repeatedly review it to make sure it looks right. There are two ways to preview your movie.

Preview from the Editing Screen

Tap the ▶ button under the preview window to play back your movie-in-progress from the playhead forward. To watch your movie from the beginning, drag the timeline all the way to the start of the first clip before tapping ▶. (The back-arrow button next to it takes you to the start of the clip or transition currently under the playhead.)

Preview Full Screen

To see your movie at its best, tap < from the Timeline screen. That brings you to the Project Info screen, the one where you can rename your movie. Tap the Play button on the movie thumbnail (noted in Figure 19-4) to see your opus full-size.

Save Your Project to the Camera Roll

Page 296 explains how to save video you shot from within iMovie to your Camera Roll. Of course, a completed project, edits and all, could be just as worthy of saving to your Camera Roll so you can share it later (see page 351). From the Project Info screen, tap ⬆ and then choose Save Video. iMovie ships it over to your Camera Roll, where it's available to other apps on your phone.

Import Projects from Other iDevices

Let's say you shoot a movie with your iPhone and put a simple rough cut together. Now you're back home and want to edit it on the roomier screen of your iPad.

The easiest way to do this, by far, is to use AirDrop, a feature that lets you share projects and movies between iOS devices. Page 353 explains the AirDrop process for iOS in detail, so flip ahead to read more. But not all iOS devices can use AirDrop. (You need an iPhone 5 or later, a fourth-generation iPad or later, any iPad mini, or a fifth-gen iPod Touch or later.)

Lucky for you, you can transfer the project between devices using iTunes. These steps describe the process from iPhone to iPad, but they work for any iOS devices going in either direction:

1. **Tap the Share button (⬆) in the Project Info screen, and then choose iTunes.**

    iMovie displays a message telling you where to find the project when you connect your iPhone to iTunes.

2. **Connect your iPhone to your computer and then open iTunes.**

    If you sync by WiFi, your iPhone may already be listed in the Devices section of iTunes. If you don't see it, connect your iPhone using the USB cable that came with the device.

3. **Select your device in iTunes.**

    Look for your gadget under Devices in the left-hand column of iTunes. It may be listed as iPhone, iPad, iPod Touch, or, if you named your device, it'll be something like "Joanne's iPhone." When you find it, click its name to select it.

4. **Choose Apps from the list of media types at the top of the iTunes window.**

5. **Scroll down to the File Sharing section of the screen. Under Apps, select iMovie.**

   When you do, iTunes displays a list of projects you can export (Figure 19-10).

6. **Choose the project you want to transfer, and then click "Save to."**

   Save the project to a spot you'll remember, like the desktop.

7. **Connect your iPad to iTunes and then repeat steps 2–6 to get to the same iMovie Documents list.**

8. **Click Add in the lower-right corner and then choose the project you saved in step 6.**

   iTunes copies the project into iMovie on your iPad.

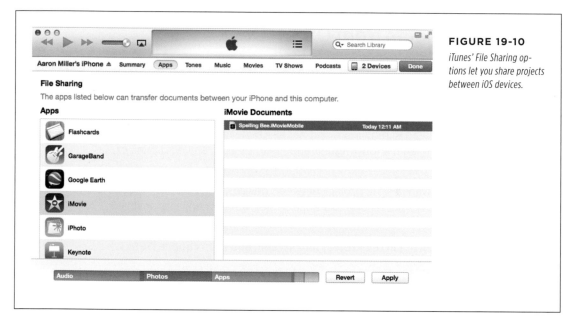

FIGURE 19-10

iTunes' File Sharing options let you share projects between iOS devices.

9. **Open iMovie on your iPad and then tap Projects at the top of the screen.**

   You'll see all your projects listed.

10. **Tap ⬇ and then choose the project you just copied from iTunes.**

    The project you originally edited on your iPhone is now an iPad project. iMovie copied all the clips, sounds, and photos you used in the project, so nothing is missing.

■ The Undo Button

You can use the Undo button in iMovie for iOS if you remember two things: First, you can only undo steps in order. Second, if you do a bunch of other things on your iDevice and then go back into iMovie, there's a good chance that your undo list will be erased from iMovie's memory.

Redoing

Unlike iMovie for the Mac, iMovie for iOS has no Redo command. The only way to redo an edit is to manually recreate it.

iMovie for iOS Themes, Titles, and Transitions

Y ou must choose a theme for every iMovie project you make on your iPhone or iPad. A theme is a collection of coordinated titles, transitions, and music that tie your shots together and make your movie look professionally done. Each theme comes with three special titles, one unique transition style, and a theme song.

Besides the titles and transitions that come as part of a theme, iMovie offers an additional eight titles and four transitions. That's not a terribly big catalog, but it includes the most popular ones. (The truth is, you should be keeping things simple most of the time anyway. It helps people focus on your *movie*, instead of your titles and transitions.)

This chapter covers theme basics and then talks more about using titles and transitions.

Themes

What does a theme actually do for you? Unless you can carry a film post-production team around in your pocket, complete with editors, animators, and musicians, a theme is the easiest way to give your project the appearance of a professionally produced movie.

iMovie for iOS offers eight themes: Modern, Bright, Playful, Neon, Travel, Simple, News, and CNN iReport. Each one has an analogous theme in iMovie for the Mac; if you want to edit the same movie on both your portable and desktop device (by transferring the movie between the two—see page 301), choose one these themes.

Theme titles and transitions behave just like non-theme titles and transitions (explained more on pages 307 and 310). Just know that you can't use a title or transition from one theme with the titles or transitions from another one. With themes, it's all or nothing.

Change a Theme

You can change the theme for a project any time. Tap ✿ from the Timeline screen and iMovie shows your eight themes again (Figure 20-1). Tap one, and iMovie updates all the theme elements in your project.

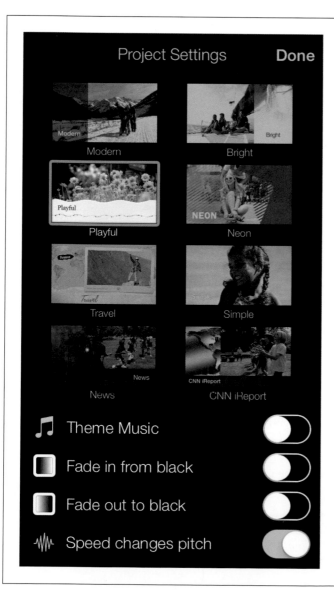

FIGURE 20-1

You can choose from eight themes in iMovie for iOS, and lucky for you the choice isn't permanent. Use this menu to change to a new theme whenever it strikes your fancy.

Turn Theme Music On or Off

Apple had iMovie's theme music professionally recorded to match the theme titles and transitions. For example, the music for the News theme sounds like what you'd hear a TV network play to introduce a breaking story.

To turn theme music on, tap ⚙ (Figure 20-1). You'll see a set of switches, one of which is Theme Music. Turn it on (tap the switch to the right), and a green band appears beneath your video clips, representing the audio. When you play back your movie, the theme music plays along with it.

NOTE Like other audio in iMovie for iOS (Chapter 21), theme music won't play longer than your movie does. If you want the music to keep playing, add more video or pictures, or a solid black image (a tip explained on page 210).

Use the same switch to turn off the theme music.

TIP Unlike titles and transitions, you can use the music from any theme in any project. If you like the titles and transitions from one theme but the music from another, choose the theme with the right visual elements and then bring in the other theme's song, as explained on page 316.

■ Titles

Pretty much every movie uses onscreen text at some point, so Apple engineers were sure to include a convenient way to title your features in iMovie for iOS.

While the titling tools are handy, they're more rudimentary than the ones in iMovie for the Mac. For example, you can't customize the font, color, or alignment of your iOS titles. Also, and more frustratingly, titles in iMovie for iOS only appear superimposed over clips; you can't see them during a transition effect, nor can you have iMovie for iOS display a black background behind titles, as you can in the Mac version of iMovie.

TIP To put titles over a black background in iMovie for iOS, you can create a black JPG image on your Mac and sync the photo to your iDevice. Or you can cover up your camera lens on the device and snap a blacked-out picture. Either way, add the image to your project as a photo (Chapter 22), and then superimpose your titles over the image using the steps that follow.

Add Titles

Follow these steps to add a title to your movie:

1. **Tap the clip where the title will appear.**

   Because titles can appear only over clips or photos, not in between clips, you have to choose a clip or a photo.

The ⓘ Button and the Toolbar

In most cases, the iPhone and iPad versions of iMovie are so much alike, there's really no need to explain the differences between the two.

One noticeable difference, however, is the ⓘ button, which only lives in the iPhone version of iMovie, and only appears when you select a video clip in your project. (It replaces the camera button.) This button gives you access to the toolbar that holds most of the features described in this part of the book.

If you're using the iPad version of iMovie, you'll go crazy looking for the ⓘ button; it's not there. An iPad has enough real estate that iMovie doesn't need to hide the toolbar when you're not using it.

So whenever you see a reference to the toolbar in this chapter, you can get to it on an iPhone with the ⓘ button. (In most cases, you can also just double-tap an item in your timeline to see the toolbar.)

2. **Tap Title in the toolbar.**

   iMovie shows you a row of tools (mostly) related to editing titles.

3. **Select the "T" icon to choose a title style.**

   When you select the Text button, iMovie opens a screen that previews the nine title styles available to your movie (Figure 20-2). The first one is theme-specific and changes depending on your movie's theme. The other eight are consistent, no matter which theme you use.

4. **Choose the title placement.**

   If you select the theme-specific title (the first choice on the titles style screen), you get three placement options: Opening, Middle, and Closing. Choose one, and iMovie places a title that matches your theme—choose Opening from the Travel theme's placement options, for example, iMovie displays a freeze frame from your movie as though it were a photo lying on a map.

   The other title styles come in two versions: Center and Lower. Center puts the title right in the middle of your frame, and Lower positions it in the bottom-left or -right corner, depending on the title style you choose.

5. **Type in your title text.**

   When you choose a title placement, iMovie previews it in the video window above, complete with placeholder text. Tap the text, and iMovie brings up the keyboard so you can replace it. Tap Done when you finish.

Change a Title

You can change any aspect of a title by following these same steps, but using the clip where you placed the title. Be aware, though, that text that looks good with one title style may not work well with another. Preview your title any time by tapping ▶.

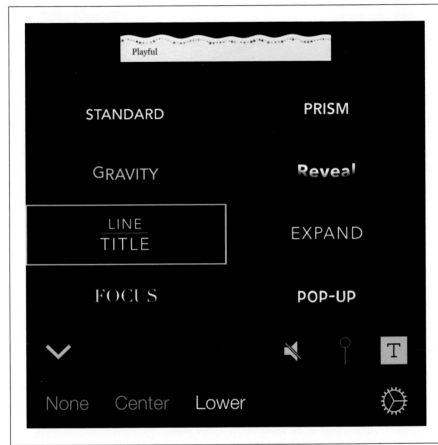

FIGURE 20-2

All these title styles are available to your projects, except the first one, which is always theme-inspired— it changes depending on the theme you chose for your project.

NOTE In iMovie for iOS, titles cover an entire clip. That's really annoying if the clip is long. To fix this, reduce the title's onscreen time by splitting the clip. Select the clip, position the playhead where you want the title to end, and then choose Split from the toolbar (on the iPhone toolbar, select the second "dot" to see the Split option). Now your title covers only the first section of the clip.

Remove a Title

If you have title regret, you can remove a title by choosing None as the title placement. (See step 4 on page 308.)

TIP In one of the themes—Travel—the custom title actually displays information about your location. Specifically, it shows the location in the letter postmark.

If you shot your footage on a location-aware device, like an iPhone or an iPad with cellular networking, the location data is embedded in the video file. iMovie uses this info to automatically choose the location for your title.

If iMovie gets it wrong, adjust the location by tapping the pin button found in the Titles toolbar. From there, tap the compass arrow to choose your current location or the magnifying glass to choose from a huge list of locations. In either case, iMovie updates the title with the new postmark.

■ Transitions

A transition occurs when your film goes from one clip to the next, even if that happens without any sort of animation (in which case the transition is called a *cut*). Of course, there are lots of other kinds of transitions, like fades and wipes. iMovie for iOS offers six transitions. (If you were hoping for more transition choices, consider editing your movie on a Mac. iMovie for the Mac offers a whopping 24 transition styles.)

You can't add a transition at the start or end of an iMovie for iOS project. If you want your movie to fade in at the start or out at the end, choose the ✿ from the Timeline screen and tap the Fade In or Fade Out switches.

Edit a Transition

iMovie automatically embeds the most popular transition, the cross-dissolve, between each of your clips. That's sometimes handy, but you might prefer one of the other five styles.

To edit a transition, go to the Timeline screen and tap the transition in your storyboard. That brings up the transitions toolbar (Figure 20-3). iMovie doesn't identify your choices with anything more helpful than a set of buttons that look like characters from an alien language. Figure 20-3 demystifies them.

With the transitions toolbar in view, you can change the style, timing, and sound of a transition:

- **Style.** Tap any of the six title styles. For Slide and Wipe, you can change the direction of the transition, and for Fade, you can fade through black or fade through white.

- **Timing.** A transition takes time, and you can edit its duration by tapping the time readout in the toolbar. Choose from 0.5, 1, 1.5, or 2 seconds.

NOTE If you can't embed a transition with a particular duration, it's likely because the underlying clips aren't long enough to accommodate the transition length. Page 88 explains in more detail.

- **Sound.** When you transition from one clip to the next, iMovie can play a sound effect to accompany the move. Each transition has its own sound. Mute or unmute it using the speaker button in the toolbar.

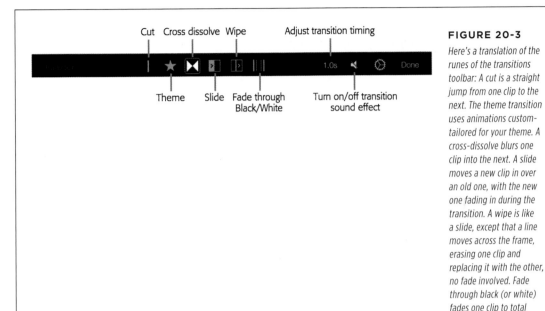

Cut   Cross dissolve   Wipe   Adjust transition timing

Theme   Slide   Fade through   Turn on/off transition
                 Black/White   sound effect

FIGURE 20-3

Here's a translation of the runes of the transitions toolbar: A cut is a straight jump from one clip to the next. The theme transition uses animations custom-tailored for your theme. A cross-dissolve blurs one clip into the next. A slide moves a new clip in over an old one, with the new one fading in during the transition. A wipe is like a slide, except that a line moves across the frame, erasing one clip and replacing it with the other, no fade involved. Fade through black (or white) fades one clip to total darkness (or whiteness) before fading the next one in the same way.

Precision Editor on an iPad

If you use iMovie on an iPad, two yellow arrows may appear below a transition when you select it. Tap the arrows and, holy smokes, you see a version of the very powerful Precision Editor found in iMovie for the Mac (page 68).

The iPad version isn't nearly as potent as the Mac's, but it's certainly useful. As you can see in Figure 20-4, your clips overlap at the point identified by the two yellow editing handles.

Drag the top handle to choose the exact spot where the top clip transitions to the bottom clip. (Pinch to zoom in on the timeline so you can find just the right spot.) The bottom handle does the same thing but chooses the transition for the bottom clip.

Tap the yellow arrows to close the Precision Editor and save your adjustment.

"Delete" Transitions Altogether

To cut from one clip to the next—that is, to have no transition effect at all—you have to select the cut icon from the transitions toolbar (Figure 20-3). iMovie for iOS always includes a transition in the timeline, even if that "transition" is a simple cut.

FIGURE 20-4

The iPad offers a mini version of the Precision Editor. Drag either of the yellow handles to reposition your cut from one clip to the next.

iMovie for iOS Music, Narration, and Sound

Professional sound mixing can be incredibly complicated. And while iMovie for iOS doesn't have a comprehensive sound tool—it's missing powerful tools like an equalizer, automatic ducking, and audio effects—it does let you do the most important types of audio editing, like fading audio, adjusting volume levels, and adding narration.

◼ Two Kinds of Audio

Every piece of audio you add to your project can live in two places in the timeline: the foreground or the background. It might seem like a strange distinction at first (why not just have all the audio in the foreground?), but there's a reason:

- **Foreground** audio clips, which appear as light-blue stripes under the video clips in your timeline (Figure 21-1), work just as they do in other video editing programs. You can drag them around and place them where you want, so they start and end at just the right moment in your movie. As you edit the video clips in your project, a detached foreground audio clip stays anchored to the spot where you left it. If you have multiple foreground audio clips, you can position them so they overlap one another. You can even make foreground audio play past the end of your video.

NOTE While you can overlap foreground audio, you get a maximum of three foreground tracks. When you try to add a fourth, iMovie tells you that the spot under your playhead is full.

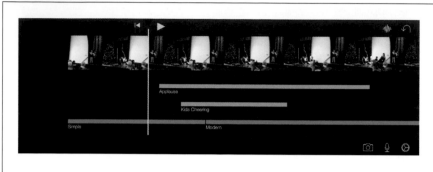

FIGURE 21-1

*The light-blue lines rep-
resent foreground audio
clips, while the green line
represents background au-
dio. Notice that the green
line starts at the beginning
of the project, while the
foreground clips can be
positioned at will.*

- **Background.** Background audio appears as a green stripe under your video clips (Figure 21-2). It's the perfect place for sound that you don't want to manage or line up to a specific spot, like background music. iMovie automatically plays background audio from the very beginning of your movie. If your clips end, so does the background track. You can't overlap background audio, so if you put multiple clips in the background, iMovie plays them sequentially. (You can reorder them by dragging them, however.)

> **TIP** When you use theme music in the background, iMovie automatically repeats it so that it plays through your entire movie.

In summary, foreground audio is for sounds you need to position in a particular spot in your movie. Background audio is the kind you want to set and forget, allowing iMovie to manage when it starts and ends so you don't have to.

Swap Foreground and Background Audio

There aren't any rules limiting what kind of audio can go in the foreground and what kind can go in the background, so feel free to switch a clip from one to the other to suit your needs. To swap a foreground (or background) clip, tap it and then choose Background (or Foreground) from the toolbar. iMovie makes the change.

> **NOTE** If you have a foreground clip positioned at just the right spot and change it to a background clip, iMovie won't remember that position if you decide to make it a foreground clip later. You'll have to line it up at the right spot again. (That is, unless you immediately tap the Undo button.)

▇ Add Audio to Your Project

All the audio you add to a project comes from the same location in iMovie: the Media screen, which you get to by tapping the Add Media button (on an iPad held on its side instead of upright, the media screen sits in the top-right corner). You used this same button when you added video clips to your project.

Tap Add Media and then choose Audio. iMovie shows you a list of sound types (Figure 21-2). Theme Music lists all the little, minute-long jingles Apple recorded to go along with your movie's theme. Sound Effects offers dozens of cool and useful sounds that augment a movie, like footsteps or a ticking clock. (Foley artists create sound effects to round out a movie's audio after the film has been shot. Quite a bit of the audio you hear in movies isn't recorded by the camera; it's recorded and added later, by foley artists.)

TIP Your movie's theme music is designed to go with your project's theme, but you can use any theme music you want by choosing it from the Media screen.

The remaining four choices—Playlists, Albums, Artists, and Songs—are just four ways to get at the music library on your device. Whether you buy your music straight from iTunes or sync it to your iDevice using iTunes on your computer, you can import any of your music into your movie (except copy-protected music you bought before 2009, when Apple still used copy protection on songs you bought; iMovie marks those songs as "unavailable.")

Use the handy search box at the top of your Songs list to find a tune quickly.

Once you have the clip you want, tap it and two buttons appear (Figure 21-3). The first one, an arrow pointing down, adds the audio to your project. The second one, ▶, previews it for you.

NOTE When you add an audio clip to your project, iMovie assumes that you want it added as background audio if it's a music file, and foreground audio if it's a sound effect. If that's not the case, you can move the clip after it lands in your timeline.

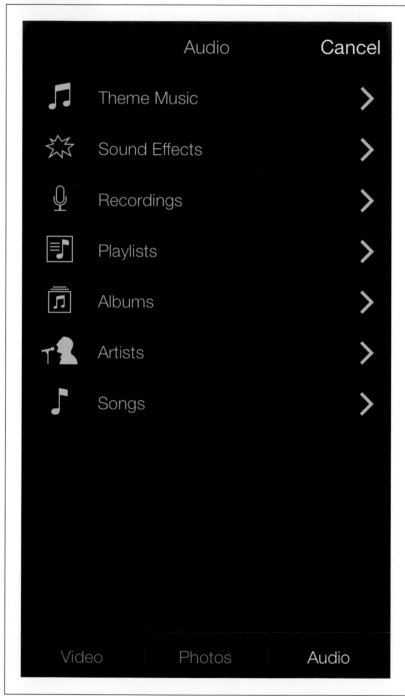

FIGURE 21-2
Tap Add Media followed by Audio to see all the sound clips you can use to enhance your movie. While Theme Music and Sound Effects offer unique audio clips, the remaining four choices (Playlists, Albums, Artists, and Songs) are just four ways to tap your device's music library.

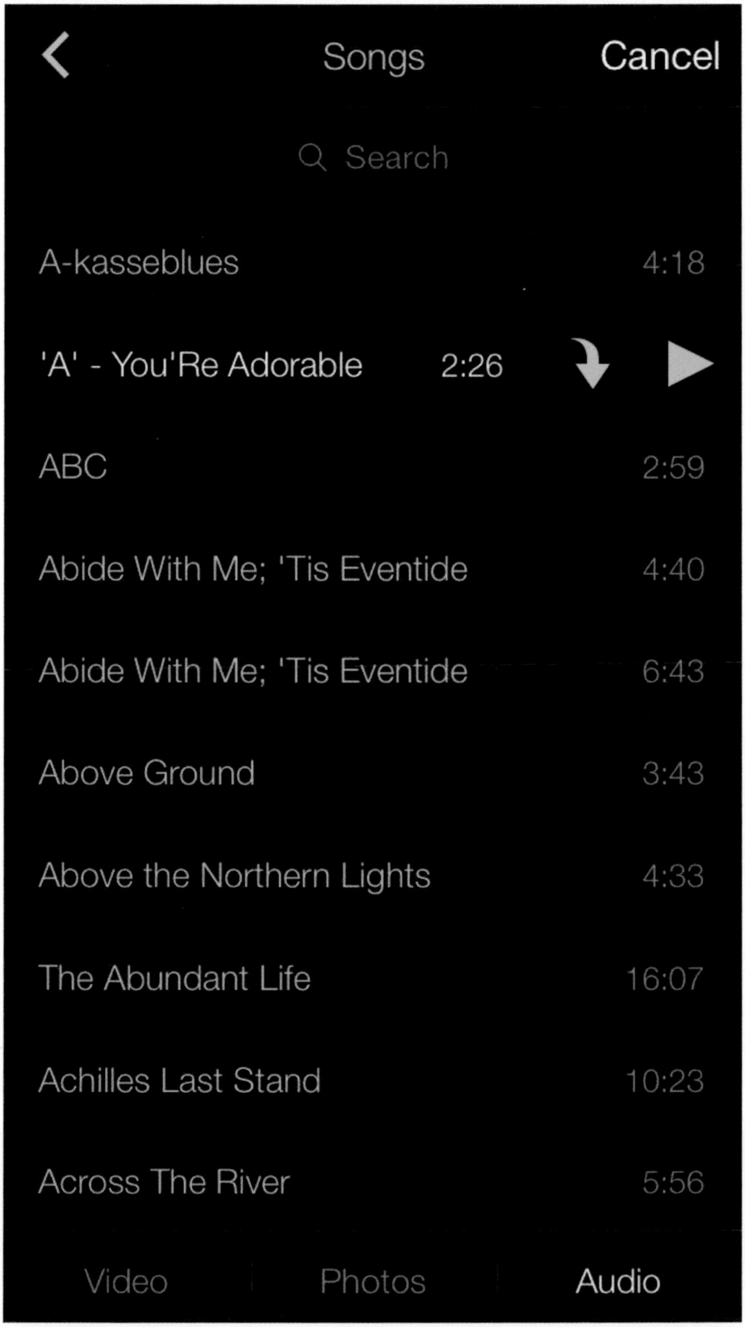

Songs	Cancel

Q Search

A-kasseblues	4:18
'A' - You'Re Adorable	2:26 ↓ ▶
ABC	2:59
Abide With Me; 'Tis Eventide	4:40
Abide With Me; 'Tis Eventide	6:43
Above Ground	3:43
Above the Northern Lights	4:33
The Abundant Life	16:07
Achilles Last Stand	10:23
Across The River	5:56

| Video | Photos | Audio |

FIGURE 21-3

When you select a song, you see two buttons. The ▶ button previews the song so you know what you're adding, while the down arrow button adds it. Also, notice the search field at the top of the list. You can use it to find the song you want quickly.

Adjust Timing

Once you add an audio clip to your project, you may want to change either its length or even its speed. In iMovie, you can do both.

TIP Before you make any audio adjustments in iMovie on the iPad, tap the squiggly button shown in Figure 21-4 to display the clip's waveform.

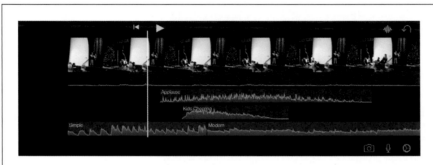

FIGURE 21-4

The iPad's waveforms button (highlighted in blue) shows you patterns in your audio, making it easier to pinpoint important moments in a clip.

■ TRIM AUDIO

To change the length of an audio clip, tap it once so the yellow border appears. Now you can drag either end to trim away the beginning or end of the audio. Once you let go, the clip is shorter.

Some useful advice for trimming audio:

- Spread two fingers outward in the timeline to zoom in on the clip (page 299) so you can fine-tune the trim.

- Keep the Undo button handy. Because iMovie on the iPhone doesn't display a clip's waveform (page 318), there's a fair amount of guesswork required to trim a clip to the right spot. (The iPad version shows you the waveform when you tap the waveform button shown in Figure 21-4.)

- If you trim to the wrong place, never fear. You can use the same yellow handles to add audio back in. You can't add more audio than was there originally, but you can add back anything you trimmed off.

■ SPEED CHANGES

To speed up or slow down an audio clip, tap the clip and then choose Speed from the toolbar. iMovie shows you a speed slider (Figure 21-5). Drag it left to slow down the audio, and right to speed it up. When you change the speed of a clip, a little tortoise or hare icon appears next to it.

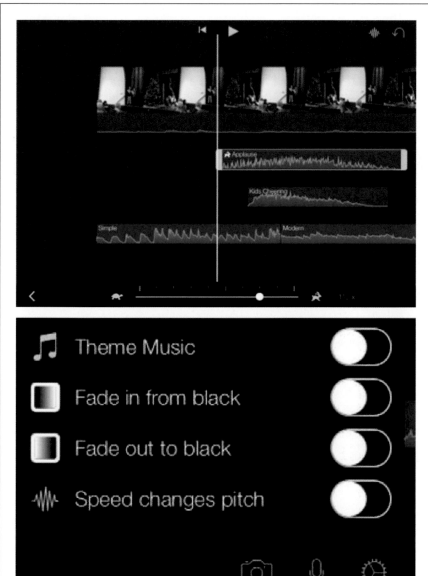

FIGURE 21-5

Top: Use the speed slider to make an audio clip faster or slower. (Notice the hare icon on the chosen clip—that means you sped it up. A tortoise icon means you slowed it down.)

Bottom: Be sure to turn off the "Speed changes pitch" setting so the audio will keep its pitch when you change the clip's speed.

Also, iMovie has a really cool ability to change the speed of a clip without changing its pitch. Normally, when you speed up audio, its pitch goes up, too, and when you slow it down, the pitch goes down. You can tell iMovie to preserve the pitch from the Project Settings menu—hit ✿ and then tap off the "Speed changes pitch" switch.

Delete Audio

Change your mind about the audio clip you added? Tap it to select it and then tap 🗑 to delete it. (You can also drag it up and out of the timeline.)

Add Narration

It probably won't be long before we see an Oscar-nominated documentary that was shot and edited almost entirely on an iPhone. When that happens, the filmmaker may end up using iMovie's built-in narration tool. Maybe that'll be you.

What makes this tool so handy is that you can film a shot and then narrate it later with as many takes as you need to get it right. Each time you record a narration, iMovie adds it as a foreground audio clip, which you can always delete to try again.

The Narration Tool

To narrate a movie, tap the microphone button in the timeline toolbar (highlighted in red in Figure 21-6). iMovie shows you a sound meter with Cancel and Record buttons (Figure 21-6, top). Tap Record and iMovie gives you a 3-second countdown before it starts recording. As it records, the storyboard turns red to mark your progress through the film (Figure 21-6, middle). Tap Stop to end your recording. iMovie asks you to make one of four decisions (Figure 21-6, bottom): cancel the recording, re-record it, review it (play it back to hear how it sounds), or accept it.

When you accept a narration, iMovie adds it as foreground audio, marking it with a lavender stripe. You can reposition it, trim it, change its speed, adjust its volume, and switch it to background audio.

Detach Audio from Video

To continue your documentary training, you need to learn how to do cutaways, where you switch from an interviewee's headshot to a shot of what she's describing, all while her voice keeps narrating.

To do a cutaway, you need to detach the audio from the video you recorded. Then you keep the audio track in place while you replace the video track.

iMovie offers two ways to detach audio from a video clip:

- **From a clip in your project.** If you already added the video clip to your project on an iPad, select it, tap the Audio button in the toolbar, and then tap Detach. For iPhones, select the clip, tap Audio, tap the second "dot" in the toolbar, and then tap Detach.

FIGURE 21-6

Top: Tap Record to start your narration.

Middle: While you record, iMovie indicates your progress through the movie with a red shadow in the timeline.

Bottom: When you tap Stop, iMovie gives you four choices for your recording.

- **From a video clip in your library.** Instead of adding a video clip from your library and *then* detaching its audio, you can add *just the sound* from a clip. Use the Add Media button to go to the Media screen, and then select the clip. You may need to tap the ••• button to see the "Add audio" button—it looks like a waveform with a + sign in it (see Figure 21-7). When you tap it, iMovie inserts just the audio as a foreground clip.

FIGURE 21-7

To add just the audio portion of a video clip to your timeline, tap the "Add audio" button.

The resulting audio stripe in your timeline is vibrant blue (see Figure 21-8). Trim the clip, move it, and adjust its speed or volume to your heart's content.

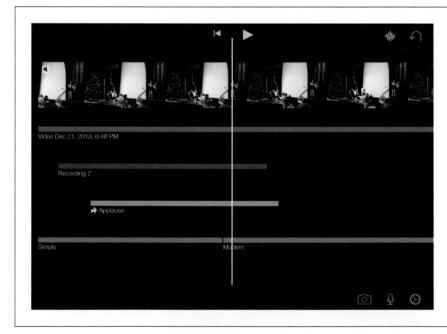

FIGURE 21-8

iMovie marks these three kinds of foreground audio in different colors. The vibrant blue stripe (top) is detached audio, the lavender stripe (middle) is narrated audio, and the light-blue stripe (bottom) is a sound effect.

■ Adjust Audio Levels

You might have a background song in your movie that's so loud that there's nothing background about it. Or there may be a moment when your annoying brother was yelling at your sister, and you'd rather not draw attention to it. In this and other cases, you need to adjust the audio volume levels.

Volume

To change the volume of a clip, select it and, if it's a video clip, choose Audio from the toolbar. iMovie shows you a volume slider (Figure 21-9). Drag it to the left for a quieter clip and to the right for a louder one.

> **TIP** You can't change the volume of just *part* of a clip, like you can on the Mac. In iMovie for iOS, you have to split the clip and then change the volume of the split part.

Unfortunately, there's no ducking feature in iMovie for iOS (page 174), so you need to be vigilant about adjusting the volume levels for different parts of your project.

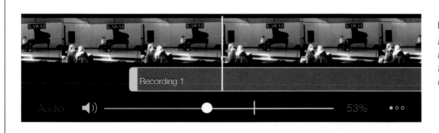

FIGURE 21-9

iMovie's audio toolbar houses a volume slider that makes the selected clip quieter or louder.

Fade Audio

To make audio slowly fade in or out, select a standalone audio clip or detach the audio from a video clip and select the detached clip. Either way, the clip sports a yellow edit border. Choose Fade from the toolbar. iMovie replaces the yellow trim handles (page 322) with yellow arrows at either end of the clip (Figure 21-10). As you drag the arrows, you lengthen or shorten the fade in (or out) of the audio. (You can't overlap the front and end fades.) You can come back and adjust the fade anytime.

■ Split Audio

Just as breaking up a video clip can help with various editing tricks, so can splitting an audio clip. For example, you might want to pause a song for dramatic effect. When the song starts playing again, you want it to pick up where it left off. In a case like that, you want to split the clip.

FIGURE 21-10

*When you use the Fade
tool, yellow arrows mark
the duration of the volume
change. Drag them around
to retime a fade.*

Choose the audio clip and position the playhead where you want the split to occur. Choose Split from the toolbar and iMovie chops the clip in two. Now you can
reposition the second part so that it picks up at the right moment in your movie.

NOTE Splitting a clip is really useful only for foreground audio, since you can reposition it. Even if you split
a background clip, you can't reposition it.

◼ Duplicate Audio

If you need to repeat the same audio clip, don't bother adding a second version
of it to the timeline. Select the clip and choose Duplicate from the toolbar. iMovie
creates a copy in the timeline.

iMovie for iOS Photos

N ot everything in a movie has to move. Sometimes a nicely placed photo tells
the best story. In an iMovie for iOS project, you can use any photo that you
take with or sync to your device.

However, if you're accustomed to iMovie for the Mac, don't expect the same photo
versatility in iMovie for iOS; you're limited in certain frustrating ways. For example,
you can't use cutaway, picture-in-picture, or side-by-side effects, nor can you apply
photo effects, like making an image appear black and white. (You *can*, however, edit
a photo in something else first, like iPhoto for iOS.) Finally, and most frustratingly,
you can add only one photo at a time to your timeline. That makes assembling a
slideshow of 100 photographs in iMovie for iOS unrealistic.

TIP iPhoto for iOS has a perfectly capable slideshow tool of its own. Consider trying that app instead to create
a quick slideshow.

That said, all the basic photo-editing tasks are here. You can rotate and zoom in on
a photo, add a title, and change its duration. This chapter covers all the ways you
can use photos in iMovie for iOS.

■ The Photo Library

What photos does iMovie use? The short answer is all the ones on your device. You
can see them using the Photos app on your iPhone, iPad, or iPod Touch.

NOTE Lots of other apps can snap and edit pictures. If you want to shoot or edit an image that you can use in iMovie, be sure that the app stores and retrieves photos to and from your Camera Roll.

But you don't need to open Photos to pick images for your movie. iMovie can display pictures from your Camera Roll and then insert them straight into the timeline (another example of Apple programs that seamlessly talk to each other).

To do that, tap Add Media→Photos. iMovie groups the photos on your device by their source (Figure 22-1). The list includes your Camera Roll, your iCloud photo stream, and the names of any photo albums you created. (If you see a bunch of photo squares instead of album names, tap < to get to the album-listing screen.)

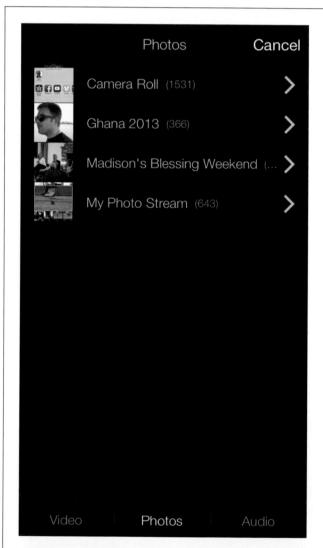

FIGURE 22-1

iMovie's Photos screen lists every photo album you have. Through them, you can access every photo on your device.

Choose any album. iMovie displays thumbnails of the photos it contains (see Figure 22-2). Don't worry, iMovie hasn't cropped your photos to fit the grid; it displays them this way to save space.

To get a better look at a photo, tap it; iMovie presents a larger version in a pop-up window (Figure 22-2). That preview uses the photo's real dimensions, too (unlike the standardized grid squares), so you can see its orientation before you add it to your project.

FIGURE 22-2

All the photos in an album show up as squares in the thumbnail grid, even if the real dimensions are different. Tap and hold on a square to preview the full photo. To add a photo to your project, tap it.

Once you find the photo you want, tap it to add it to your project. iMovie inserts it at the end of the clip under the playhead. (iMovie won't split a clip to insert a photo.)

Once inserted, a photo plays for 3 to 6 seconds, depending on the length of the transition on either side of it (different transitions take different times to fade to and from a photo). In addition, iMovie automatically applies the Ken Burns effect to each photo. (To change that, see page 330.)

■ Shoot with Your Camera

Of course, your iPhone, iPad, or iPod Touch comes with a built-in camera, and you can use it to take pictures and add them straight to your timeline.

To add photos directly into iMovie, open the Camera app and then slide the capture choice to Photo, as shown in Figure 22-3. You can't use some advanced features like HDR and effects, but you can focus with a screen tap, shoot flash photography, and flip between the front and back cameras.

FIGURE 22-3

You can use the camera on your iPad, iPhone, or iPod Touch to add pictures directly to your timeline.

After you snap a photo, tap Use Photo, and iMovie inserts it into your project at the playhead.

NOTE When you use the camera in iMovie to record video, you can save those videos to your Camera Roll (see page 324). You can't do the same with iMovie-shot photos, however—they work in your movie projects only. To save and access a photo for other uses, take the picture with the Camera app and then import it into iMovie.

■ Video Freeze Frames

Sometimes the best photo is trapped in a video. To freeze a frame of a clip and save it as a photo for use in iMovie (see the Note that follows), position the playhead on the perfect moment. Tap the video clip to highlight it and then choose Freeze from the toolbar (Figure 22-4). When you do, iMovie splits the clip at the playhead and sticks in the still image.

NOTE You can't create a still image using the freeze frame trick described here and then use that image in another app. iMovie for iOS doesn't store the image anywhere; it simply adds it to your timeline, making the pic inaccessible to other apps.

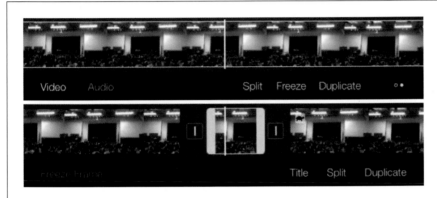

FIGURE 22-4

iMovie's Freeze features creates a still image from a frame in a video.

Top: To "snap" the frame, position the playhead and then tap Freeze in the toolbar.

Bottom: The frozen frame acts like any other photo in your timeline, except that you can't apply the Ken Burns effect to it, and you can split it.

You can treat the captured image pretty much like any other photo in your time-line—move it around, change its duration, add a title, or duplicate it. Oddly enough, though, you can't apply a Ken Burns effect to it, even though iMovie automatically applies that effect to other photos. And you *can* split the photo, which iMovie doesn't allow with other photos. Go figure.

TIP While you can't apply the Ken Burns effect to a freeze frame, you *can* zoom in on it—see page 299.

■ Adjust Photos

Odds are, a photo you dropped into your timeline won't behave exactly the way you want it to. You may not like its timing, its rotation, or how iMovie automatically applied the Ken Burns effect to it. And you might want to add a title. Once a photo is in your timeline, you can change all these attributes.

Duration

Altering a photo's duration works just like trimming a video clip (page 298), except that you're not trimming the image; you're telling iMovie how long to display it.

Tap a photo in your timeline so the two yellow highlight handles appear at either end. Drag an end left or right to shorten or lengthen the duration of your photo. (It doesn't matter which handle you drag.)

When you let go, your photo retains its new timing. If you want to time the duration just right in relation to the shots that come before and after it, zoom in on the timeline so you can precisely position the yellow handles. If you're editing to sound and you're on an iPad, turn on the waveform (tap the squiggly line button) to edit to the audio pattern.

Rotation

You can rotate the photos in iMovie just as you can rotate the video (see page 300). With a photo selected and displayed in the preview window, put two fingers on the window, and twist them right or left. With each twist, iMovie rotates the clip a quarter-turn in that direction.

Adjust the Zoom Level and Ken Burns Effect

iMovie on the Mac made the famous panning zoom effect created by documentarian Ken Burns even more famous. That's when a movie gradually zooms in on and slides across a photo to make it appear more dynamic and interesting. What used to take special camera equipment, you can now do on your handheld Apple device.

iMovie automatically applies the Ken Burns effect to all the photos you add to your timeline. If you don't like what iMovie did, you can always change it.

Tap a photo in your timeline to select it. When you do, the preview screen includes options to set the start and end points of the Ken Burns pan and zoom (see Figure 22-5). To "remove" the Ken Burns effect, position the start and end points to be exactly the same, showing all your photo. Your photo will stay still in the movie. (To zoom in on or out of a photo, pinch it; to reposition a photo, drag it.)

To show just part of a photo, zoom in on it until just the part you want people to see is visible, and then make sure the start and end points are the same.

To create your own Ken Burns effect, set the start and end points differently. iMovie automatically creates the pan and zoom effect that moves the shot from one position to the other. For example, if you want to zoom out during the effect, start with a zoomed-in point and end with a zoomed-out one. If you want to pan across a photo, zoom in the same amount for both points, but position the photo at one side for the start point and the other side for the end point.

FIGURE 22-5

To adjust the start of the Ken Burns effect, choose the top arrow, and then drag and zoom in on (pinch) the photo. To adjust the end, choose the bottom arrow and then position and zoom in on the photo again. Tap ▶ to preview your work.

Add Titles

Add a title to a photo the same way you add a title to a clip, as explained on page 307.

■ Delete Photos

Deleting a photo from your timeline couldn't be easier. Tap to select the photo, and then tap 🗑. Poof. The photo is gone. (But not gone from your device, necessarily. Anything you added from a photo album is still in that album, safe and sound. Only photos you shot from within iMovie are gone forever.)

iMovie for iOS Trailers

T railers, the 1- to 2-minute previews you see before a movie, have become a
form of entertainment on their own. Today, it's common for an action-movie
trailer on YouTube to get millions of views before the film even hits theaters.

iMovie for the Mac pulls off super cool, complex tricks with its trailers feature (Chapter
13). Using high-quality animations, titles, and music, it lets you easily create a preview
featuring your family, friends, or, heck, even your pets. With over two dozen trailer
styles to choose from, you're sure to find one that tells your story.

iMovie for iOS does the same thing, albeit with fewer styles (14 instead of 29). But
it also offers something iMovie for the Mac can't: the ability to both shoot and then
build your trailer on your handheld device. This chapter explains how to do that and
everything else trailer-related.

NOTE Before you get too deeply into building an iOS trailer, note that you can't convert it to a project and
tweak it with custom edits on an iPhone, iPad, or iPod Touch.

■ Create a Trailer

To build a trailer, open the iMovie app, tap the + button, and then choose Trailer from
the New Project screen. When you do, iMovie shows you a range of trailer styles, each
with a unique thematic flair (Figure 23-1). Apple thoughtfully put together a preview
for each trailer style so you can imagine what your story will look like. To preview a
preview, select a style and then tap ▶. Tap Create Trailer when you find one you like.

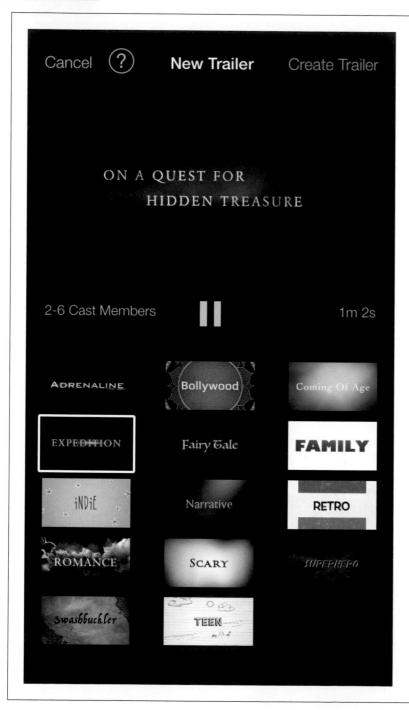

FIGURE 23-1

When you create a trailer, you can choose from 14 styles. Select one and then press ▶ to preview it.

You can build and edit a trailer two ways. In the first, you supply basic facts about your movie, and iMovie feeds that information to the trailer storyboard, which, in turn, dictates the shots you need for a great trailer. Alternatively, you can go straight to the storyboard and film your trailer "live," by shooting scenes and having iMovie save them directly to your trailer. Both methods are described next.

◼ The Outline

Great filmmaking almost always starts with an outline. It helps you organize your story before you ever focus a camera lens. iMovie for iOS's trailer-builder's outline feature works something like that. You record details about your movie—its name, the names of your cast members, and so on—and it uses that info later on, when you assemble clips and photos in the storyboard (Figure 23-2). For example, if you list two actors in the outline, the trailer storyboard will call for closeups of each of the actors.

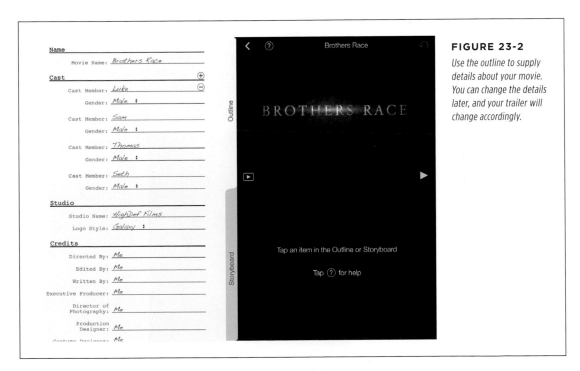

FIGURE 23-2

Use the outline to supply details about your movie. You can change the details later, and your trailer will change accordingly.

Fill in the Details

After you click Create Trailer, iMovie takes you to a screen with two tabs, labeled Outline and Storyboard. Tap the Outline tab.

iMovie lists the info it wants using dummy text: Name, Cast, Studio, and so on. To change the placeholder text, tap it. iMovie brings up the keyboard so you can type in your own info. Tap Done when you finish.

Some questions, like the gender of your actors, require you to choose from a drop-down menu. Tap the item to call up the menu.

Other questions, like how many actors appear in your movie, need a number for an answer. Tap the + and – buttons to add or subtract items to and from the list (see Figure 23-2).

NOTE iMovie adds new items, like an additional actor, to the top of the list, not to the bottom. (Subtracting items also removes items from the top of the list, not the bottom.) This matters if you want the names of your actors in a particular order. The best way to achieve that is to first add the correct number of actors to the outline. Then change the dummy text to list your actors from most important to least important, beginning with the topmost item. iMovie preserves that order in the trailer.

Once you fill in the outline, tap the Storyboard tab to go to the trailer's timeline, where you'll add video clips, photos, and titles to your preview-in-progress.

The Storyboard

The trailer storyboard looks nothing like a typical project timeline (see Figure 23-3). Instead of a blank slate that moves horizontally, the trailer storyboard looks more like a bunch of standalone frames you fill up with video clips and photos.

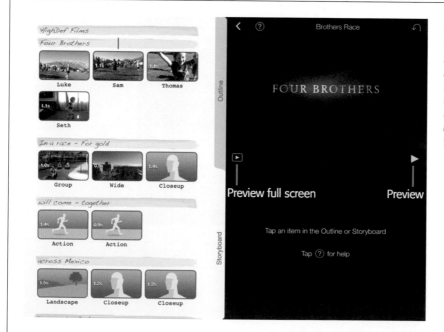

FIGURE 23-3

The trailer storyboard is a unique way to build a movie. Each of these frames represents a clip that will play in your trailer, and each recommends the kind of shot you should insert.

The frames appear in the order they play during the trailer, and each recommends a particular style of shot. For example, some call for a closeup, while others recommend a landscape scene. These suggestions are purposeful—Apple designed the trailers to be fast-paced and visually interesting. (They're actually like lessons in storytelling.) Of course, iMovie won't refuse a clip that doesn't match the frame's label, so it's up to you to follow (or not) the advice.

Each clip has a fixed duration, which you can't change, but that minor limitation is a small price to pay for having iMovie do so much of the trailer-building work.

Add Clips or Photos to the Storyboard

To add video or photos to a trailer, tap any empty frame to launch the Media screen. To see a particular type of media, tap Video or Photos in the toolbar. You can use the media selection tools described on page 294 for video (so you can sort your footage) and page 326 for photos (to get access to all your device's photo folders).

Choosing the right video clip is a little tricky, because you want to display just the right moment in the few seconds the trailer gives you. First, select a clip. That calls up the yellow highlight box with the edit handles, but this time the handles are immobile—you can't drag them to change the clip's length—remember, trailers use clips of fixed duration. But you *can* drag the entire yellow box, and that's the trick to getting the shot you want: Drag the box until the right section of the clip sits within it (Figure 23-4).

As you drag the border around, iMovie previews the clip in the viewer. Tap ▶ to play the selection as it will appear in your trailer. When you're satisfied, tap ⬆ to add your selection to the storyboard.

For photos, the selection process is simple: Find the photo you want, and then tap it to add it to the storyboard.

Film Straight to the Storyboard

Perhaps the coolest thing about making trailers on your iPad, iPhone, or iPod Touch is not having to capture a frame of movie footage before you build your trailer. You can start a new trailer project and film the shots as you go.

When you tap a frame to add a shot, choose Camera instead of Video or Photos. iMovie displays a special camera screen above your storyboard (see Figure 23-5). Use this camera to film a shot, and iMovie saves it straight to the trailer. Talk about on-the-fly editing! iMovie at its best, really.

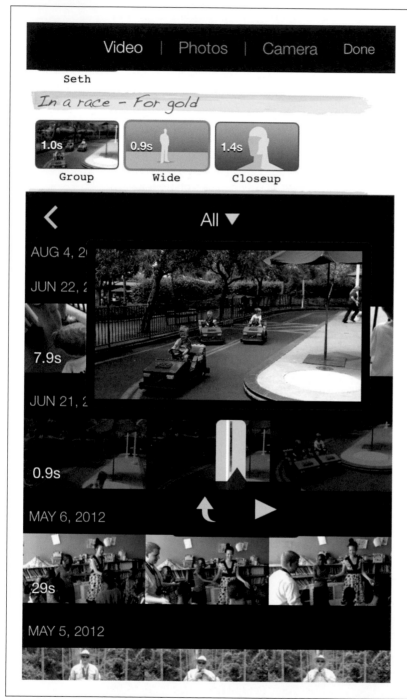

FIGURE 23-4

When you select a clip for your trailer, iMovie limits how long it plays. Drag the yellow selection border to choose the right moment.

FIGURE 23-5

Use this special camera screen to shoot footage or photos and save them straight to your trailer. (The top image shows the iPhone version, and the bottom image is from an iPad.)

The video version of the camera has a few unique features. It displays the destination frame for your footage right below the camera, and it lists the clip's duration in the frame, so you can better plan your shot.

When you hit the Record button, the camera counts you in and displays an elongated destination frame (Figure 23-6). That frame has the trailer shot at its core, and room on either side that serves two purposes: It lets you prepare to shoot—as the red "playhead" moves across the frame, you can see where your trailer shot goes "live." And second, it gives you some extra footage in case you need to fine-tune the shot later (read on).

FIGURE 23-6

When you record video, iMovie counts you in and displays an elongated destination frame. As you can see from the frame, iMovie films extra footage on either side of the core trailer shot so you can fine-tune the clip later.

The photo version of the trailers camera is really simple. Just point and shoot. The photo you take fills the trailer frame.

Adjust Clips and Photos

The video clips and photos you put in a trailer frame will sometimes be off a little. Video clips might be off because of timing, with the wrong moment displayed in the frame. Photos might be off because the Ken Burns effect iMovie automatically applies doesn't look quite right. You can fix both issues easily.

If, after you shoot a clip, your timing is a little off, you don't have to retake the shot. Tap the frame that has the errant footage. iMovie opens the Edit Shot window. It displays the clip as a filmstrip, with the trailer shot highlighted in yellow. To adjust the shot, drag the filmstrip until the section you want sits within the yellow box (Figure 23-7).

You can also unmute a clip here, and delete it if you want to start over.

The Edit Shot screen for trailer photos is different (Figure 23-8). iMovie applies the Ken Burns effect to photos, so the edit screen lets you set the start and end points for the zoom and pan.

iMovie displays the image in a yellow highlight box. Just under that, tap Start and then use the preview screen above to position (by dragging) and zoom in on (by pinching) the photo. When you finish, tap End and do the same thing. iMovie uses the difference between the two positions to determine how to apply the Ken Burns effect. (For a description of the process, see page 330.) Press ▶ to preview the shot. Tap Done when you finish, or the trash can to delete the photo and start over.

> **TIP** Notice the Next button in Figures 23-7 and 23-8? It takes you from one trailer shot to the next. Rather than stepping in and out of the Edit Shot screen, start with the first trailer frame and then tap Next when you finish with each one. You can edit your entire trailer this way.

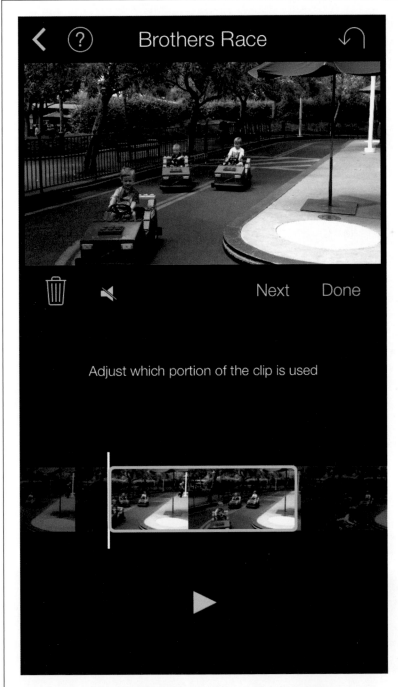

FIGURE 23-7

To edit a trailer clip, drag the filmstrip around to position it at just the right moment. You can also mute or unmute the clip using the speaker button. (iMovie mutes trailer clips by default.) Tap ▶ to preview the shot before you tap Done. Tap the trash can if you want to delete the footage and start over with a different shot.

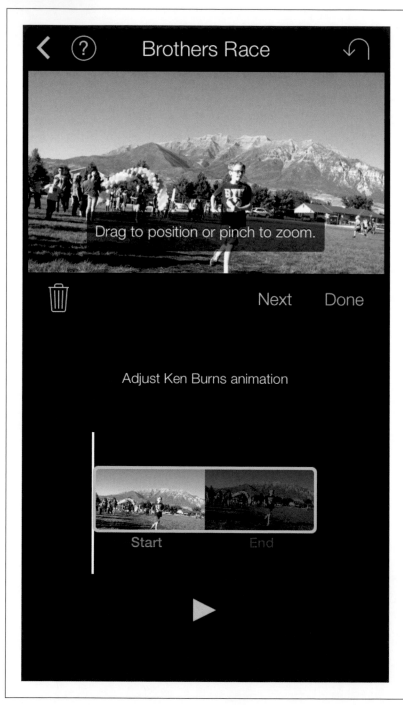

FIGURE 23-8

Editing a trailer photo is a matter of dragging and pinching it to set its start and end points for the Ken Burns effect. Press ▶ to preview your work, or the trash can to delete the photo and start over.

Change Titles

Part of what makes trailers so great are the impressive titles Apple designed for them. They make your movie look like you spent a lot of money on animators and designers. The fact that you can type in whatever you want and have it look so good is amazing.

To change the text of a title, tap it in the storyboard (be sure to tap the title itself, not the frame under it). iMovie launches the keyboard (Figure 23-9). Type in the new text and see what it looks like in the preview window. Tap Done to save your changes.

FIGURE 23-9

To change a trailer title, tap it in the storyboard. Use the keyboard to type in new text, and the preview window shows what it will look like. Tap Done to save your changes.

Be sure to take the time to update all the text in the trailer. Although iMovie provides placeholder copy, odds are you can come up with something better that will make the trailer your own.

■ Preview Your Trailer

Once you finish your trailer, press either the Preview or "Preview full screen" buttons (see Figure 23-3). Review your work to see if you want to make any more edits.

When you finish, share your trailer with the world—to do that, see the next chapter.

iMovie for iOS Sharing

Unless you're gathering your loved ones around your iPhone or iPad screen, you probably want to share your hard work far and wide. How does the entire Internet sound? You can upload your movie straight from your iDevice to Facebook, YouTube, Vimeo, and even CNN's citizen-reporter website, iReport. As long as someone has a web browser and an Internet connection, he's part of your audience.

If you care less about web stardom and more about getting your movie onto another device, like an iPhone, a Mac, or an Apple TV, iMovie can accommodate you there, too.

Read on to discover all the ways you can share your movies from iMovie for iOS.

■ Share Movies, Trailers, or Clips

A word before getting into the details of sharing. On page 245, you can read how iMovie on the Mac is a little stingy when it comes to sharing footage in your Events library; you can't share it until you move it into a project.

iMovie for iOS is much more generous. It lets you share not only projects (movies or trailers), but individual video clips, too. That saves you the time and hassle of building a new project just to share a single clip.

To share a project, use the Share button on iMovie for iOS's Project screen, shown in Figure 24-1, left. To share an individual clip, go to the Media screen for videos (click Videos from iMovie's main screen), and use the Share button shown in Figure 24-1, right.

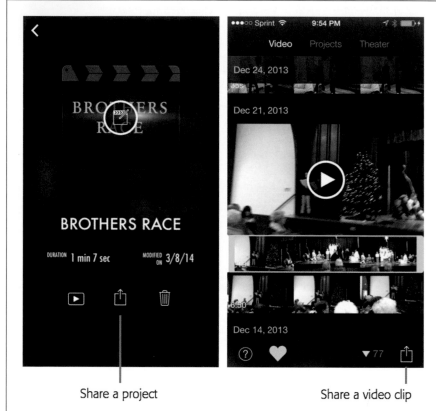

FIGURE 24-1

Left: Share a project (movie or trailer) from the Project Info screen using the Share button (the rectangle with an arrow sticking out of it).

Right: Share a clip from your video library by selecting it and using the same button.

Share a project

Share a video clip

▇ Share to the Web

Facebook, YouTube, Vimeo, and CNN iReport are four far-reaching websites for distributing your movies. You'll find them covered in detail in Chapter 15, so, to save some trees (and pixels, if you're reading electronically), this chapter covers only the aspects of sharing unique to iOS devices. For details on using each service, refer to the information starting on page 248.

> **NOTE** Each of these websites requires an account—complete with user name and password—before you can share anything. To set up an account for any of them, see the instructions in Chapter 15.

Facebook

When you tap the Share button from the Media screen, Facebook is one of your destination choices (Figure 24-2). iOS has some pretty deep integration with Facebook, so you set up your account from the Settings app on your iDevice. (Figure 24-3). Open Settings, scroll down to Facebook, and then tap the panel to open Facebook's Share Project screen.

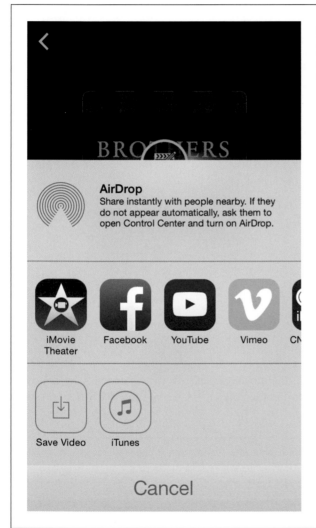

FIGURE 24-2
The Share menu lists all your choices for distributing your movie. Drag to the left to see options that don't fit in the window.

If you haven't signed into Facebook yet, fill in your user name and password. If you have, be sure you can share your movie to Facebook. Under "Allow these apps to use your account," turn on iMovie access. Then click the Settings button on the same screen and turn on Upload HD, as shown in Figure 24-3. If, for some reason, you don't see iMovie listed under "Allow these apps..." go back into iMovie and try sharing a movie to Facebook. Your device asks your permission to share movies with Facebook.

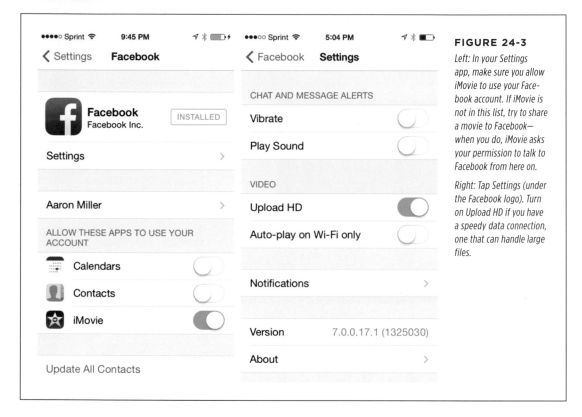

FIGURE 24-3

Left: In your Settings app, make sure you allow iMovie to use your Facebook account. If iMovie is not in this list, try to share a movie to Facebook— when you do, iMovie asks your permission to talk to Facebook from here on.

Right: Tap Settings (under the Facebook logo). Turn on Upload HD if you have a speedy data connection, one that can handle large files.

With your account information entered and access granted, tap the Share button from iMovie's Media screen to launch the Share Project screen (Figure 24-4). Tap Facebook, and then enter the movie or clip's name and description, choose a movie quality, and decide who can see your video. (See page 251 for more on these choices.) Then tap Share.

> **NOTE**   See the "Add to Theater" switch on the Share Project screen? It shows up on all the Internet sharing screens. Its purpose is to add your video to iMovie Theater, explained on page 257.

iMovie exports your video, uploads it, and then gives you a chance to visit it or tell a friend where to find it. Don't worry if you forget the exact web address. You can always get to it by tapping to share the same thing to Facebook again. When you do, iMovie reminds you that you've already shared it, and you can go see it or tell a friend about it again. You can publish the same project a second time (if, for example, you made changes to it), but that doesn't replace the old version; it just uploads a new one.

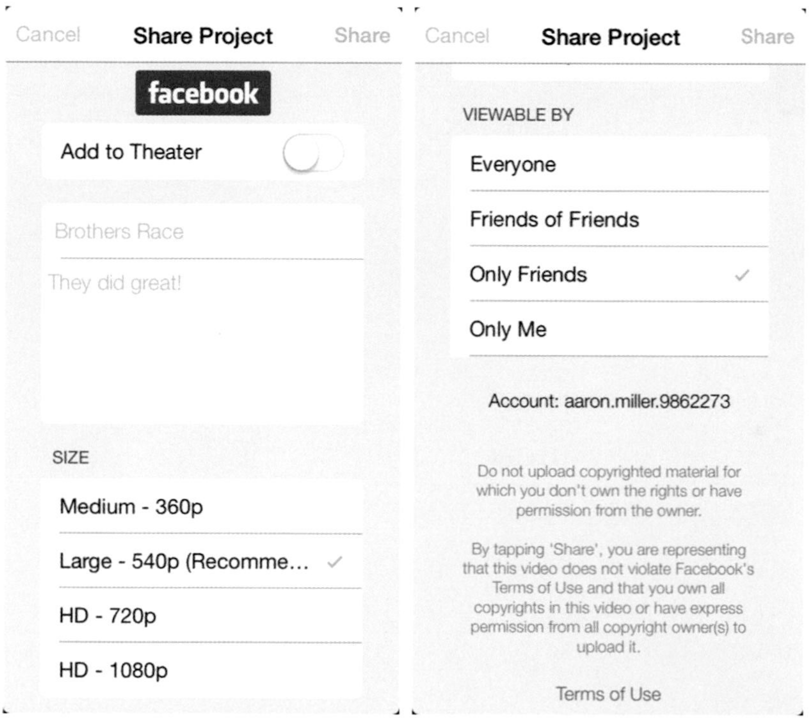

FIGURE 24-4

Left: When you share to Facebook, the first half of the screen asks for your video's name and description and lets you choose a file size.

Right: The other part of the Facebook screen lets you decide who can see your video.

NOTE For reasons unknown, when you visit your video from iMovie, it opens your iDevice's Safari browser and sends you to the web version of Facebook instead of to the Facebook *app*. If you prefer to use the app, you can find your video by looking in your account timeline.

iMovie doesn't help you manage a video once you upload it, so editing or deleting your video requires a trip to Facebook.

YouTube

The first time you share to YouTube, you have to log into your account (YouTube isn't integrated with iOS the same way Facebook is). Enter your user name and password, and you see the YouTube Share Project screen (Figure 24-5).

Fill in the details about your movie, including the size of the file you want to upload and who can see it (choose Public to make it available to the world). Tap Share once you decide.

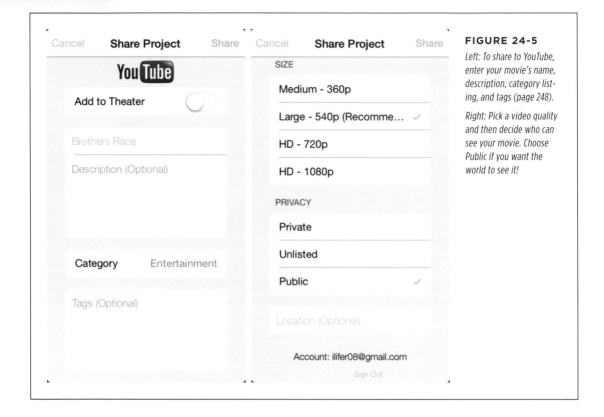

FIGURE 24-5

Left: To share to YouTube, enter your movie's name, description, category listing, and tags (page 248).

Right: Pick a video quality and then decide who can see your movie. Choose Public if you want the world to see it!

> **NOTE**   iMovie repeatedly recommends 540p quality for your videos. That's fine, but uploading in HD format (720p or 1080p) is worth the trouble if you have the time and a speedy connection that can handle hefty HD files. After all, you want your friends watching your movie in the highest quality possible.

iMovie uploads your movie and tells you where you and your friends can find it. As with Facebook, trying to share the file to YouTube again results in a reminder that you've been this way before. And again, to edit or delete your video, you have to log into YouTube itself.

Vimeo

iOS integrates your Vimeo account the same way it does for Facebook, so you need to take a trip to the Settings app to enter your login details. (iMovie sends you there if you haven't signed in yet.)

Once that's done, Vimeo sharing is almost identical to YouTube sharing. The only difference is that you choose Anyone instead of Public to share your video with the world.

CNN iReport

Like YouTube, CNN iReport is not integrated into iOS, so iMovie will prompt you to log into your account. Once done, fill in the details about your movie.

Note that iReport doesn't offer a privacy setting—iReport videos are, by design, public. In addition, you *can't delete them*. Short of persuading someone at CNN to remove a video you've uploaded, it's going to stay there.

■ Share to Other Devices

Sharing between devices is covered in detail in Chapter 16. In keeping with the spirit of conservation, only new information related to iOS devices will make the cut here.

The Camera Roll

All kinds of apps can tap into an iDevice's Camera Roll, the shared photo library explained in detail on page 324. That includes apps for third-party file-sharing services like Dropbox, making it easy to upload a video from your Camera Roll to Dropbox so you can share the Dropbox folder with family and friends.

To share to your Camera Roll, tap the Share button and then choose Save Video. Once you select a file size (Figure 24-6), iMovie processes your movie and sticks it in the Camera Roll, nestled among all the other video clips and photos found there. Now any app that can access your Camera Roll can see your video.

iMovie Theater

iMovie Theater is a convenient way to share videos among all the devices on the same iCloud account. This includes Macs, iDevices, and AppleTVs. You can share full 1080p HD movies, too, making this a really slick setup.

Chapter 16 discusses iMovie Theater at length (starting on page 257). All you really need to know here is that you can share any clip or project to iMovie Theater from your iPhone, iPad, or iPod Touch by choosing iMovie Theater from the Share menu, or by turning on the Add to Theater switch anytime you share a video to the Internet.

Once you upload a video, tap Theater in your iDevice's toolbar to see it. Unlike in iMovie for the Mac, you don't need to worry about uploading the video to iCloud—iMovie for iOS automatically does that when you share a movie to iMovie Theater.

iMessage

iMessage is Apple's free messaging service for all Mac and iDevice owners. Not only can you send messages, but you can also send photos, videos, and other files.

Because iMessage's maximum file size is 100 MB, iMovie automatically exports your movie at a video quality that's, well, low—360p, in fact. If you need to transfer something of higher quality, like HD, consider using AirDrop (described on page 353) or iTunes.

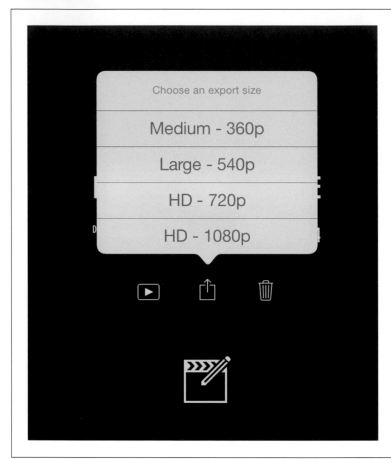

FIGURE 24-6

To share a video to the Camera Roll, tap Share and then Save Video. iMovie asks you to pick an export size. It's usually best to go big and later export a smaller movie if your first choice ends up taking too long to share.

When you choose Message from the Share window, iMovie automatically converts your project and starts a new message ("Check out my video!") with your movie attached to it (Figure 24-7). (You can, of course, edit the message.) Type in your recipient's contact information and then tap Send.

Mail

Mail's data limits, as noted in Chapter 16, are dramatically lower than iMessage's for most email accounts. When you choose Mail from the Share menu, iMovie generates the same low-quality video (360p) it does for iMessage and opens a new mail message with your video attached. Type in the name of your recipient and a message, and then tap Send.

FIGURE 24-7

*When you share using iMessage, it automatically attaches
a low-res version of your video to a new message. Just
type in the recipient(s) and then tap Send.*

AirDrop

If you've been underwhelmed by the sharing options thus far, get ready to be
impressed. AirDrop—discussed in detail on page 285—is a tool that lets you share
files between iOS devices.

AirDrop for the Mac works only between Macs; AirDrop for iOS works only between iOS devices. There's no way to use AirDrop to share between a Mac and an iOS device. To do that, you need to use one of the other sharing methods discussed here.

Before you use AirDrop, you need to know a few things:

- You have to have two iOS devices, both of them running iOS 7 or later and both of which support AirDrop. That includes an iPhone 5 or later, iPad fourth generation or later, any iPad mini, and an iPod Touch fifth generation or later.

- You need to turn on both WiFi and Bluetooth on each device. You can do this in the Settings app.

- The devices need to be within at least a couple dozen feet of each other; the closer the better.

- The receiving device needs to be AirDrop-available to the sending device. Do this by swiping up from the bottom of your screen to show the Control Center. Tap AirDrop and choose Contacts Only if the other person has an iCloud address that's in your address book. If not, choose Everyone. (You can easily come back and change this later if you want.)

If you've covered these bases, AirDrop sharing works this way:

1. **Tap ⬆ on the sending device.**

   The Share screen appears, with an AirDrop logo at the top. Wait a moment or two, and your friend's device should show up, replacing the logo (Figure 24-8).

2. **Tap your friend's name.**

   When you do, your friend's device displays a message asking him to accept the file.

3. **Tell your friend to tap Accept.**

   After accepting the file, AirDrop starts copying it from one device to the other. Both devices show the progress using a blue circle (Figure 24-9).

When AirDrop finishes, your friend's device posts a message telling you the transfer is finished and invites you to check out the file you sent.

TIP As noted on page 285, AirDrop works for sending full-blown *projects* in addition to standalone videos. That's really convenient. You can piece together a basic video on your iPhone, and then use AirDrop to send it to your iPad, where you have more elbow room to work. Or you could use AirDrop to share a project you're handing off to a friend for finishing.

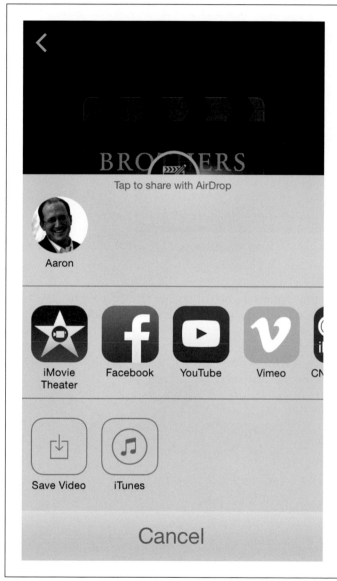

FIGURE 24-8

When you have your devices set up right for an AirDrop share, your friend should show up on the Share screen in place of the AirDrop logo. Tap his picture to transmit your movie.

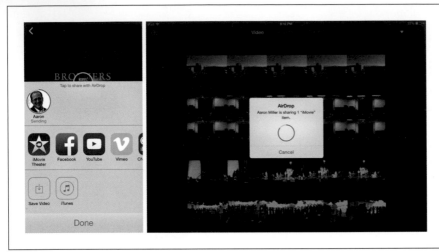

FIGURE 24-9

Left: An iPhone is sharing a video to Aaron's iPad.

Right: The iPad is receiving the video. The blue circle on both screens indicates how far along the transfer is.

iPhoto or Aperture

Every iDevice has a camera. That means both iPhoto (which is free with every Mac) and Aperture ($80 in the Mac App Store) can import your gadget's photos and videos just as it can any other camera's photos and videos. To make that happen, you first have to save your images and movies to the Camera Roll (see page 296 for the details). Once there, you can import them into iPhoto, Aperture, or any other compatible photo-management program on your Mac or PC.

Appendixes

iMovie, Menu by Menu

As you've certainly noticed by now, iMovie doesn't look like a standard Mac program. Part of its radical charm is that it uses such a unique interface to edit movies, unlike any other software out there.

While a lot of what it does happens in the main movie window, some of its cooler features—like One-Step Effects (page 125)—require a trip to the menu bar.

> **NOTE** You don't *have* to go to the menu bar if you've got a good memory. Just about every menu item in iMovie has a keyboard shortcut. Appendix B lists them all.

Here's a rundown of the commands in iMovie's menus:

iMovie Menu

In OS X, Apple names the first menu (the one after the menu) for the program you're using—in this case, iMovie.

About iMovie

This command opens the About box, containing the requisite Apple legal information. There's really only one good reason to open this window: It's the easiest way to find out exactly which version of iMovie you have.

Preferences

Opens the Preferences window (Figure A-1). No, your eyes do not deceive you. iMovie's preferences consist of two checkboxes, nothing else. If you thought this must be a mistake, it's probably because you're accustomed to applications that have dozens of preference settings. In iMovie, there really are just two.

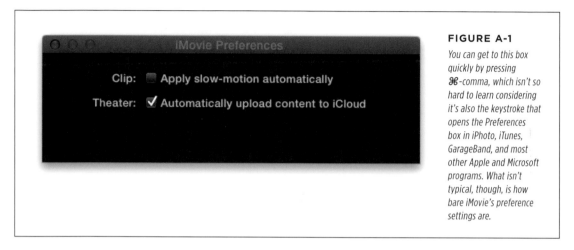

FIGURE A-1

You can get to this box quickly by pressing ⌘-comma, which isn't so hard to learn considering it's also the keystroke that opens the Preferences box in iPhoto, iTunes, GarageBand, and most other Apple and Microsoft programs. What isn't typical, though, is how bare iMovie's preference settings are.

Here's what they do:

- **Clip: Apply slow-motion automatically.** If you shot footage with an iPhone or iPad capable of shooting slow-motion video (filmed at 120 frames per second), iMovie will automatically slow it down to quarter-speed (30 frames per second, the standard frame rate for movies) when you stick it in your project. If you turn off this checkbox, you have to do the speed adjustment yourself, as explained on page 110.

- **Theater: Automatically upload content to iCloud.** Page 257 tells you all about iMovie Theater, a way to share your iMovie projects with other Apple devices that use the same iCloud account. But iMovie doesn't have to upload your movies to iCloud if you don't want it to. Instead, it can store them just in the iMovie Theater tab on your Mac. You can always manually upload them to iCloud from there. But if you want that to be automatic, make sure you turn on this checkbox.

Provide iMovie Feedback

This command takes you to a web form on Apple's website where you can register complaints, make suggestions, or gush enthusiastically about iMovie.

Services

Services are like mini tools in OS X for doing simple tasks on things like pictures, snippets of text, or other random things on your Mac. There aren't any built for iMovie, so this menu won't help much. But if you want to know more about it for other uses, choose the Services Preferences to see what's offered there.

Hide iMovie, Hide Others, Show All

These aren't iMovie commands—they're OS X's.

In any case, they determine which of the various programs running on your Mac are visible onscreen at any given moment. The Hide Others command is probably the most popular of the three. It zaps away the windows of all other programs—including the Finder—so that the iMovie window is the only one you see.

> **TIP** If you know this golden OS X trick, you may never need to use the Hide Others command: To switch into iMovie from another program, hold down the Option and ⌘ keys when clicking the iMovie icon in the Dock. Doing so simultaneously brings the software to the front and hides all other programs you have running, producing an uncluttered, distraction-free view of iMovie.

Quit iMovie

This command closes iMovie after offering you the chance to save any changes you made to your project file. The next time you open iMovie by double-clicking its icon, the program reopens whatever project you were working on.

◼ File Menu

As in any Mac program, the File menu serves as the program's interface to the rest of the Macintosh world. It lets you import movies and video, manage events, create or duplicate projects, or quit the program.

New Movie/Trailer

Creates either a new movie or a new trailer project, ready for filling with video snippets from the Event browser.

New Event

Creates a new event in the Event list, which you can do before you import any video. This also lets you reorganize your events just how you want them (page 29).

Import Media

This is just another way to bring up the Import screen you read about on page 15.

Open Library

Libraries, explained on page 31, contain both events and projects. The idea is that you can keep different libraries for different parts of your life, like home and work. Use this menu to open past libraries, make new ones, or open libraries others have shared with you.

Close Library "[Library Name]"

If you want a selected library to get out of your way in iMovie, use this command. It's grayed out if you have only one library open.

Copy to Library/Move to Library

These commands also work only with more than one library open. Select any event, project, or clip and you can copy it to another library (so it lives in both libraries) or move it (so it leaves one library and lives in the new one). You can also use these menus to create a new library.

Merge Events

iMovie sticks imported video into events—which you can choose as explained on page 29. You may sometimes find it useful, however, to combine several events into one, like an entire family reunion you originally broke into events for each day.

To use this command, first highlight the events you want to merge. (Click one, and then ⌘-click each additional one.) Then choose this command. iMovie names the new event after the first event you folded into this one, going alphabetically.

Consolidate Library Files/Project Media

Sometimes you might end up using footage from one library in a project that's stored in another library. Because iMovie edits by reference (page 35), your project won't have the footage it needs if the original library isn't available. This would happen if you copied a library to another computer, for example, and then deleted it from the first computer.

Choose Consolidate Project Media so all the files iMovie needs are available in the same library where you stored the project itself. Select Consolidate Library Files to do the same thing for *all* of a project's files, not just footage.

Share

What fun is iMovie if you can't share your work with the world? This menu contains all the same sharing options as the big Share button in the iMovie toolbar. Each is explained in Chapters 15 and 16.

Convert Trailer to Movie

If the constraints of the trailer-builder are holding you back, this option turns a trailer into a normal movie project, but the trip is one-way—you can't later change the project back into a trailer.

Reveal in Event

This handy option lets you click a clip in the storyboard and then jump to the corresponding raw footage in the Event browser. Seeing the original clip gives you a lot more information; for example, you can see how much of the clip you've used or whether or not you've used pieces of the clip elsewhere in the project (as indicated by the orange stripes).

Reveal in Finder

Although iMovie hides all the individual video files in a big, single library file (explained on page 41), you can still get access to them. Select any clip and choose this command. Your Mac opens a new Finder window and highlights the file.

Update Projects and Events

When you first open iMovie, the software offers to import and update projects and events from a previous version of iMovie. Because this process can take a long time, you can skip this step. If you decide to import all of these events and projects later, use this menu command.

Move to Trash

To delete most things in iMovie, like transitions, titles, or sound clips, you just click the item and then press the Delete key. All you're really doing when you delete these things is to remove them from your project. But that's not the same as moving things to the trash.

The trash is for things that take up space in your iMovie library, like projects, events, and imported video. When you move them to the trash, they go in one of two places: the internal iMovie trash you never see, or the Macintosh Trash in the Finder. Page 80 explains the process.

◼ Edit Menu

The Edit menu contains many of the basic tools you need to build your movies.

Undo

In iMovie, you can take back not only the last edit you made, not only the last 10, but an infinite number of steps, all the way back to the last time you opened iMovie. The ability to change your mind, or to recover from a particularly bad editing decision, is a considerable blessing.

The wording of this command changes to show you which editing step you're about to reverse. It might say Undo Adjust Volume, Undo Split, and so on.

Redo

We're only human, so it's entirely possible that sometimes you might want to undo your Undo.

For example, suppose you just used the Undo command a few times, retracing your steps back to a time when your movie was in better shape, and then decide that you've gone one step too far. That's when the Redo command is useful; it tells iMovie to undo your last Undo, so you can step forward in time, redoing the steps you just undid. (If you haven't yet used the Undo command, then iMovie dims Redo.)

Cut, Copy, Paste

You can use the Cut, Copy, and Paste commands just as you would in any other program: to move stuff around. You can cut, copy, and paste whatever you select: entire filmstrips or just chunks of them.

For example, you can cut a selection from a clip and paste it into another spot, or you can copy a selection and paste it into another project.

Cut, Copy, and Paste also work when you edit text, such as the names of your clips or the text for your credits and other titles.

Paste Adjustments

Once you painstakingly edit the look of a clip (to correct its color, for example), a photo (to direct a Ken Burns effect, for example), or some audio (to boost the volume, for example), you can rapidly enhance a bunch of other footage the same way. Just copy the first clip, and then, after selecting the other clips, use the Paste Adjustments commands. You have a lot of options:

- **Color:** Color changes
- **Crop:** Crop, fit, or Ken Burns changes
- **Stabilization:** Stabilization and zoom changes
- **Rolling Shutter:** Rolling shutter setting changes
- **Volume:** Volume changes
- **Video Effect:** Video effect changes
- **Audio Effect:** Audio effect changes
- **Speed:** Timing changes
- **Cutaway Setting:** Unique characteristics (such as fade and opacity) of cutaway, picture-in-picture, and side-by-side clips
- **Map Style:** Type of map changes

Delete (Reject)

More ways to get rid of stuff. If it's anything in a project, Delete removes it (but not from your Event library).

In the Event browser, this command says Reject instead of Delete, but only because rejecting, in iMovie, is the first step toward deleting footage for good. Page 80 has the details.

Delete Keyframes

When you animate a picture-in-picture clip, you do it with keyframes (page 122). This command deletes those keyframes so you can start over.

Duplicate

In the Event browser, makes an exact copy of whatever project or clip you selected.

Select All

Use this to select everything, at least everything in one part of iMovie.

- If you select a clip (or part of a clip) in an event, it selects all the clips in that event.

- If you select a project in an event, this highlights all the projects in the same event.

- If you highlight something in the storyboard, the command selects everything in the project storyboard.

- If you highlight some text in a text box, this selects all the text in the box.

Select Entire Clip

When you hover your mouse pointer over a clip, this surrounds the whole thing with a selection border.

Select in Movie

You have even more options available to you under Edit→"Select in Movie." If you want to make changes to all your transitions, for example, you can use this command to *select* all your transitions first. Use this to select all video clips, transitions, photos, maps, and backgrounds.

Deselect All

Removes any selection.

Add to Movie

Inserts a selected clip (or a selected part of a clip) in the Event browser to the end of your movie.

Connect

Inserts a selected clip (or a selected part of a clip) in the Event browser as a connected clip (page 112), starting at the position of your playhead.

Insert

Splits the clip under your playhead and inserts the Event browser selection between the two pieces.

Add Cross Dissolve

iMovie's preferred transition is the cross dissolve. How do you know? It's the only one that gets its own menu item and keyboard shortcut, saving you a trip to the Transitions library.

Find

If the clips you import into an event have custom names to tell them apart, you can use the Find command (or the search field at the top of the Event browser) to search for these clips by name. Most often, this is useless because cameras tend to name clips with meaningless combinations of numbers or letters.

Start Dictation

This is a standard menu item in all OS X apps. It makes your computer read back selected text with one of the built-in text-to-speech voices. If you haven't noticed, there's not a lot of text in iMovie to dictate.

Special Characters

You're creating a subtitle for an interview with the CEO of "I've Got a ¥en™" Productions. But how the heck do you type the ¥ symbol—or the ™ symbol? Easy. Choose this command and then double-click the symbol you want from the palette arrayed before you.

■ Mark Menu

The Mark menu holds a pretty short list of items, related to either categorizing your footage or flagging important moments in it for other uses.

Favorite/Delete/Unrate

There are three categories of footage in iMovie: favorite footage, rejected footage, and unrated footage (neither favorited or rejected). Select a clip in the Event browser and choose one of these three to decide a clip's fate. (Or use these to change its fate if you categorized it wrong.)

Add Marker

Page 66 explains how video markers work. This command adds a marker at the playhead.

Delete Marker

After you click a video marker to select it, this command removes it.

■ Modify Menu

This menu offers various tools for making changes to the video clips in your project.

Enhance

This does the same thing as the Enhance button in the iMovie toolbar. The software analyzes your selected clip and improves its appearance and sound automatically.

Fade to Black & White/Sepia/Dream

These three video effects are explained on page 125. These commands split a clip at the playhead, apply the chosen effect to the second piece, and transition smoothly into the effect you chose.

Add Freeze Frame

Does the trick explained on page 126.

Mute Clip

This completely silences a clip, or restores the volume setting if you'd already muted the clip.

Trim to Playhead/Selection

Use this command to trim excess footage off a storyboard clip, the part of the clip that follows the playhead's current position. If you have selected part of a storyboard clip, this cuts off everything outside the selection border.

Split Clip

It's often convenient to chop a clip in half; this command splits a clip at the playhead.

Join Clips

If, having split a clip as just described, you want to *rejoin* the pieces, place them consecutively in the storyboard, and then use this command. (You can't join clips that were never part of one clip to begin with.)

Detach Audio

This handy command takes the sound from the selected project clip and puts it in as a sound effect (page 191), still synced up with the clip. The source clip itself is now soundless.

Slow Motion/Fast Forward/Instant Replay/Rewind

These next four menu items in the Modify menu are covered in detail starting on page 126. Go there to learn what each of these does.

Reset Speed

If you've made any speed changes to a project clip (page 110), this undoes them all.

Adjust Clip Date and Time...

You'll use this command to fix any event footage that just didn't happen when iMovie thinks it happened.

■ View Menu

This menu is mostly about changing the way iMovie displays your video while you work.

Play

Starts previewing a clip from the playhead.

Play Selection

Plays whatever you've selected, from the beginning of the selection.

Play from Beginning

Previews a set of event clips or a project from the start.

Play Full Screen

Fills your screen with a preview of whatever you're working on (event footage or a project).

Show Separate Days in Events

By default, iMovie lumps all the footage in an event together. This command visually distinguishes them by the days they were filmed, using the embedded date and time.

Loop Playback

When you're playing something, turn this on and iMovie will go back to the beginning and play it again automatically.

Sort By

As explained on page 27, this command lets you view event clips in a different order.

Show/Hide Waveforms

This is how you can visualize the audio in your video and sound clips, as Chapter 11 explains.

Show/Hide Used Media Ranges

If you don't like seeing the orange stripes telling you what footage you've already used, this makes them go away.

Show/Hide Skimmer Info

When you turn this option on, a balloon pops out of the playhead when you move it over event footage, displaying the clip's file name.

Wrapping Timeline

If you want your project clips to flow more like text in a word processor, making use of vertical screen space, turn this on. (Page 43 explains how it works.)

Zoom In/Out

Shows longer or shorter filmstrips representing your footage (page 50).

Zoom All Clips

Displays all your event clips as single frames. (This basically zooms all the way out.)

Snapping

Snapping is when the playhead is "magnetically" drawn to nearby markers or clip ends, saving you tedious hand-positioning. You'll need this feature if you want to follow the useful advice on editing to a beat (page 182).

Audio Skimming

When you skim (see page 52), iMovie plays the audio simultaneously, which may sound fragmented and disturbing. Turn off this option if you'd rather skim in silence.

■ Window Menu

This Window menu is fairly standard in OS X programs. The Minimize and Zoom commands are almost always present; they let you minimize iMovie (hide its window by collapsing it into a Dock icon) or expand the window to fill your screen.

But iMovie's Window menu is quite a bit more detailed.

Go to Library/Theater

These commands give you access to the same parts of iMovie that the Library and Theater tabs in the middle of the iMovie toolbar do.

Show Adjustments Bar

You've seen the Adjustments bar a million times by now. It's where you make all kinds of adjustments, like video and audio effects. This command does the same thing as clicking the Adjust button in the iMovie toolbar.

Hide/Show Libraries

If the Libraries list on the left side of iMovie is cramping your style, make it go away with this command.

Content Library

This command offers direct access to any of the Content libraries that live in the lower-left corner of iMovie when you're editing a project: Transitions, Titles, Maps & Backgrounds, iTunes, Sound Effects, and GarageBand.

Show/Hide Clip Trimmer

This option opens the Clip Trimmer tool described on page 67.

Show/Hide Precision Editor

This command opens the Precision Editor tool described on page 68.

Sports Team Editor

The really cool Sports theme provides you with a team roster you can customize with player names and other information. This is where you edit the roster. Page 101 explains.

Record Voiceover

Shows the voiceover tool, covered on page 188.

Movie Properties

This changes the Viewer to show information about your project. You first see basic information about the video quality, length, and share status of your project. Click Settings in the Viewer (Figure A-2) and you can adjust the following:

FIGURE A-2

Your project's settings determine basic behavior for your movie.

- **Photo Placement.** This pop-up menu tells iMovie how to handle photos that don't exactly fit the aspect ratio (proportions) of your movie project. It can either crop them (enlarge them to fill the frame), fit the frame ("Fit in Frame") by adding letterbox bars, or execute the Ken Burns effect (perform a slow zoom and pan across them).

- **Theme.** Here you can change the theme choice you made when you started your project.

- **Automatic Content.** If you want theme titles and transitions automatically inserted, make sure you turn on this checkbox.

- **Clips.** When adding clips from the Event browser, you can just position the playhead and hit the letter E key, without actually selecting any part of a clip. This slider determines how much of the event clip will be added from the playhead forward.

- **Transitions.** Drag this slider left or right to determine how long a newly added transition takes.

- **Trim Background Music.** With this box checked, any audio clips placed in the background (page 170) of your project will automatically stop playing at then end of your last video clip.

Swap Project and Event

This command flips the top and bottom halves of the editing screen, so that the storyboard is now on the bottom. The advantage is that there's no Viewer window taking up the bottom of iMovie's screen, so you get a more expansive workspace.

Revert to Original Layout

If you've monkeyed with your window layout in iMovie using any of the previously described commands, this command returns it back to the way it looked on first launching iMovie.

Enter Full Screen

Uses iMovie in the full screen format available to all apps in OS X.

◼ Help Menu

iMovie doesn't come with a manual—if it did, you wouldn't need this book. Instead, you're expected to learn its functions from the online help.

Search

This search box does two things when you type in text:

- If the text appears in a menu command, the command shows up in the resulting list. Pointing to the list item will even open up and highlight the corresponding command.

- If the text appears in the Help documentation, it provides a link to the corresponding help article, which opens in the Help window (read on).

iMovie Help

Choose this command to open the iMovie Help Center window, where you'll see a list of help topics (Figure A-3).

You can use the Help Center in either of two ways:

- Keep clicking colored links, burrowing closer and closer to the help topic you want. You can backtrack by clicking the left-arrow button at the top of the window, exactly as in a web browser.

- Type a search phrase into the top window, such as *cropping*, and then click Search (or press Return), as shown in Figure A-3.

Either way, you'll probably find that iMovie's online assistance offers a helpful summary of the program's functions, but it's a little light on "what it's for" information, illustrations, tutorials, speed, and jokes.

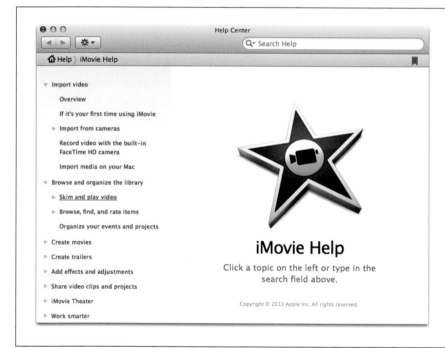

FIGURE A-3

The Help Center's first screen offers a large, browsable outline. Most people, however, start by typing a phrase into the search box. (If you do, double-click a topic in the search results to read the corresponding help page. Click the Back button at the top of the screen to return to the list of topics.)

Keyboard Shortcuts

This is really just another link into the Help Center, but a particularly valuable part of it. It takes you to a table showing about 50 keyboard shortcuts in iMovie. (They're among the listings in Appendix C: Master Keyboard Shortcut List of this book.)

Supported Cameras

This takes you to a handy web page Apple designed to list all the cameras iMovie supports. You can use this to plan your next camera purchase.

Service and Support

Opens your web browser and takes you to Apple's iMovie help website. Which, by the way, is a pretty great resource for asking questions and getting answers.

■ The Shortcut Menu

If you Control-click clips in the Event browser or the project storyboard, iMovie offers quick access to some common commands. Figure A-4 shows you what they look like.

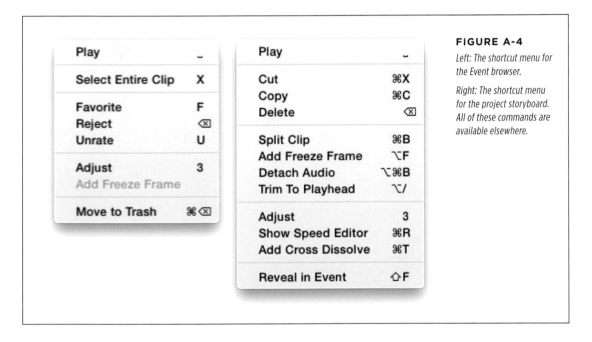

FIGURE A-4

Left: The shortcut menu for the Event browser.

Right: The shortcut menu for the project storyboard. All of these commands are available elsewhere.

Troubleshooting

Apple does amazing things with each new version of iMovie. It adds features new not just to iMovie, but to consumer video editing, period. And you know what happens with brand-spanking-new features, right? Right: glitches.

Here's an impressive compendium of the problems you may run into—and the world's best attempts at solving them.

The Golden Rule

If there's any common wisdom at all about iMovie, here it is—the golden rule that will stave off a huge number of problems down the road:

- **Use the latest version.** Each ".01" or ".1" iMovie upgrade zaps a whole host of bugs and glitches. The updates are free, so when your Mac App Store advises you that one is available, jump at the chance to install it.

General iMovie Troubleshooting

Let's start general, shall we?

Keep Your Hard Disk Happy

Remember the old expression "If Mama ain't happy, ain't nobody happy"? Well, if your hard disk isn't happy, iMovie won't be happy, either.

Here's a short list of maintenance suggestions. A little attention every week or so may help keep minor hard drive problems from becoming major ones:

- After installing or updating any software, use Disk Utility to repair permissions. (Disk Utility is in your Applications→Utilities folder. Click the First Aid tab, select your hard drive, and then click Repair Permissions.)

- Back up, back up, back up. Oh, and have a good backup. Use, for example, the Time Machine backup software built right into OS X. It can back up your entire hard drive onto another hard drive, automatically, hourly, completely. Since hard drives are dirt cheap these days—a $60 drive would probably cover you—there's little reason not to set up this automatic backup system.

TIP Don't worry about arcane things like defragmenting your hard drive or manually running the background maintenance jobs. Modern Macs do all this on their own.

Starting Up and Importing

Trouble getting going? Here's some advice.

iMovie Doesn't See the Tapeless Camcorder

First, note that some camcorders refuse to enter PC connection mode unless you plug them into a power outlet. They won't even consider entering PC mode when running on battery. (The camcorder's fear is that it will run out of battery power in the middle of the transfer, possibly corrupting and ruining some of your video scenes.)

Next, try plugging the USB cable into one of the USB jacks on the Mac itself, rather than into the USB jack on the Mac's keyboard. (The one on the keyboard is for low-powered gadgets only.)

If you double-check these conditions, quit iMovie and reopen it. Now, at long last, the Import screen should appear.

iMovie Doesn't See the Tape Camcorder

Try these checks, in this order:

Make sure you set your camera to VCR or VTR or whatever the setting is called that plays back your tape. Check the FireWire cable connections. Turn the camcorder off and then on again. Quit iMovie, turn the camcorder on, and then reopen iMovie. Restart the Mac. Try a different FireWire cable.

Do you have a high-def tape camcorder (one that uses the so-called HDV format)? If so, delve into the menus and make sure that the camcorder's output matches what you recorded.

See, these camcorders can record either standard-definition or high-definition video on the same tape. But when you connect the camcorder to a TV or a Mac, it has to know which format to transmit.

Usually, you get a choice of DV (which means standard definition, 4:3), HDV (high definition, widescreen, 16:9), and Auto. But Auto doesn't always work. If you're having problems, choose DV or HDV manually.

Video Looks Interlaced

You know the cool iMovie Preview window (page 16), where you get to see and even play the thumbnails for the video on tapeless camcorders before you actually import any video? Sometimes that preview playback looks awful. It might be jerky or have nasty interlace lines, for example.

Rest assured that this is all just a problem with the preview. Once you actually import this footage, it'll look fine.

No Sound from Tape Camcorder

If you're used to the old, old iMovie, you might wonder why you can't hear anything as you import footage from your tape camcorder. That's because iMovie no longer plays audio through the Mac when you import. If you want to hear the soundtrack as you import, leave the camcorder's screen open so you hear the audio from the camcorder itself.

iMovie Crashes on Startup

If you can't even make it past the startup phase, you can try deleting iMovie (just drag the app to the Trash) and reinstalling it from the Mac App Store. Don't worry; deleting the app doesn't delete all your movie files. Those are stored elsewhere.

Also consider rebuilding your iPhoto library; iMovie checks in with iPhoto every time you open it, and if there's something wrong with your iPhoto library, iMovie chokes. To rebuild the iPhoto library, quit iPhoto, and then reopen it while holding down the ⌘ and Option keys. In the resulting dialog box, you see several diagnostic options. Choose the Rebuild button, and then wait a very long time. When it's all over, iMovie should be much happier about doing business with a clean, fresh iPhoto library.

Can't Import from DVD Camcorder

See the Note on page 22.

Dropouts in the Video

A *dropout* is a glitch in the picture. DV dropouts are always square or rectangular. They may be blotches of the wrong color or may be multicolored. They may appear every time you play a particular scene or may appear at random. In severe circumstances, you may get lots of them, such as when you try to capture video to an old FireWire hard drive that's too slow. Such a configuration may also cause tearing of the video picture.

Fortunately, dropouts are fairly rare in digital video. If you get one, it's probably in one of these three circumstances:

- **You're using a very old cassette.** Remember that even DV cassettes don't last forever. You may begin to see dropouts after rerecording on the tape 50 times or so.

- **You're playing back a cassette that was recorded in LP (long-play) mode.** If you recorded the cassette on a different camcorder, dropouts are especially likely.

- **It's time to clean the heads on your camcorder.** The electrical components that actually make contact with the tape can become dirty over time. Your local electronics store sells head-cleaning kits for just this purpose.

If you spot the glitch at the same moment on the tape every time you play it, then the problem is on the tape itself. If it's there during one playback but gone during the next, the problem more likely lies with the heads in your camcorder.

NOTE Different DV tape manufacturers use different lubricants on their tapes. As a result, mixing tapes from different manufacturers on the same camcorder can increase the likelihood of head clogs. It's a good idea, therefore, to stick with tapes from one manufacturer (Sony, Panasonic, or Maxell, for example) when possible.

Editing

Once you learn the program's ins and outs, there's not much that can go wrong during editing.

Can't Drag Certain Photos into the Movie

If you open the iPhoto library and try to drag an iPhoto photo into your movie but you get a "The file could not be imported" error message, you're probably working with a RAW image file. (That's a high-end photo file format created by semiprofessional SLR cameras and intended for processing later on a computer.)

The solution: Return to iPhoto. Make a tiny change to the photo, like a small crop or brightness adjustment. When you exit editing mode, iPhoto applies the change and, in the process, turns the RAW photo into a JPEG or TIFF format photo, which iMovie can import.

Can't Use Audiobooks in Soundtrack

Yep, you can't use an audiobook as an iMovie soundtrack. They show up in the Media browser, all right, but if you drag them into iMovie, nothing happens. Them's the breaks.

■ Where to Get Help

You can get personal iMovie help by calling Apple's help line at (800) 500-7078 for 90 days after you buy either iMovie from the Mac App Store or on a new Mac. After that, you can either buy an AppleCare contract for another year of tech-support calls ($170 to $350, depending on your Mac model), or pay $50 per individual call!

Beyond 90 days, however, consider consulting the Internet, which is filled with superb sources of fast, free technical help. Here are two of the best places to get your questions answered:

- **Official iMovie help pages.** Apple doesn't freely admit to bugs and problems, but there's a surprising amount of good information in its official iMovie answer pages (*www.apple.com/support/imovie*).

- **Apple's own iMovie discussion forum.** Here you can read user comments, ask questions of knowledgeable iMovie fanatics, or hang out and learn good stuff (*https://discussions.apple.com/community/ilife/imovie*). Some of the most knowledgeable and friendly people—like AppleMan1958 and Karsten Schlüter—take time to help out and answer questions.

Master Keyboard Shortcut List

As you know, iMovie was conceived with a single goal in mind: speed, baby, speed. And part of gaining speed is mastering keyboard shortcuts, so you don't waste time puttering around in the menus. So here it is, by popular, frustrated demand: the master list of every secret (or not-so-secret) keystroke in iMovie for the Mac. Clip and post it to your monitor (unless, of course, you got this book from the library).

> **TIP** There are also a million shortcut menus—the contextual menus that appear when you Control-click (or right-click) almost anything on the screen. Most of the time, the commands you find there just duplicate what's in the menus. Learning the keyboard shortcut is still faster.

■ Panes, Panels, and Windows

Go to Library View (where you edit video)	1
Go to iMovie Theater	2
Show/Hide adjustments bar	3
Show/Hide Libraries list	Shift-⌘-1
Show Transitions browser	⌘-1
Show Titles browser	⌘-2
Show Maps & Backgrounds browser	⌘-3

Show iTunes library	⌘-4
Show Sound Effects browser	⌘-5
Show GarageBand browser	⌘-6
Open Precision Editor	⌘-/
Open Clip Trimmer window	⌘-R
Show/Hide Voiceover window	V
iMovie Preferences window	⌘-, (comma key)
Movie Properties	⌘-J
Import Window	⌘-I
Speed Editor	⌘-R
Minimize iMovie	⌘-M

■ Event Browser and Storyboard

Scroll to top/bottom	Home/End
Scroll up/down	Page Up/Page Down
Show skimmer info	Control-Y
Movie Properties	⌘-J
iMovie Help	Shift-⌘-?
New project	⌘-N
New trailer	Shift-⌘-N
New event	Option-N
Reveal in event	Shift-F
Reveal in Finder	Shift-⌘-R
Move to trash	⌘-Delete

■ Playback

Play from playhead	Space bar
Play selected footage	/
Play project (or event) from start	\ (backslash)
Play full screen	Shift-⌘-F
Exit full-screen mode	Esc

Loop playback	⌘-L
Move the playhead one frame forward	Right arrow
Move the playhead one frame backward	Left arrow
Move to next clip in Event browser	Down arrow
Move to beginning of Event browser clip (or previous clip if at start of clip)	Up arrow

▪ Editing

Import	⌘-I
Select all (or whole filmstrip)	⌘-A
Select entire clip	X
Deselect all	Shift-⌘-A
Cut, Copy, Paste	⌘-X, ⌘-C, ⌘-V
Paste color adjustments only	Option-⌘-A
Paste crop/Ken Burns adjustments only	Option-⌘-R
Paste stabilization adjustments only	Option-⌘-Z
Paste rolling shutter adjustments only	Option-⌘-T
Paste volume adjustments only	Option-⌘-O
Paste video effect adjustments only	Option-⌘-L
Paste audio effect adjustments only	Option-⌘-O
Paste speed adjustments only	Option-⌘-S
Paste cutaway, green screen, or picture-in-picture adjustments only	Option-⌘-U
Paste map style adjustments only	Option-⌘-M
Undo	⌘-Z
Redo	Shift-⌘-Z
Delete	Delete
Delete keyframes	Option-Shift-Delete
Turn on/off snapping	N

■ Working with Clips

Add selection to storyboard	E
Add selection as connected clip	Q
Insert selection at playhead	W
Add cross-dissolve	⌘-T
Mark selection as a Favorite	F
Mark selection as a Reject	R (or Delete, in Event browser only)
Unmark selection	U
Add marker	M
Delete marker	Control-Shift-M
Trim to Playhead/Selection	Option-/
Split Clip	⌘-B
Join Clips	Shift-⌘-B
Open Precision Editor	⌘-/
Open Clip Trimmer window	⌘-\
Enhance Clip	Shift-⌘-E
Add Freeze Frame	Option-F
Speed Editor	⌘-R
Reset Speed	Option-Shift-R
Zoom in on clips (one step)	⌘-=
Zoom out on clips (one step)	⌘--
Zoom all the way out on clips	Shift-Z
Turn on/off snapping	N
Undo	⌘-Z
Redo	Shift-⌘-Z

■ Music and Audio

Show iTunes library	⌘-4
Show Sound Effects browser	⌘-5
Show GarageBand browser	⌘-6
Detach audio	Option-⌘-B
Show/Hide Voiceover window	V
Audio during skimming on/off	Shift-S
Mute/unmute clip	Shift-⌘-M

■ Editing Titles

Show/Hide Titles browser	⌘-2
Cut, Copy, Paste	⌘-X, ⌘-C, ⌘-V

Visual Cheat Sheet

As you've probably gathered, iMovie is completely different from any other program you've seen before—including previous versions of iMovie. You'll find it filled with handy visual cues as to what's going on. But, especially at first, learning all those cues can seem like a full-time job.

iMovie is teeming with banners over and under your filmstrips (in green, blue, or purple); horizontal lines drawn right across them (in red, green, and orange); buttons galore; and on and on.

You practically need a cheat sheet to remember what they're all for—and Figure D-1 is where you'll find it.

Libraries list   Project   Used footage   Favorite footage

Library

Event

Event
with
current
project

Marker   Playhead

Adjustments bar

Viewer

Connected clip
(cutaway)

Title

Transition

Connected
audio

Background
audio

Index

iMovie

THE MISSING CD

There's no
CD with this book;
you just saved $5.00.

Instead, every single Web address, practice file, and
piece of downloadable software mentioned in this
book is available at *missingmanuals.com*
(click the Missing CD icon).
There you'll find a tidy list of links,
organized by chapter.

Don't miss a thing!
Sign up for the free Missing
Manual email announcement
list at missingmanuals.com.
We'll let you know when we
release new titles, make
free sample chapters available,
and update the features and
articles on the Missing Manual
website.